For Wes,

with esteem and good wishes,

Rob 4/22/68

The Changing World of Anthony Trollope

The Changing
World of
Anthony Trollope

ROBERT M. POLHEMUS

University of California Press
Berkeley and Los Angeles   1968

University of California Press
Berkeley and Los Angeles, California

Cambridge University Press
London, England

Library of Congress Catalog Card Number: 68–16111
Printed in the United States of America

for Elizabeth

Acknowledgments

I wish to thank those who helped me with this book. Professor John Henry Raleigh supervised the research and writing in an early form. Professors Thomas Parkinson, Wilfred Stone, Lawrence Ryan, George Guttridge, Thomas B. Flanagan, Douglas Bush, Bradford Booth, W. Bliss Carnochan, and Thomas Moser, along with Mr. Herbert Mann, Mr. Robert Hass, and Mr. Robert Burroughs, have all read this manuscript (or parts of it) at some stage and provided me with encouragement and invaluable suggestions. I am indebted to my editors Mrs. Gladys C. Castor and Mrs. Lynda S. Bridge, and to Mrs. Eva Nyqvist and Mrs. Betty Brereton for typing the final manuscript. Last, but by no means least, I am grateful to my friends, colleagues, and students at Stanford for indispensable practical and moral support during the time of writing.

Author's Note

There is no standard or complete edition of Trollope. Therefore in the notes, I have included chapter as well as page
numbers in citing him. Unless otherwise noted, all quota-
tions and citations are from the Oxford University Press,
The World's Classics editions of his novels, because so many
of them are in print and readily available. Many of the
novels in *The World's Classics* editions which were formerly
printed in two volumes are now printed under one cover
as "double volumes." In "double volumes" all chapters are
numbered consecutively, but the two sets of page numbers
used when each novel was printed in two volumes are retained. The Roman numeral I or II following page numbers
in the notes denotes the first or second sequence of pagina-
tion.

The reader may turn to the index of Trollope's work to
find where a particular work is discussed at some length.
He will, however, find no index of subject matters. After
struggling for days to prepare one, I had little more than a
list of my chapter titles arranged in alphabetical order. I
concluded that the book simply does not lend itself to such
an endeavor. By way of consolation to the reader, I can only
suggest that he turn to the Contents for an indication of the
various aspects of Victorian and modern life that are discussed in this book.

A Chronology
Of Trollope's
Novels

Date of Composition	(the year of publication in book form appears in parentheses)
1843–1845	The Macdermots of Ballycloran (1847)
1847	The Kellys and The O'Kellys: A Tale of Irish Life (1848)
1849	La Vendée: An Historical Romance (1850)
1852–1853	The Warden (1855)
1855–1856	Barchester Towers (1857)
1857	The Three Clerks (1858)
1857	The Struggles of Brown, Jones and Robinson begun
1857–1858	Doctor Thorne (1858)
1858	The Bertrams (1859)
1859	Castle Richmond (1860)
1859–1860	Framley Parsonage (1861)
1860–1861	Orley Farm (1862)
1861	The Struggles of Brown, Jones and Robinson finished (1870)
1862–1863	The Small House at Allington (1864)
1863	Rachel Ray (1863)
1863–1864	Can You Forgive Her? (1864)
1864	Miss Mackenzie (1865)
1864	The Claverings (1867)
1865	The Belton Estate (1866)
1865	Nina Balatka (1867)
1866	The Last Chronicle of Barset (1867)

Contents

1

An Approach to
Trollope's Fiction

Anthony Trollope is a great novelist, but his greatness is
not fully recognized or accepted. The immediate purpose of
this book is to make clear the range, skill, and accomplish-
ment of Trollope as an interpreter of social change. Its larger
aim is to gain for him the kind of attention and critical reas-
sessment which his great contemporaries Dickens and George
Eliot have received in the last generation. I want to consider
the whole span of Trollope's career and to discuss, in the
order in which he wrote them, his best and most representative novels—particularly the Barset and Palliser series. Obviously no single study can do more than touch on the more
significant aspects of his incredibly long shelf of books. But
by pointing out the thematic development in his work and by
quoting liberally from him, I hope to show what he actually
achieved in chronicling imaginatively the forms of historical
and psychological change. His fiction can bring us to a
deeper understanding of changing Victorian life and of the
modern world which has grown out of nineteenth-century
experience.

Despite distinguished criticism concerning him by Henry
James, Michael Sadleir, Anthony Cockshut, Arthur Mizener,
Bradford Booth, B. C. Brown, Walter Allen, and Hugh
Sykes Davies, among others, his subject matter, his creative
powers and methods, and his unique vision have often been
slighted, misinterpreted, or ignored. "All in all," concludes

Donald Smalley in a recent guide to research, "Trollope's particular qualities . . . continue to evade definition."[1] Lord David Cecil expresses the prevalent critical opinion of him: "Only now and then does he manage to transmute the dross of reality into the gold of art. Here it is that Trollope falls short of his contemporaries as an artist. The fact that his imagination was a relatively weak one means that his books are, compared with the greatest novels, deficient in quality. And since it is this artistic quality that most distinguishes the great from the lesser novelist, Trollope is, compared with the very greatest, a lesser novelist."[2]

The point is that Trollope did not see or imagine that reality *is* drossy, and critics who can talk about "the dross of reality" can never really appreciate his artistic imagination. Look hard at reality, his fiction seems to say, and you find that the lives of so-called "ordinary" people are in fact extraordinarily interesting and important. The particular quality which makes Trollope a major writer is his outstanding ability to make us intensely aware both of the special predicament of individual Victorians and of the universal human condition: the fate to live in the midst of historical flow and to struggle with the demands of one's own uncertain times.

We take it for granted that we live in a time of revolutionary change, but for the Victorians the concept of the world radically transforming itself was still fresh and exciting. The discovery and analysis of the "otherness" of the past and, implicitly, the future had the kind of emotional and intellectual impact on consciousness in the nineteenth century that our growing awareness of technology with all its wonderful and terrible possibilities has in the twentieth century. Trollope made change his predominant subject

---

[1] Donald Smalley, "Anthony Trollope," in *Victorian Fiction,* ed. Lionel Stevenson (Cambridge, Mass., 1964), p. 213.

[2] David Cecil, *Victorian Novelists* (Chicago: Phoenix Books, 1958), p. 247.

matter, and it not only gives unity to his huge body of work, it also puts his single novels in perspective. At one time or another he wrote about almost every part of his changing world that stirred middle-class minds. In different periods he stressed certain themes and patterns of change, and the chronology of his writing lets us see how closely he tied his art to the constantly changing conditions of his era. For example, his novels from the "hungry 'forties" deal with the tragic power of historical determinism, and his comedies of the mid-fifties tend to express the expansive, boom-time psychology of those years. He was the first Victorian novelist of stature who consistently set his stories in "the present"; unlike Dickens, Thackeray, and George Eliot, he nearly always made the time in his fiction correspond to the real time when he was writing. Not for nothing did he call his novels "chronicles."

At the end of a typical Trollope novel such as *The Warden* or *The Duke's Children,* society, or the atmosphere of that society, is in some crucial way altered from what it was at the beginning, and this change projects or foreshadows the actual movement of the Victorian world. In most novels, even in many very great novels like *Emma, Vanity Fair,* and *Ulysses,* the characters change in some way, but the world in which they live is virtually the same at the end as it was in the beginning. For Trollope, however, the whole world moved.

Nevertheless, the heart of his novels is not the world, but the particular men and women in it who both produce and are products of the fluctuating society and who must face change individually. The best moments in his work come when he makes his characters realize the world's uncertainty and the conflicting forces of tradition and innovation in their lives. Moral crises and questions of conscience occur when his people feel the pressure to give up conventional assumptions and act in new ways.

Trollope's sympathy for humanity is marvelously broad.

He has a rare talent for imagining the kinds of people that other novelists usually find dull, inconsequential, or morally tainted, forming them into sympathetic characters, and showing how they collectively shape the nature of an age. He understood that inconspicuous people are victimized by history and circumstance, but he knew also that they make history.

If Trollope, as Professor Smalley says, "seems still in the process of being discovered," it is time that he was.[3] His novels convey a sophisticated understanding of the communal nature of life and, at the same time, a remarkable sense of the dignity of individual human beings. George Eliot wrote to Trollope: "In all the writings of yours that I know—it is that people are breathing good bracing air in reading them—it is that they are filled with goodness without the slightest tinge of maudlin. They are like pleasant public gardens, where people go for amusement and, whether they think of it or not, get health as well."[4] She did not mean that Trollope tamely inculcated a simple morality of goodness. She meant that he, with his great tolerance for all sorts of characters, even morally flawed ones, and his strange but passionate reverence for ordinary middle-class life, could make people realize that their own ordinary lives have value and consequence. He can show us that we do not always have to bear that traditional middle-class burden of justifying our existences to ourselves.

Trollope's best fiction is subtly passionate and humane, though it sometimes seems deceivingly restrained. It is true that he is a self-effacing writer. His novels lack the powerful authorial voice that we find in a Dickens, a George Eliot, or a Dostoyevsky. He does not have a gaudy style which calls attention to itself, nor does he assume a sage-like tone. He does not force us to submit to his point of view with an

---

[3] "Anthony Trollope," *Victorian Fiction*, p. 213.
[4] *The George Eliot Letters*, ed. Gordon S. Haight, 6 vols. (New Haven, 1955), IV, 110.

overwhelming rhetoric. But his unobtrusive technique can be extremely effective, and we need to see how it works.

Comparison with Dickens is revealing. Though all fiction is make-believe, every good novelist must convince his readers to accept his imaginary world as somehow a true reflection of reality. Dickens does this by overpowering us with his imagination, by making us see his world through the high-powered glasses of his own originality. The force of his description, his metaphorical exploration of moral and psychological forces in society, and his startling use of language open up a striking new perspective for us. By exaggerating and by jolting us, he almost bullies us into believing that he is showing us reality as no one has ever perceived it before. He seems to shout at us to look at things his way, and we do.

Trollope is different. He poses as nothing special and pretends that he looks at the characters and circumstances in his novels in the way any reliable person would. By using a plain style he tries to lessen the distance between author and reader. He wants to give the illusion that he is just as objective toward his material as we would be—in fact, that he is our agent, our stand-in who tells us about people and events as a sensible friend might. Dickens's fiction attracts attention to his brilliant style and genius of invention. The effect of Trollope's fiction is usually to turn us away from much concern about the author at all and to plunge us into the lives of his characters. He wants us to think of them, not as creatures of his imagination or as the expression of his view of life, but as autonomous people whom we can talk about and judge as if they were real. The greatest moments in Dickens usually come when he is describing things for us in his own narrative voice or when his characters, the best of whom seem to have their own language, declaim their fantastic, inimitable soliloquies, not to communicate with others, but to create and define their identities and worlds in original tongues. Trollope, however, excels at writing dialogue so natural that it almost gives us the illusion of eaves-dropping. In his view the most important times in life come when people talk to each other, and many of his best passages are simply long conversations in which the author seems to fade out and the characters go on talking, drawing each other out, revealing themselves and their world, inter-acting, and consciously or unconsciously changing each other's minds and habits.

When Trollope is writing well, he can make it seem that he comes as close to transcribing reality as a novelist can come, and that, given the circumstances, people really would talk and act the way they do in his books. Relatively speak-ing, he lacks interest in plots, and the exigencies of con-ventional plotting sometimes bother him. Generally he tries to make his readers believe that his characters are so real that they cannot be manipulated to satisfy an author's whim. When, for example, he intrudes in his own voice in *Bar-chester Towers* and announces that Eleanor will marry neith-er of her suitors, he is trying to show that her life is inviolable and that he could not make her marry anyone she did not choose for herself, even if he wanted to.[5] We may find him—in weak moments, for the sake of a rigid story-line or a simplistic moral code—contradicting the rich complexity of his characters' own voices and the unpredictability of life that comes through in what they say to each other. But usually his best characters do not seem to spring out of his psyche (though of course they do), nor do they seem pro-jections of social attitudes or psychological states (though they very often are); rather they seem to be whole people who come out of the historical reality of the age. His great rhetorical trick is to make us think that he is simply report-ing the truth about the privileged-class Victorians; and bring-ing off this sort of trick is much harder than it looks.

---

[5] See Wayne Booth, *The Rhetoric of Fiction* (Chicago, 1961), p. 206.

Yet Trollope makes heavy demands on our imagination. In order to succeed, his fiction must persuade us to share his sympathy for "average" middle-class life of the nineteenth century and to value people and areas of experience which intellectuals of the last century-and-a-half have tended to disparage—for both good and bad reasons. He fails ultimately if he cannot convince us that what we normally consider the adventurous or romantic life is neither superior to nor more interesting than what we call "everyday life." He sees a world in which nothing is more important than how an "ordinary" man gets along with his wife, or how he comes to a moral decision about his profession, or how these commonplace personal matters affect the whole community. Even if we reject his view, we ought to recognize how challenging and important it is.

Sometimes Trollope has been ticked off as a kind of Victorian journalist. Actually, he is the very opposite. Journalism normally consists of some form of sensationalism, but Trollope's great virtue, as Henry James said, is his "complete appreciation of the usual."[6] He is never bored by life. A tabloid interest in experience, the craving for news of the bizarre person and the dramatic event, eventually cheapens life. For instance, if you think that a murderer and a prostitute are intrinsically more interesting than a bureaucrat and a housewife, in effect you slander humanity. Trollope cares deeply about the common processes, problems, and kinds of relationships which make up the lives of most middle-class people, even when he disapproves of these people. He is the explorer and poet of that complex shaper of the modern world, middle-class mentality.

His often understated fiction requires that we go deeper into ourselves to see what we have in common with the Victorians, but it also requires us to get out of ourselves. To appreciate him we must see that he gives us a world at once

---

[6] Henry James, "Anthony Trollope," in *The Future of the Novel*, ed. Leon Edel (New York, 1956), pp. 233-260.

like our own and very different from it. He writes so informa-
tively about Victorian manners and morals that historians
of the age, such as Asa Briggs and Walter Houghton, find
him invaluable. No one shows us better than Trollope what
it was like and how it felt to be alive in the nineteenth
century. For this reason, he has sometimes been read for
escape—most notably in World War II. His books are,
however, anything but escapist in the way that the usual
historical novel and detective story are. His world, especially
the world of Barset, may at first seem quiet and even stable
if we compare it with our own; his fiction is so rooted in the
slow-developing lives of his people and their individual
predicaments that, like Jane Austen's, it can give the illusion
of taking place in an enclosed, almost idyllic milieu. But
sooner or later, necessity, in the shape of passing time and
historical change, threatens and moves almost all of Trollope's characters and their communities.

For the whole century, change was a two-faced Janus, a
benefactor and a devouring tyrant at the same time. But
Trollope personally had even more reason to be sensitive to
change than other Victorians, and there are clues in his
autobiography which help explain its place and its patterns
in his novels.[7] His wretched, lonely early life, with the uncertain, worsening conditions of his family, gave him feelings
of insecurity that lasted a lifetime. His father's mental deterioration and financial ruin, his mother's neglect of him
while she tried to repair the family fortunes in America, and
the day-by-day descent into poverty and despair in those
years shook his imagination. As a boy, he learned to know
and fear change because things for him just kept getting
worse all the time. Yet if he was ever going to get out of his
misery, he had to hope for and count on change, too. The
traumatic shock of those days and his obsessive insecurity
comes out in his autobiography even when he is talking

---

[7] See Anthony Trollope, *An Autobiography* (London, 1953),
chaps. I–IV.

about the comfortable happiness of his adult life: "But all is not over yet. And mindful of that, remembering how great is the agony of adversity, how crushing the despondency of degradation, how susceptible I am myself to the misery coming from contempt,—remembering also how quickly good things may go and evil things may come,—I am often again tempted to hope, almost to pray, that the end may be near."[8]

It was in his cherished fantasy life, he tells us, that he could both transform his craven little self into a fine fellow and escape from the nightmare of his own changing world. There in his imagination he could preserve an illusion of permanence and security. Not only his subjects but his very vocation as a writer are thus linked to his early experiences with change.

All writers are misers of perception and experience, and in the act of writing they save up for the rainy day when memory fails and their minds can no longer recapture the past. Yet Trollope's sense of impermanence and his compulsion to fix life by "getting it down" are extraordinary even for a novelist. A man who writes forty-seven novels and millions of words, who creates thousands of characters, personal relationships, and conversations, is a man who fears that the blurring flux of life will obliterate all that he has known and thought important. Trollope wanted desperately to record his imaginative insight into the passing scene, and he reacted against the transience of his world by trying to get as much of it as he could down on the page. The power of change took hold of his creative being and never let go.

---

[8] *Ibid.*, chap. IV, pp. 51–52.

2
The Clutch of History

From the beginning Trollope insisted on what Arnold Kettle calls "the inter-relatedness of social life."[1] Few if any English novelists before him had conveyed as explicitly as he does in *The Macdermots of Ballycloran* the interdependence of private lives and political conditions. His steady interest in the effects of history and of power relationships on everyday life made him essentially a political novelist.

He saw the individual human will circumscribed by the demands of time and place, and he allowed free will less play than most contemporary novelists. The idea of historical inevitability is very strong in his early work. History figures in his books as an omnipotent god of change, a judge of men on earth whose decisions are beyond appeal, just as it does in Carlyle's *French Revolution*, Macaulay's *History of England*, and various works by Marx—all of which were written in the ten-year period during which Trollope began his career (1843).

His first three novels, *The Macdermots, The Kellys and The O'Kellys*, and *La Vendée*, have generally been ignored or dismissed as false starts, but they shed indispensable light on his mind and art. He set the first two in Ireland and the third in Revolutionary France; they have nothing directly to do with the anatomy of English life on which he made

---

[1] Arnold Kettle, *An Introduction to the English Novel*, 2 vols. (New York, 1960), I, 190.

his reputation. Yet in them emerges the typical Trollopian situation of people unwillingly caught up and menaced by change. He found he could represent broad historical changes by a few carefully drawn characters rooted in a particular environment. Also, there began to develop the conflict between his emotional conservatism and his intellectual, pragmatic liberalism, which animates so much of his writing.

I

The little-known *Macdermots of Ballycloran* (1843–1845)[2] is one of the few novels by an early Victorian that contains a genuinely tragic sense of life. Though it has its share of trashy verbiage, it also has passages of undiluted tragedy and pessimistic honesty which Trollope never surpassed and which are hardly equaled in all Victorian fiction. A deep strain of pessimism was always part of his nature, and from down-and-out Ireland, where he lived in the forties, and the woeful Irish he took a subject matter that could have no happy ending.

Trollope's biographers Richard and Lucy Stebbins claim that with good editing *The Macdermots* "could have ranked among the very finest of English novels."[3] The story is about the abasement and final disintegration of the Macdermots, an Irish Catholic family. All in all, Trollope tells it without flinching from the terrible consequences which have logically to follow once he sets the grim circumstances. Despite the long irrelevant scenes of "comic relief," he does not compromise the grisly fate of the Macdermots and the miserable Ireland in which they live.

Thady Macdermot, a well-meaning but bewildered young

---

[2] Dates of composition for Trollope's novels are given in parentheses when the novels are introduced for discussion. See Michael Sadlier, *Trollope: A Commentary* (London, 1951), pp. 406–413, for a complete chronology of Trollope's life and the composition and publication of his writings.

[3] Richard and Lucy Stebbins, *The Trollopes: The Chronicle of a Writing Family* (New York, 1945), p. 117.

man, has to bear all the family responsibilities. His sister Feemy, a passionate and ignorant girl, loves the caddish Protestant neighborhood police captain, Myles Ussher. Thady is the first of Trollope's characters to feel the threat of the future and the crushing power of change. Like so many characters to follow, he tries to defend the status quo, in this case the relatively high position of his family in the community. In order to maintain a semblance of family honor and respectability, Thady has to perform two tasks. First, he must keep the estate from falling outright into the hands of the creditors, either by collecting rent from tenants who cannot pay, or by persuading the creditors to give the family some sort of face-saving bargain. Also, he feels he must keep his wild sister Feemy from running off with Ussher before he can make Ussher marry her.

But Thady fails completely. He has too much heart to evict the peasants, and his stupidly stubborn father, Larry, will not make the necessary compromise that would stave off ruin. Finally, in trying to protect his sister he brings about his own death. One night he finds Captain Ussher carrying off Feemy. Thinking Ussher is kidnapping her—she is actually going off willingly as his mistress—Thady accidentally kills him. Because Ussher was a policeman, the authorities prosecute Thady severely as an example to the rebellious peasantry. For an acquittal he needs the testimony of his sister, but before she can testify she dies of a pregnancy complication—Ussher had gotten her with child. After Thady's conviction, they hang him. The only surviving Macdermot at the end is old Larry, the father, indignantly sipping his grog and living in a shell of imbecility. Trollope sets down this bleak tale in a matter-of-fact way without any moralistic hand-wringing, and the novel still has shocking force.

From a decade's experience in Ireland (1841–1851), he learned something he never forgot: the course of social history sometimes moves inexorably, seemingly untouched by individual or collective human will; men with the best intentions in the world can be helpless in determining the future. History was grinding the Irish down. Nobody wanted Ireland to be in misery, but no one seemed able to do anything about it. According to the historian R. B. McDowell, "Irish history, for the first half of the nineteenth century, was characterized by failure."[4] The terrible plight of the country gives the novel its form. The fall of the Macdermots leaves the whole countryside around them in chaotic desolation. Trollope took a huge conglomeration of historical facts about the Ireland of 1835–1845 and put it all in his first book.

In the introductory chapter he indicates that the Macdermot estate, Ballycloran, will embody the Irish condition. It "brought into my mind," Trollope says, "thoughts of wrong, oppression, misery, and despair"[5]—thoughts, in other words, that any sensitive, well-informed Victorian might have if he thought about Ireland. But the story of the Macdermots does more than loosely allegorize Irish history; it also shows how historical process can implacably determine human life. Trollope creates characters of depth, but he makes them impotent in a tragedy of circumstances. Historical determinism rules the whole moral and physical environment in which they live, and once we grasp that fact and all it implies, we can see how remarkable this first novel was for its time.

The poor Macdermots remind us sometimes of those trapped people in Thomas Hardy's world. But in Trollope it is the clutch of history, rather than, as in Hardy, some hostile cosmic fate, that breaks lives. He stresses the changing conditions of Ireland and links his story to the reality of the times. It is almost certain that a family in debt, like the Macdermots, will not be able to get out of debt in a declining economy; that ill-educated people cannot gain under-

[4] R. B. McDowell, *Public Opinion and Governmental Policy in Ireland 1801–1846* (London, 1952), p. 15.

[5] *The Macdermots of Ballycloran* (London: John Lane, The Bodley Head, 1906), chap. I, p. 5.

standing about their lives in an impoverished culture; that
a policeman like Captain Ussher, who is picked for professional ruthlessness in dealing with a class of people, will be
ruthless in his personal relations with that class; that violence
will break out in an unstable land; and that a man who kills
a law officer in a place where authority feels threatened will
be severely punished.

Trollope gives a frank and sympathetic treatment of coarse
people and their brutal lives which is exceptional in a Victorian novel and, for that matter, in almost any previous
English novel. There is little of the typical Victorian passing
of moral judgment upon characters and their actions, because
Trollope conceives of these people as prisoners of history
without the freedom of moral choice. He describes one scene
in which Feemy, having bound herself tightly in a corset so
that no one will see that she is pregnant, passes out from the
pain. His quiet neutral tone makes this all the more convincing and terrible. He points no literary finger of guilt at
the girl. A trapped animal, he implies, will act desperately.

In the world of *The Macdermots* the social and moral fervor of mid-century England, with its ethical and religious
conviction, and its theories of self-help, progress, and reform,
have little or no meaning. Trollope was trying to understand
and explain a kind of life whose essence was necessarily
tragic. He wanted his own countrymen to realize that Ireland
was not England and that the uniqueness of the Irish historical experience meant that the life in this book could not
be measured and judged by English values. Unlike most
contemporary novels describing suffering and misery—novels
such as *Oliver Twist, Sybil,* and *Alton Locke—The Macdermots* has no black and white characters, no polemics, and
no solutions.

II

Unfortunately for Trollope, influential reviewers decided
that the genteel reading public ought not to waste its time on

an un-English country and a depressing tragedy of determinism. *The Athenaeum* castigated him for writing "miserable Irish stories," and *The Spectator* said: "The subject is not well-chosen . . . the morale is indifferent. The persons are too coarse and sordid, the incidents too low to inspire sympathy. . . . The matters of the story should excite an interest which we cannot feel for the characters, either as gentry or peasants, because they belong to neither."[6] There is one incident of special horror for which, presumably, *The Spectator* felt no sympathy. The evicted tenants of Ballycloran avenge themselves on the new owner by waylaying him and hacking off his foot with an axe:

> The instrument fell on his leg, just above the ankle, with all the man's force; the first blow only cut his trousers and his boot, and bruised him sorely, for his boots protected him; the second cut his flesh, and grated against the bone; in vain he struggled violently and with all the force of man struggling for his life; a third, and a fourth, and a fifth descended, crushing the bone, dividing the marrow, and ultimately severing the foot from the leg.
> . . . He got up and hobbled to the nearest cabin, dragging after him the mutilated foot which still attached itself to his body by some cartileges which had not been severed.[7]

No wonder the provincial guardians of the Victorian bourgeoisie objected! This passage is no fantasy of revolution to titillate middle-class sensibilities, such as we sometimes find in Disraeli and Dickens. It shows the very basis of revolutionary feeling: such a clear, naked will to personal vengeance against an exploiter that the most cruel act can come to seem a simple matter of justice. Trollope shows no indignation over this crime. Yahoos though these tenants may be, he imagined that history had victimized them. The immediate brutality of life in the novel is probably unequaled in

---

[6] See Launce O. Tingay, "The Reception of Trollope's First Novel," *Nineteenth-Century Fiction* (Dec. 1951), pp. 195–236.

[7] *The Macdermots*, chap. xxv, p. 447.

Victorian literature, and it was too much for squeamish British readers—especially since hundreds of thousands of Irishmen were starving to death when *The Macdermots* was published (1847).

Trollope himself was struck by this land and people so different from his own. Ireland was a place where change meant only change for the worse for the great majority, where each new year brought deepening depression instead of hope. One of the most original and impressive parts of the novel is Thady's escape after the murder to the peasants who hide him out. Trollope's sullen peasants seem unique in English fiction. They are neither the sometimes picturesque, often warlike peasants of Scott, nor the comic and practical peasants of Maria Edgeworth, but a surly, idle, hunger-numbed lot who live completely fogged in by ignorance and poverty. They have nothing left to do but brew illegal potheen, harass the police, and cadge or steal potatoes. Some, like Thady's old host, just stay inside, stare at four walls, and wait for death. They blend perfectly into the mood of the book. Like the Macdermots, they are doomed to live in a world whose ghastly conditions have been unalterably predetermined for them.

Michael Sadleir complains that Trollope, in *The Macdermots*, "lapses readily into either sociology or politics" from "the thoughts and doings of his men and women."[8] But in the novel Trollope is contending that the lives of individual men and women cannot be separated from the sociology and politics of their time and place. For example, what happens to the people in this story depends on the fact that Ireland is, in effect, a British colony. Because an irresponsible absentee landowner sucks the wealth out of the town of Mohill, the peasants of Mohill must live in degrading poverty, hatching up sedition. Thady dies because the ankle-

---

[8] *Trollope: A Commentary*, p. 141.

chopping affair makes the colonial "magistrates and the government imagine that the country was in a disorderly state generally, and that it was therefore necessary to follow up the prosecution with more than ordinary vigor."[9] *The Macdermots* is one of the most powerful indictments of colonialism written in the nineteenth century.

The tremendously insecure society in which the characters exist destroys the power of civilization. This failure of rationality and the triumph of chaos in the book help explain Trollope's emotional conservatism. The Macdermots and their tenants have nothing to build on because they cannot be sure of their land from one day to the next. Everyone, even the authorities who fear the people, dreads some sudden and disastrous change. Trollope does not think real civilization is possible under such unstable conditions. People menaced by violent change will react violently to keep what they have, as they do in the novel. Tradition and custom can give at least a little of the stability on which civilization rests.

But the characters in *The Macdermots* have no way of controlling their unstable world, and that is why Trollope has such great pity for them. He shows a compassion here that he never lost. In all of Trollope, we find fewer cheap moral victories over "wicked" characters than we find in any other Victorian novelist. He was the most tolerant writer of his time because he knew so well that historical circumstances alter cases. Here is the way he describes Thady sitting in his cell waiting for trial:

From the years to which his earliest memory could fall back, he had been fighting an earnest, hard battle with the world's cares, and though not thoroughly vanquished, he had always been worsted. . . . Few men in any rank of life had known so little joy as he had done, or had so little pleasure; his only object in life had been to drive the wolf from

---

[9] *The Macdermots*, chap. xxv, p. 448.

his father's door and to keep a roof over him and his sister.

Had patient industry and constant toil been able to have effected this, he would have been perhaps not happy, but not discontented; this however, circumstances had put out of his power, and he felt that the same uncontrollable circumstances had now brought him into his present position. He knew little of the Grecian's doctrine of necessity; but he had it in his heart that night, when he felt himself innocent, and was at the same time assured that all the kind efforts of his friends would not save him from his fate—a hangman's rope. . . .[10]

No one would call this distinguished prose, but in context it is extremely moving; it states with flat finality the unfairness of life and the inability of a good man to master the conditions of his existence.

The spirit of the whole book and Trollope's view of Irish life probably are best represented in old Larry Macdermot. A babbling, incoherent man, he symbolizes the common human response of befuddlement to a changing world. He takes on the proportion of a mythic creation. When life gives him new and unpleasant terms on which to live, he cannot adjust. Shutting the real world out and withdrawing inwardly, he lives in the past, builds up fantasies, believes only what he wants to believe, loses all judgment, escapes into drunken dreams, and wallows in lethargic incompetence and finally insanity. His life serves as a tragic pattern of waste both in this novel and in the Ireland of that age, but it serves also as a pattern for the defeat which mutability can inflict on man at any time.

Trollope would never again write such an absolutely tragic book, and he would seldom give determinism such a complete tyranny over human affairs. He would always, however, write about people caught up in the changing currents of their own times, and link these characters to the major forces and issues of the real contemporary society.

---

[10] *Ibid.*, chap. xxix, p. 529.

III

When he began his second book, *The Kellys and The O'Kellys* (1847), he set out to write a historical novel in the manner of Scott. *The Kellys* opens with a long and absorbing account of O'Connell's trial in 1844 and its rousing effects on the Irish, much as *The Heart of Midlothian* begins with an account of the Porteous Riot. Within this historical framework Trollope set up a conflict between Kelly, a poor Irish Catholic, and Lynch, a Protestant, Irish-hating Anglo-Irishman. At first he skillfully relates their action to the historical patterns of Irish and English behavior. But he soon drops historical reality and lets the novel degenerate into a stereotyped love story. We find no coherent connection between the lives of his people and the setting in which they live. What they do or undergo often defies all logic. At one point the pathetic, mistreated Irish girl Anty Lynch lies on her deathbed—hopelessly ill, Trollope tells us. For half the novel she suffers from the greed and hardness of the Irish world. Living in a doomed land, she herself is doomed by her environment, and Trollope exclaims about her inevitable fate, "Necessity how stern she is." But suddenly, like a miracle-healer, he cures her! When she blithely gets up to go off, marry, have children, and live happily ever after—all this in a ruined land—"Necessity" just fades away into fantasy, and the novel loses all credibility. If, at the end of *The Idiot*, Prince Myshkin were dusted off and sent happily away to marry Cinderella, the effect would be the same. Trying for better sales with his second book, Trollope hoped to flutter hearts with the loveliness of love and the goodness of good. Instead, he spoiled a promising book.

But *The Kellys*, though much inferior to *The Macdermots*, was important in Trollope's development. He learned to populate a whole fictional world with all kinds of people—aristocrats, Protestant ministers, lawyers, doctors, hunting people, as well as Joyce-like racing touts, cronies, and hangers-on—as he would later do in the Barset series. He found he could exploit the clash of incongruous values and social attitudes between all these different types and generations for comic purposes, something he would do over and over in his novels about English life. He also began articulating the pet myths of the literate middle classes, such as the wickedness of the nobility, the pushing incivility of the lower classes, and the idea of the female as moral savior.

It becomes obvious in *The Kellys* that, to be compelling, Trollope's characters need to be bound up intimately with an actual environment. Barry Lynch is the most impressive character in the book largely because, in his savage drunkenness, his backbiting, and his obsessive greed, he seems a totally convincing figure in his frightful Irish world. On the other hand, Lord Ballindine has no reality about him whatsoever, and he soon palls. Nothing that is particular to his Irish community touches him, nothing shows that he experiences anything different from what an English lord might. Few of Trollope's people can stand out of context like a Don Quixote or a Mrs. Gamp. They must live in a realistic and changing world.

IV

Trollope's third novel, the historical romance *La Vendée* (1849), is the worst book he ever wrote, but surprisingly it shows clearly the characteristic world view that shapes his fiction. What matters about it is not the story, but Trollope's interest in political power and historical movement. The western French province Vendée refused to accept the French Revolution and, after the execution of Louis XVI, rebelled against the First Republic. Trollope sympathetically follows a band of heroic royalists from the beginning of the uprising to its final suppression by the government.[11]

---

[11] See *The Memoirs of the Madame de La Rochejacquelein*, trans. David Wilson (London, 1827), on which Trollope relies heavily in *La Vendée*.

The conservative, tradition-loving Vendéeans hate the revolutionary changes of the republicans and react violently. But of course the real Vendéeans were destroyed; and so their cause in the novel is lost, and most of the characters die as victims of history.

What happens in *La Vendée* is not very different in form from what usually happens in Trollope's novels about British life: the forces of change pour over those who try to wrap themselves in the security of the past, no matter how noble they and their aims may be. Men must somehow recognize change and adapt themselves to it whether they want to or not. His interest in this particular historical episode reveals a special quality of mind. He wrote *La Vendée* during the disturbed late forties, a revolutionary period in Europe. It shows the contemporary English fear that the French Revolution might be transplanted across the channel. What is remarkable is that Trollope, a foe of revolution and a supporter of conservatism, chose this time to write about a chapter of history in which the traditionalist, counterrevolutionary force fails abysmally. He had a deep distrust of the tide of change and a simultaneous awareness that this tide ineluctably touches and sometimes overwhelms the world.

There is a strong parallel between his choice of a rural, conservative people as his subject here and his customary choice later on of clergymen, landowners, and government officials. Love for old-fashioned life and the virtues of the country, fear of democracy, and belief in responsible hierarchy appear in *La Vendée* as they do in his English novels, but so does his conviction that mutability somehow always wins.

The conflict in *La Vendée* between a feudal provincial group and the cold force of national centralization undoubtedly owes much to Scott. But Trollope had none of Scott's gifts for historical epic, and the difference between the two writers is important. As recent criticism has shown, Scott's stories and heroes often have intrinsic allegorical interest.

He creates at certain moments metaphors which make clear
crucial points in the whole sweep of European history. The
typical hero of the Waverly Novels is not a realistic man,
but something larger than life—almost a symbol for Western
consciousness at a given period of history. Trollope at times
may also write symbolically, but he is good only when he
shows empathy for an individualized, quirky human being
living in a contemporary historical context. *La Vendée* fails
because, though the action has symbolic significance, the
characters are not interesting in themselves. They have no
more real substance than balloons with painted faces.

The one exception is Robespierre, the destroyer of La
Vendée. In his characterization, Trollope shows a glimmer-
ing of the balanced tolerance that afterwards distinguishes
his work. For the British privileged classes in the nineteenth
century, Robespierre was a bloody bogeyman, the incar-
nation of revolutionary butchery. Trollope imagines him as
a well-meaning man whose brutality is largely determined
by eighteenth-century history. It is not fair to call him a
moral monster for crushing La Vendée, Trollope says, since
he really did not have the freedom to do otherwise.

Trollope had no talent for costume history, but he had
great skill at interpreting the interplay between a man and
actual historical circumstance. Near the end of his life he
said that his two favorite novels were *Ivanhoe* and *Henry
Esmond* (though in his autobiography he tells us that a
publisher said to him: "Whatever you do don't be historical;
your historical novel is not worth a damn").[12] What he admired in an author and what he brought to his own Victorian world was the knack of putting human nature in a
specific setting and then showing how human nature both
defines and is defined by that setting.

In his first three novels, Trollope follows Scott and Maria
Edgeworth in working to develop a sense of fixed time and

---

[12] Anthony Trollope, *An Autobiography* (London, 1953),
chap. VI, p. 95.

place and in stressing that men are what they are because
of history. He recognizes that things at any minute will
necessarily be different from what they were before, and
that, paradoxically, it is just this mutability that gives universality to human experience. Men are alike because they
all face the ordeal of change.

He sees in this early work—especially in *The Macdermots*
—the pain which historical change causes. The inescapable
tragedy of particular victims of history cannot for him, as
it could for Scott, be redeemed by any notions of general good
or national progress. Change is inevitable, but with change
comes terrible loss for some poor souls. George Eliot said
affectionately of Trollope that he was a man "clinging to
whatever is."[13] The man who clings is a man who feels himself being pulled, and in his first writings Trollope wanted
to make his readers understand how people could be and
were pulled down by history. When he finally turned to
English life, the clutch of history, though less deadly, would
be just as powerful.

-----

[13] *The George Eliot Letters*, ed. Gordon S. Haight, 6 vols.
(New Haven, 1955), IV, 81–82.

3
Changing England: Problems, Compromise, And Comic Possibilities

G. M. Young has said, "Of all the decades in our history, a wise man would choose the eighteen-fifties to be young in."[1] Returning home from Ireland in 1851, Trollope looked around him at the great transformation that was taking place in English life. Change brought difficulties to England, but unlike the change in Ireland, it was also bringing prosperity and hope. Exactly how, where, and why was the Victorian world moving, and what was all this sweeping social change likely to mean for typical Englishmen? Barsetshire gives us Trollope's answer.

In *The Warden, Barchester Towers*, and *Doctor Thorne*, he realized the comic potential of his world. Barset, where he set these three of his first four complete novels of English life, may be, as Hawthorne put it, "just as real as if some giant had hewn a great lump out of the earth and put it under a glass case, with all its inhabitants going about their daily business";[2] but it is also a miniature England being hurled forward by the gigantic forces of history. The changing times of the fifties provided wonderful opportunities for

---

[1] See George H. Ford, "The Victorian Age," *The Norton Anthology of English Literature*, 2 vols. (New York, 1962), II, 636–637, for this quotation and for corroboration of Young.

[2] See Anthony Trollope, *An Autobiography* (London, 1953), chap. VIII, p. 125.

social comedy. There is something inherently funny in the clash of newfangledness with old fashions, in a meeting, for example, between a freethinking bohemian and a staid bishop. In Barset, the new and the old continually jangle against each other, but somehow, the jarring of the past and future improves the quality of life.

Especially in his books written from 1853 to 1858, Trollope developed and became a master of the comedy of change. He liked to juxtapose radically different kinds of behavior in the face of changing conditions and to show the folly, the variety, and the joy of mid-Victorian life. His novels of the period have their black—sometimes very black—moments. We find in them, as in so much of Victorian literature, an elegiac note for a way of life that was passing. He made no attempt to gloss over the problems or the maladjustments of the times. But for the middle classes, at least, the decade was promising, and happy endings seemed realistically possible. The Barsetshire of these early books makes the phrase "Victorian compromise" come clear; it is a place where the claims of the world and the individual conscience can be reconciled, where, in Crane Brinton's words, "Victorian civilization is more than a mere struggle."[3]

I

"The function of the nineteenth century," writes G. M. Young, "was to disengage the disinterested intelligence, to release it from the entanglements of party and sect . . . and to set it operating over the whole range of human life."[4] We find a perfect example of Trollope's "disinterested intelligence" in The Warden (1852–1853). He took the public controversy over ecclesiastical income and the larger issue of reform and turned it into a novel of poise and beauty. Journalistic reports—including one in Dickens's Household

---

[3] Crane Brinton, English Political Thought in the Nineteenth Century (New York, 1962), p. 87.

[4] G. M. Young, Victorian England, Portrait of an Age (London, 1960), p. 186.

Words[5]—about Church abuse of endowment funds made him wonder just what impact an impersonal reform movement might have on the people directly affected. *The Warden* gets at the complexity of motives and feelings involved in reform. In his unassuming way Trollope makes clear the moral dilemma that progress can bring.

With all its light and sometimes awkward playfulness, *The Warden* is a very serious novel. Trollope barely does allow the comic possibilities in the story to win over its tragic potential. We have here, in its simplest form, the typical Trollopian situation of a man whose mode of life is suddenly challenged by changing conditions in his world. "[Harding] felt that he would give almost anything—much more than he knew he ought to do—to relieve himself from the storm which he feared was coming. It was so hard that the pleasant waters of his little stream should be disturbed and muddied by rough hands; that his quiet paths should be made a battlefield; that the unobtrusive corner of the world which had been allotted to him, as though by Providence, should be invaded and desecrated, and all within it made miserable and unsound."[6] The problem which Trollope poses for Mr. Harding lies at the heart of all of his best fiction: "Now that I must rearrange my life, what should I do in these new circumstances?" How his characters go about resolving this question forms the most valuable part of his writing. *The Warden* is a prologue to all of Trollope's work in tone, subject matter, and particular concerns. The balance, the stress on conciliation, the fear of dehumanizing utilitarianism, the celebration of modest private life that we find here, remain constant in his writing.

Harding, a clergyman and warden of Hiram's Hospital for old workingmen, is one of his great creations. He is both a unique figure and a kind of unheroic hero for modern times:

---

[5] See Michael Sadleir, *Trollope: A Commentary* (London, 1951), pp. 164–165.
[6] *The Warden* (London, 1961), chap. v, p. 65.

an often ineffectual and ridiculous man who has little control over his era, but who conscientiously faces up to the
necessity of making moral choices. The backers of reform
charge that he unwittingly takes money which the Church
ought to give his wards. Archdeacon Grantly, his domineer-
ing son-in-law, orders him to stand firm against this attack
on Church privilege. Harding always tries to do the right
thing, but ambitious men, irresistible social forces, and his
family constantly push and pull him about. Knowing that
new times make new demands on one, he finally chooses, a
bit wistfully, to do what best seems to reconcile his ethical
standards with the world around him.

Not only Harding's plight, but the concrete difficulties of
reform and change in the story give us a shock of recognition.
Personal and party motives determine the sides over the
hospital dispute, and the real merits of the case get lost. John
Bold leads the attack on Harding's revenue. A young, enthusiastic reformer who loves ideal justice, he botches things
because he knows nothing about the lives of those he wants
to change. He understands neither himself nor the way he
affects others. Trollope calls him a good man, but one characterized by "arrogance of thought, unsustained by first-rate
abilities, and that attempt at being better than his neighbors
which jarred painfully on the feelings."[7] The other moving
spirit of change, Tom Towers, an editorial writer for *The
Jupiter*, loves reform issues because they help him build his
own power and the power of the press. On the other side of
the question stand the worldly Grantly, who cares above all
about family dignity and Church prerogative, and the ruthless, efficient attorney-general, Haphazard, who despises
idealism of any kind. Trollope makes narrow-mindedness,
selfishness, dogmatism, professionalism, and the inability to
sympathize with others the major obstacles in dealing properly with change.

---

[7] *Barchester Towers* (London, 1960), chap. II, p. 13.

Of all the Victorian novelists, Trollope best understands the relationship between a man and his work. The sanctification of work by the Victorian middle classes, and their professional pride, caused new problems. Neither Grantly nor Tom Towers, for example, can separate his opinion as a private citizen from what he considers to be good for his professional status. In *The Warden*, Trollope begins developing his theme that work comes more and more to determine identity, that what a man does tells him who he is. Clergymen in all the Barset novels are tempted to regard the ministry as a job rather than a calling and to see themselves as a worldly professional class. The drive for professional prestige muffles individual conscience. In Trollope occupational loyalties sometimes outweigh all other loyalties. The parody of Burns in *The Three Clerks* (written in 1857 between *Barchester Towers* and *Doctor Thorne*) shows the hold that he felt a man's job had come to have on him:

> My heart's at my office, my heart is always there:
> My heart's at my office, docketing with care,
> Docketing the papers and copying all day,
> My heart's at the office, though I be far away.[8]

With his satire on the journalist Towers, Trollope declared his running war against a wayward press and the whole Victorian band of would-be mass-circulation sibyls and Cassandras. He realized both the potential force of public opinion and the tyrannical hold which the press was gaining on it. Towers says, " 'The public is defrauded whenever private considerations are allowed to have weight'," but Trollope continues in his own voice: "Quite true, thou greatest oracle of the middle of the Nineteenth Century, thou sententious proclaimer of the purity of the press—the public is defrauded when it is purposely misled. Poor public! how often it is misled!"[9] In *The Three Clerks* he blasts the moral presump-

---

[8] *The Three Clerks* (London, 1959), chap. XXII, p. 241.
[9] *The Warden*, chap. XV, p. 190.

tion of the press: "'It's the intention of the *Daily Delight* [says a character], always to uphold a career of virtue to the lower classes as a thing that pays. Honesty, high wages, and hot dinners. Those are our principles'."[10] Tom Towers actually knows nothing about Harding's affair, but ignorance does not stop him from pronouncing judgment in *The Jupiter*. Trollope hated the press for its sensationalism, inaccuracy, and arrogant pomposity.

His witty parodies of Carlyle and Dickens as Dr. Pessimist Anticant and Mr. Popular Sentiment also satirize the self-righteousness and oversimplified morality of the Victorian sages. Mr. Sentiment writes a novel called *The Almshouse* with a caricature of Harding: "What story was ever written without a demon? What novel, what history, what work of any sort, what world, would be perfect without existing principles of both good and evil? The demon of *The Almshouse* was the clerical owner of this comfortable abode. He was a man well stricken in years, but still strong to do evil: he was one who looked cruelly out of a hot, passionate, bloodshot eye."[11]

Trollope is insisting in *The Warden* that moral questions in an age of transitions are not easy. The secular pundit for the masses forgets sometimes that he pontificates, not about abstractions or statistics, but about flesh and blood. In solving complex problems, it does no good to set up wicked straw men to hate or to propose simplistic answers. Trollope wanted to show the harm that the high priests of public opinion can do. The individual human being often gets lost in their generalizations, and polemics blur the uniqueness of each case.

What Anthony Cockshut calls Trollope's "deep-rooted emotional conservatism"[12] shows through in his satire on

---

[10] *The Three Clerks*, chap. XXII, p. 242.

[11] *The Warden*, chap. XV, pp. 192–193.

[12] Anthony Cockshut, *Anthony Trollope, A Critical Study* (London, 1955), p. 177.

the zealous reformers and most obviously in his fearful attitudes toward urban power. Bold, Towers, *The Jupiter*, the success-happy parvenu, Haphazard, and all the rest of the dynamic men who disrupt Harding's placid Barchester life come out of London. The growing influence of London over country life and the physical and moral ugliness of the city impressed Trollope. The city, with its horror, becomes a new Chapel Perilous through which Mr. Harding must pass in trying to set his life in order. His visit to London turns into a comic nightmare:

A slipshod girl ushered him into a long back room, filled with boxes for the accommodation of parties, in one of which he took his seat. In a more miserably forlorn place he could not have found himself; the room smelt of fish and sawdust, and stale tobacco smoke, with a slight taint of escaped gas; everything was rough, and dirty, and disreputable; the cloth which they put before him was abominable; the knives and forks were bruised, and hacked, and filthy; and everything was impregnated with fish. He had one comfort, however; he was quite alone; there was no one there to look on his dismay; nor was it probable that any one would come to do so. It was a London supper-house.[13]

Harding passes his test of courage and is able to retreat into the comparatively wholesome life of Barset, but London power has changed Barset at the end of the book. It is not as cozy for Harding as it was in the beginning. *The Warden* has a touch of the pastorale about it, as do all the novels of this period. But the pastorale is a genre which blooms, after all, in times of urbanization, and it almost always shows man's irrepressible will to fashion for himself "the good old days." Trollope's whole image of Barset shows that he both longs for the communal comforts of county provincialism and recognizes the slow, inevitable suburbanization of modern life.

---

[13] *The Warden*, chap. XVI, p. 208.

The conservative's deepest fear is that change will be for the worse, and this sad kind of change takes place in the novel. At the beginning Trollope writes, "Hiram's Hospital . . . is a picturesque building. . . . A broad gravel walk runs between the building and the river, which is always trim and cared for. . . . Further from the water . . . are the pretty oriel windows of Mr. Harding's house, and his well-mown lawn."[14] At the end, we get another view: "The whole place has become disordered and ugly. The warden's garden is a wretched wilderness, the drive and paths are covered with weeds, the flower-beds are bare, and the unshorn lawn is now a mass of long damp grass and unwholesome moss. The beauty of the place is gone; its attractions have withered."[15] The change in the landscape symbolizes the change for the hospital residents. The ignorant workingmen find themselves at the close with no Mr. Harding to take care of them. They have been mere pawns in a political controversy. No one has seen them as individual men, except Harding, and when he goes they become wretched, lonely, old people, still hoping vainly for more money, but finding only emptiness.

II

And yet despite the low-key tragedy of the hospital, the comic possibilities of this world *are* realized. The marriage of John Bold and Harding's daughter Eleanor shows human affection triumphing over party spirit. But the real comic affirmation in the novel is Harding himself. Mr. Harding, a single man, matters more to Trollope than the hospital community, and *The Warden* becomes one of the best expressions of Victorian faith in individualism.

Harding's gain overshadows the communal loss. By resigning quietly when he does not have to, and giving up his income against the advice of Haphazard and Grantly, he

---

[14] Chap. I, pp. 6–7.
[15] Chap. XXI, p. 261.

gains self-respect and asserts the integrity of his conscience.
The pressures of change give him the opportunity to live up
to the ideals of his religion and put moral concerns before
his own worldly interests. For Trollope, the health of society
and peace of mind rest ultimately on the strength of personal
conscience and the ability of men to act unselfishly. As long
as he sees the force of changing circumstances leading to a
victory of moral conscience, his comic vision prevails.

The rhetoric of Trollope's fiction works here in a delicate
and effective way. It ought to convince us, in the end, how
successful, if unlikely, a man Harding is in becoming what
the existentialists call an "authentic" human being. For a
good part of the novel Trollope makes Harding a sometimes
weak, bumbling, and laughable creature. We tend to think
of him as amusing and kind but ineffectual—his habit, when
things go wrong, of letting his hands play imaginary dirges
on an imaginary cello sums up his harmless futility. Yet by
the end of the novel, if we understand what Trollope tells
and shows us, we have to stop patronizing Harding or we
stand convicted of serious moral failings. If we think of him
as inconsequential, then we identify ourselves with the point
of view of the cold materialistic Haphazard, which reduces
human worth to a matter of cash balances and Who's Who
listings. If Harding seems too slight a figure to be significant,
then we find ourselves agreeing with Tom Towers that only
the sensational surfaces of life with headline potential
count. If we think that Harding's qualms about staying at
the hospital are foolish, then we take the dogmatic Grantly
view that makes private conscience seem unimportant. Unlike Grantly, Harding can act against narrowly parochial
interests; unlike Haphazard, he does not need worldly status
and success to prove to himself that he is worthy; and unlike
Towers, his ego does not require power over others: he can
make his decision about the hospital without insisting that
everyone else think as he does. Harding is sure enough of
himself to respect the freedom and conscience of others.

Trollope's moral rhetoric works in two ways. First of all,

it persuades us that almost anybody has, like Harding, the capacity for independent, conscientious moral action; Harding, after all, is often ridiculous, and he has no great genius or force of character. But the rhetoric also shows us how hard it is for a man to resist outside pressures and *use* that capacity. To act independently and morally can mean upsetting the whole pattern of one's life. A passage that comes after Harding has just told Grantly that he is resigning reveals Trollope's subtle rhetoric: "Had he not cause for triumph? Had he not been supremely successful? Had he not for the first time in his life held his own purpose against that of his son-in-law, and manfully combated against great odds —against the archdeacon's wife as well as the archdeacon? Had he not gained a great victory and was it not fit that he should step into his cab with triumph?"[16]

At first it appears that Trollope is being ironical. Standing up to Grantly may be a moral victory for timid little Harding, but for anyone else it would be a small triumph, and his pride is comic. Our next reaction ought to be to ask ourselves what kind of thing an act of conscience is. Moral courage does not usually mean making a grand gesture of universal significance or championing some cause that everyone around you believes in. Most often, it means upholding a point of view when those close to you, who have power to hurt you, disagree. Harding is funny—a few proud thoughts and a splurge on a cab can make a celebration for him—but he is also admirable. He can do that difficult thing of "holding his own purpose." In this characterization, Trollope challenges and broadens our conception of what it is to be a superior person.

The problems of change loom large in *The Warden*, but he saw how the changing world could help to make a man aware of his individuality and free his "disinterested intelligence." Harding not only makes a satisfactory moral adjustment to the times, he positively changes his own life for the

---

[16] Chap. XIX, p. 238.

better. Out of the Barchester clash between impersonal reform and stand-pat rigidity comes his hard-won, faintly
comic, yet beautiful serenity at the end.

Mr. Harding is still precentor of Barchester; and it is very
rarely the case that those who attend the Sunday morning
service miss the gratification of hearing him chant the litany
as no other man in England can do it . . . . Mr. Harding, we
say, is not an unhappy man: he keeps his lodgings, but they
are of little use to him, except as being the one spot on earth
which he calls his own. His time is spent chiefly at his daughter's or at the palace; he is never left alone, even should he
wish to be so; and within twelve months of Eleanor's marriage his determination to live at his own lodging had been
broken so far through and abandoned, that he consented to
have his violoncello permanently removed to his daughter's
house.
    Every other day a message is brought to him from the
bishop. "The bishop's compliments, and his lordship is not
very well today, and he hopes Mr. Harding will dine with
him." This bulletin as to the old man's health is a myth; for
though he is over eighty he is never ill, and will probably die
some day, as a spark goes out, gradually and without a
struggle. Mr. Harding does dine with him very often, which
means going to the palace at three and remaining till ten;
and whenever he does not the bishop whines, and says that
the port wine is corked, and complains that nobody attends
to him and frets himself off to bed an hour before his time.
    It was long before the people of Barchester forgot to call
Mr. Harding by his long well-known name of Warden. It had
become so customary to say Mr. Warden, that it was not
easily dropped. "No, no," he always says when so addressed,
"not warden now, only precentor."[17]

But he really is still warden—a self-deprecating warden now
of the discriminating private conscience on which personal
and communal happiness rest.

---

[17] Chap. XXI, pp. 263–264.

III

Barchester Towers (1855–1856) is the story of a community rather than of one man. It is Trollope's finest comic novel and one of the best in English. In *The Warden* he had begun to discover the comic possibilities in the lives of churchmen and their families, and by expanding Barchester he shaped a comic interpretation of his whole middle-class Victorian world. Barsetshire becomes a little England; outwardly calm and secure, it seethes with ambition, passion, contradictions, idealism, banality, and change of all sorts. In *Barchester Towers*, Trollope helps define for us the special richness and value of Victorian civilization.

His comedy takes as its starting point the incongruity between the ideal of the Church as a spiritual entity and the reality of the Church as a temporal organization—a going concern, in fact, in which people like the Proudies and Mr. Slope can shove their way to the top. Nothing is surer about the Victorian age than the power of religion and the church. Ecclesiastical affairs probably mattered more to a larger percentage of the people than they had for two centuries. Since organized religion was so important a part of the middle-class Victorians' search for meaning and stability, so interfused into the texture of national life, Trollope felt that the behavior of clergymen and the workings of Church institutions would inevitably reveal the tone and substance of English society.

Paradoxically the Church was becoming more and more secular. There is a lot of fervor about religious decorum and policy in *Barchester Towers*, but none of that mystical force of faith which stabs into men's minds. A cleric dedicated to preserving the mysteries of religion remarks, " 'Everything has gone by I believe. . . . The cigar has been smoked out and we are the ashes'." He then goes on to predict the workings of the modern secular state: " 'The Government is to find us all in everything and the press is to find the government'."[18]

---

[18] *Barchester Towers*, chap. XXXIV, p. 330.

Trollope was out to prove that the influential clerical establishment, like any other institution, was made up of comic
and worldly people. As men and women came to understand
the huge power that could be exerted through the various
moral and theological establishments, they found a major
outlet for their instinct to dominate others. Where there is
power to be had, people will struggle, and though power
struggles are sometimes frightening, they can be funny too.
Self-important people trying to live up to a lofty position
nearly always behave affectedly, and affectation, as Fielding
says, is the mother of comedy.

Two comic figures, Archdeacon Grantly and Mrs. Proudie,
domineer in the book. They seem to divide between them
the effective worldly power—the power to move and influence other people. Though they battle each other for suprem-
acy, they have a great deal in common. Each characterizes
the era.

Trollope begins with a wonderful scene in which Grantly
waits by the bedside of his dying father, the old bishop. Who
the new Bishop of Barchester will be depends on whether
the old man dies before or after the impending fall of a Conservative Ministry in "July in the year 185—" (Trollope carefully gives the book a realistic setting in moving time).[19]
Grantly knows that if his father dies quickly the Conservatives will probably appoint him bishop:

The ministry were to be out within five days; his father
was to be dead—No, he rejected that view of the subject. . . .
He tried to keep his mind away from the subject, but he could
not. The race was so very close, and the stakes were so very
high. . . . He knew it must be now or never. He was already
over fifty, and there was little chance that his friends who
were now leaving office would soon return to it. No probable British prime minister but he who was now in, he who
was so soon to be out, would think of making a bishop of Dr.
Grantly. Thus he thought long and sadly, in deep silence, and

---

[19] Chap. I, p. 1.

then gazed at that still living face, and then at last dared to ask himself whether he really longed for his father's death. ... The proud, wishful, worldly man, sank on his knees by the bedside, and taking the bishop's hand within his own, prayed eagerly that his sins might be forgiven him.[20]

Trollope, in a short space, gets at the immense polarities and ambivalence in the single human personality and marvelously deepens Grantly's character. The novel opens, then, with a son's wish for his father's death, a guilty conscience, and an example of that drive for power in human nature which can appear at any unseemly time. The longing for place overcomes, for the moment, the churchman's Christian principles. Grantly typifies a whole Victorian state of mind: torn by the wish to rise high in the world's eye and the wish to live within the strict bounds of Christian decorum, he suffers from the knowledge that he fails to live up to his own ideals.

After this beginning, Trollope does something that only a very skillful novelist could successfully do. Without denigrating the bishop's death or Grantly's emotion, he makes comedy out of the situation. When the old man finally dies, Grantly rushes to send a telegram to the government, hoping that the Conservatives will give him the job. But out of propriety, he makes Mr. Harding sign and send it. In the scene of this dutifully grieving son looking after his own bread-and-butter before he arranges the funeral, Trollope sees humor. This is a good instance of what Suzanne Langer calls comic rhythm—the amoral impulse of life asserting itself in the presence of death. Grantly represents one of the great comic paradoxes of nineteenth-century life, the extremely worldly man walking around in clerical garb. He does very well as a metaphor for the whole Victorian age.

So, however, does that apostle of Evangelical thought and action, Mrs. Proudie. Grantly's telegram is too late, and the new Liberal government sends the Proudies down from

---

[20] *Ibid.*, pp. 3–4.

London to Barchester where they derange the old life. Mrs.
Proudie, with her sense of moral duty, her reforming obsession, her Grundyism, her earnest certitude, and her utter
lack of humor, also stands for a whole side of Victorian life.
Like Grantly, she can rise to heights of moral indignation,
but she has more kinetic force than he does—she wants to
change more things.

The growing moral awareness of the nineteenth-century
lay public was slowly but surely causing a secularization of
morality. Trollope shows us the comedy in this when he
imagines his virago, Mrs. Proudie, browbeating the clerical
Barset society. In her unctuous language he parodies the
Evangelical zeal: " 'I fear there is a great deal of Sabbath
travelling here . . . I see that there are three trains in and
three out every Sabbath. . . . Don't you think Dr. Grantly,
that a *little energy might diminish the evil?* Surely we should
look at it differently. You and I, for instance in our position:
surely we should do all that we can to control so grievous a
sin . . . surely, surely,' continued Mrs. Proudie, 'Surely . . . ' "[21]
And on she goes, turning morality into something petty.
Moral awareness had been nurtured and guided by the
Church. Mrs. Proudie lets us see how the Church itself was
coming under the control of a secular society that was obsessed with institutionalizing virtue.

She and Grantly not only give us insights into their age,
they also help us recognize the eternal human comedy of
moral affectation in which earnestness and righteous postur-
ing mask the aggressive will to dominate others. Especially
in Mrs. Proudie, Trollope catches and makes ridiculous that
insufferably offensive tone that always marks the smug
proselyte of a "higher morality."

She also stars in Trollope's comic Victorian version of the
Samson theme in *Barchester Towers*. Never before or since
the Victorian age have strong, public-minded women so con-

---

[21] Chap. V, pp. 33–34, italics mine.

sistently been the butt of comedy in fiction. The reason is obvious: women were taking over more power and influence than they had ever had before, particularly in determining and judging moral conduct. In the age of Queen Victoria and Florence Nightingale the changing role of women was striking. From *The Pickwick Papers* to *The Way of All Flesh* comic Delilah avatars romp through English fiction, cowing men. In Barchester a formidable group of females, Mrs. Proudie, the Stanhope girls, Mrs. Quiverful, and others, shears away strength from docile male relatives. Nor is it accidental that all of these women have close ties with the Church; out of the evangelical spirit of nineteenth-century religion developed the moral insistence and will to power of Victorian females.

IV

Trollope adds a whole new dimension to his comic anatomy of mid-Victorianism by bringing in the radical and provocative Stanhopes. Lacking earnestness and moral ambition, they just want to get through life as best they can. They are neither moral nor immoral but amoral, standing apart from the conventional middle-class morality and idealism of the age. Bertie and his sister Madeline do not take life seriously; they keep looking for comfort and amusement—mainly amusement. Since they will not conform, they affront Barchester and undermine its way of life. Trollope stresses their good nature, but he calls them heartless, which means, as he uses it, that they cannot love or feel deeply. The Stanhopes are literary ancestors of Evelyn Waugh characters. Through them, Trollope went a long way toward making the scandalous frivolity and hollowness of upper-class life a major subject in British comic fiction.

Signora Madeline Stanhope Vesey Neroni, with her overt sexuality, is one of the more intriguing females in Victorian literature. Trollope uses her as an antiheroine—the first of his highly intelligent women who contrast sharply with his pure, often passive heroines. His antiheroines are not very nice or sweet, but they make perfect tools for destroying sacred cows with iconoclastic wit.

Through Madeline we can see the uncomfortably ambivalent attitudes that the Victorians were developing about sex. She is one of the most brazenly sexual creatures in a Victorian novel and one of the few characters before the last decades of the century who consciously sets out to trap men with her sex appeal (she insists on receiving her gentlemen callers while languishing, courtesan-like, supine on a sofa). She marries unhappily because a man got her pregnant: "Why she had chosen Palo Neroni . . . need not now be told. When the moment for doing so came, she had probably no alternative. . . . After a prolonged honeymoon among the lakes, they had gone together to Rome. . . . Six months afterwards, she arrived at her father's house, a cripple and a mother."[22]

Madeline is neither villainess, pathetic victim, nor a social problem. For a popular Victorian novelist to impute the equivalent of a shotgun wedding to such a character was unheard of. The proper men of Barset love her ostentatious sexuality; Slope proposes to her, and Bishop Proudie, Arabin, and Squire Thorne all hover around her couch. But the fact that she is a cripple shows the pressure that Victorian efforts to repress sex could exert. An internal moral censor evidently told Trollope that the flaunting of sex must be punished, and so he imagined her with one leg shorter than the other. A robust Madeline who could get up off her couch and run off with some sex-starved parson would be too dangerous for Barchester's equilibrium. She had to be kept immobile and relatively harmless. Her letters, Trollope says, "were full of wit, mischief, love, latitudinarian philosophy, free religion, and sometimes, alas! loose ribaldry." That "alas!" has an ironical and plaintive quality, as if he envied

---

[22] Chap. IX, p. 67.

her liberty to indulge in "ribaldry." But her freedom must be in her letters and not her life—she must be an invalid.

Madeline nevertheless cracks the rigid façade of Barchester's moral propriety, and Mrs. Proudie, the voice of codified prudery, immediately sees her as a deadly enemy: "Mrs. Proudie looked on the signora as one of the lost—one of those beyond the reach of Christian charity, and was therefore able to enjoy the luxury of hating her, without the drawback of wishing her eventually well out of her sins."[23] " 'Is she [Mrs. Proudie] always like this?' said the signora. 'Yes—always—madam,' said Mrs. Proudie, returning, 'always the same—always equally adverse to impropriety of conduct of every description.' " The signora's response to this speech—"She laughed loud, and set the sound of it ringing through the lobby and down the stairs after Mrs. Proudie's feet,"[24]—shows the weakness of Proudieism, and the motive behind much of Trollope's comedy in the book becomes clear. People were beginning to resent pleasure-denying tyrannies of people like Mrs. Proudie, and they found that comic ridicule could best express their feelings. When we see how easily Madeline can vamp the staid clerics of Barset, we see also how shaky Mrs. Proudie's hold on her society is getting to be and how ready human nature is to mock the claims of moral system.

Madeline plays the role of social outlaw. Trollope sees her as a kind of revolutionary. Not only does she reject Proudie propriety, she also makes fun of social rank and class. The meeting of the signora with the blood-proud Countess De Courcy, whose place in the aristocracy intimidates other characters, is extremely important:

Lady De Courcy . . . taking her glass to investigate the Signora Neroni, pressed in among the gentlemen who surrounded the couch . . . and as she did so she stared hard

---

[23] Chap. XXXVII, p. 360.
[24] Chap. XI, p. 97.

at the occupant. The occupant in return stared hard at the countess. The countess who since her countess-ship commenced had been accustomed to see all eyes, not royal, ducal, or marquesal, fall before her own, paused as she went on, raised her eyebrows, and stared even harder than before. But she had now to do with one who cared little for countesses. It was, one may say, impossible for mortal man or woman to abash Madeline Neroni. She opened her large bright lustrous eyes wider and wider, till she seemed to be all eyes. She gazed up into the lady's face, not as though she did it with an effort, but as if she delighted in doing it. She used no glass to assist her effrontery, and needed none. The faintest possible smile of derision played round her mouth, and her nostrils were slightly dilated, as if in sure anticipation of her triumph. And it was sure. The Countess De Courcy, in spite of her thirty centuries and De Courcy castle, and the fact that Lord De Courcy was grand master of the ponies to the Prince of Wales, had not a chance with her. At first the little circlet of gold wavered in the countess's hand, then the hand shook, then the circlet fell, the countess's head tossed itself into the air, and the countess's feet shambled out to the lawn. She did not however go so fast but what she heard the signora's voice asking—

"Who on earth is that woman, Mr. Slope?"

"That is Lady De Courcy."

"Oh, ah. I might have supposed so. Ha, ha, ha. Well, that's as good as a play."

It was as good as a play to any there who had eyes to observe it, and wit to comment on what they observed.[25]

This is a perfectly-achieved piece of drawing-room comedy (note, for example, the effects of the lustrous eyes, the dilated nostrils, the circlet of gold, the shaking hand, and the signora's use of the word "woman," in creating the comic intensity of the scene); but it is also revolutionary comedy. The target is the aristocracy's pretentious claim that the lower classes must automatically flatter its own pompous

---

[25] Chap. XXXVII, pp. 356–357.

self-importance. Madeline behaves even more subversively than a character like Stendhal's Julien Sorel, who at least thinks the aristocracy of his world important enough to hate and envy. But her laughter is not the forced laughter of bitterness. She laughs genuinely at what she considers the ridiculous presumptions of a rude woman whose social rank matters not at all. The spirit of comedy in the signora's eye turns the countess into a silly and impotent old woman. A social hierarchy based on class and heredity was beginning to disintegrate because many people could no longer take it seriously. When Madeline chooses her name, Vesey Neroni, just because she likes the sound of it, and makes the claim that her child by the Italian is "the last of the Neros," she subverts polite society and turns the presumptions of gentility into a huge joke.

Trollope both loves and despises Madeline. He had that peculiar tendency of Victorian men—a tendency which he, unlike Thackeray, was later able to throw off—to regard moral virtue and critical intelligence in a woman as somehow incompatible. He explicitly condemns the signora's lack of principle and religion and her neglect of her child. But he loves her when she strips away the hypocritical pretenses of his society and demolishes its cheap platitudes. When Chaplain Slope, for example, talks of love's sacredness, she shows him how often it is a passing whim based on sex and egotism. And when he, a self-righteous minister of the Church, makes love to her, a married woman, she makes him appear a foolish epitome of canting hypocrisy. At times she expresses the deepest urges of the mid-Victorian to rebel against the idealistic mythology of his age, declaiming, for instance, against the sentimental nonsense about the bliss of wedlock:

" 'I hate your mawkish sentimentality. . . . You know as well as I do in what way husbands and wives generally live together; you know how far the warmth of conjugal affection can withstand the trial of a bad dinner, of a rainy day, or of the least privation which poverty brings with it; you know what freedom a man claims for himself, what slavery he would exact from his wife if he could! And you know also how wives generally obey. Marriage means tyranny on one side and deceit on the other.' "[26] Trollope could never put a statement like this in his own voice, but a part of him obviously agrees with it.

When he reproves Madeline for exploiting her little daughter as a kind of pretty prop to win sympathy, he is interestingly ambivalent. She is a terrible mother, but through her he satirizes the gullibility of people who sentimentalize children. He saw in his age the growth of a child-cult which was to have its apotheosis in Freud. At one point he describes Eleanor Bold's baby-worship as she plays with her son: " 'Diddle, diddle, diddle, diddle, dum, dum, dum,' said Eleanor. . . . 'H'm'm'm'm'm'm'm', simpered the mama, burying her lips also in his fat round short legs. 'He's a dawty little bold darling, so he is.' "[27] Compare this with the signora's insincere outburst to Bishop Proudie about her child: " 'Oh! my lord . . . you must see that infant—the last bud of a wonderous tree.' " The Madeline side of Trollope parodies the sentimentalization of childhood in both passages.

The signora speaks for the sophisticated, analytic Victorian intelligence that more and more came to detest the complacency, maddening provincialism, and simplistic morality in the culture. Madeline and Bertie, a generation younger than Grantly, Harding, and the Proudies, have a new outlook on life. They seem called into being in some dialectical fashion to give the old Barchester society what it lacks—a critical spirit of mind, a love of pleasure, and a touch of frivolity.

Bohemianism, that fascinating feature of modern life, really began to flourish in the nineteenth century. Bertie is even more bohemian than his sister. A charming, idle dilet-

---

[26] Chap. XV, p. 129.
[27] Chap. XVI, p. 131.

tante who flits about Europe dabbling in art and religious philosophy, he cuts a silly figure; and Trollope satirizes through him the latter-day British Romantics, pseudoartists, and Pre-Raphaelite hangers-on who were always trotting off to Europe to waste time. But bohemianism, as the Stanhopes show, can mean comic gaiety, unexpected insight, and tolerance, as well as irresponsible arrogance and cultivation of the ego. Bertie conveys even more successfully than Dickens's Harold Skimpole the siren-song appeal to the Victorians not to be moral and responsible. The widow Eleanor Bold finds Bertie very attractive because he never preaches sermons, and he dispels some of Barchester's stuffiness. The funniest scene in the novel comes when he meets with the Proudies and the other Barchester clerical dignitaries.[28] Ingenuously he asks them about their salaries, tells the bishop, " 'On the whole I like the Church of Rome best,' " starts recounting his religious experiences—" 'I was a Jew once myself' "—tears Mrs. Proudie's dress, and makes fun of a fat rector. An age which demands duty and moral earnestness must sooner or later discover in itself a hedonistic longing for pleasure and jokes.

V

Trollope carefully balances the Stanhopes' rebellious modernity and dismissal of traditional values with another brother-and-sister pair, the pleasantly anachronistic Thornes of Ullathorne. Unashamedly reactionary, the Thornes try to shut out all change by refusing to acknowledge it. They link the changing present to the past and show strong resistance to change in the Barsetshire world. Trollope sympathizes with their fear of change and their love of security. He treats them affectionately because he realizes that in any good civilization there must be people who dedicate themselves to preserving the ideals of the past as the Thornes

---

[28] Chap. XI, "Mrs. Proudie's Reception—Concluded."

do. At the end of a slightly patronizing chapter on them he writes, "Such, we believe, are the inhabitants of many an English country house. May it be long before their number diminishes."[29] But he knew he was being nostalgic: neither of the Thornes marries; they have no descendants.

He ironically uses one of Miss Thorne's attempts to revive feudalism to get at the problem of social changes. She plans a Fête Champêtre for the neighborhood and decides to seat the upper classes in one section and the lower classes in another. The trouble is that it is not clear just where some people ought to sit: "It is in such definitions that the whole difficulty of society consists. To seat the bishop on an arm chair on the lawn and place Farmer Greenacre at the end of the long table in the paddock is easy enough; but where will you put Mrs. Lookaloft whose husband, though a tenant on the estate, hunts in a red coat, whose daughters go to a fashionable seminary in Barchester, who calls her farm house Rosebank, and who has a pianoforte in her drawing-room?"[30] Miss Thorne learns that even a benevolent reactionary cannot escape the difficulties of a changing world.

Early in the book the atmosphere of change is unpleasant. Young, modern, ambitious Dr. Slope and the old, puzzled Harding have a gloomy interview:

"You must be aware, Mr. Harding, that things are a good deal changed in Barchester," said Mr. Slope.

Mr. Harding said that he was aware of it. "And not only in Barchester, Mr. Harding, but in the world at large. It is not only in Barchester that a new man is carrying out new measures and casting away the useless rubbish of past centuries. The same thing is going on throughout the country. . . . New men, Mr. Harding, are now needed, and are now forthcoming. . . ."

Trollope then comments:

---

[29] Chap. XXII, p. 204.
[30] Chap. XXXV, p. 334.

A man is nothing now unless he has within him a full appreciation of the new era; an era in which it would seem that neither honesty nor truth is very desirable, but in which success is the only touchstone of merit.[31]

This prediction comes true in his later work, but in *Barchester Towers* he sees the possibilities for solving the problems of his world. The novel moves from the loss of equilibrium at the old bishop's death to a new equilibrium with the marriage of Eleanor and Arabin, Arabin's installation as Dean, and the tacit truce between Mrs. Proudie and Grantly that leaves them both with a share of the spoils of the diocese. Barchester in the end can assimilate and support a great variety of life without losing communal identity and integrity, and it becomes a better place for having accommodated itself to change.

VI

Trollope's key figure in achieving finally a harmony between worldliness and idealism is Mr. Arabin. He is even more important than Grantly and Mrs. Proudie in giving the novel shape and meaning. He is the one character who combines idealism, religious dedication, energy, and intellectual curiosity. If Barchester is to be anything more than an amusing but trivial place, he must flourish there. The book would be satirical and pessimistic if he did not thrive. It would say, in effect, that the best people could not live a good life in Barchester—or in Victorian England.

We need to see exactly what happens to Arabin. When Grantly brings him into Barset in order to counteract the Proudie influence, he is unhappy and discouraged with life. For religious reasons he has rejected the world, and his celibacy leaves him dissatisfied: "He was tired of his Oxford rooms and his college life. He regarded the wife and children of his friend with something like envy. . . . And now, if the

---

[31] Chap. XIII, p. 106.

truth must out, he felt himself disappointed. . . . The day-dream of his youth was over, and at the age of forty he felt that he was not fit to work in the spirit of an apostle. He had mistaken himself, and learned his mistake when it was past remedy."[32] He not only becomes happy, he becomes a better churchman by loving and winning Eleanor and accepting joy as a good in itself. When Harding learns his daughter is to marry Arabin, he arranges for him to be dean, thus increasing Arabin's moral influence. The way of the world in Barchester can further the cause of idealism.

Significantly Madeline, the spirit of intelligence and radicalism, brings about the love match. In a funny and brilliantly penetrating conversation with Arabin—too long to quote in full—she teaches him to value the world and to understand his real feelings about Eleanor. She also expands his whole conception of life.

"Is not such the doom of all speculative men of talent?" said she. "Do they not all sit apart as you now are, cutting imaginary silken cords with their fine edges, while those not so highly tempered sever the every-day Gordian knots of the world's struggles, and win wealth and renown? Steel too highly polished, edges too sharp, do not do for this world's work, Mr. Arabin. . . ."

"The greatest mistake any man ever made is to suppose that the good things of the world are not worth the winning. And it is a mistake so opposed to the religion which you preach! . . . You try to despise these good things, but you only try; you don't succeed. . . .

"There is the widow Bold looking round at you from her chair this minute. What would you say to her as a companion for life."

. . . "You cross-question me rather unfairly," he replied, "and I do not know why I answer you at all. Mrs. Bold is a very beautiful woman, and as intelligent as beautiful. . . . One that would grace any man's house."

"And you really have the effrontery to tell me this," said

[32] Chap. XX, p. 177.

she; "to tell me, who, as you very well know, set up to be a beauty myself, and who am at this very moment taking such an interest in your affairs, you really have the effrontery to tell me that Mrs. Bold is the most beautiful woman you know."

"I did not say so," said Mr. Arabin; "you are more beautiful—"

"Ah, come now, that is something more like . . ."

"You are more beautiful, perhaps more clever . . ."

"But Mr. Arabin, I am dying with hunger; beautiful and clever as I am, you know I cannot go to my food, and yet you do not bring it to me."[33]

Barchester needs Madeline's wit and critical detachment, and Trollope makes her his agent in overturning Arabin's stiffness. She draws out his humanity.

All the trends and factions in the community somehow finally work together for his good. The invasion of the Proudies causes Grantly to bring him to Barchester where such diverse forces as the signora's skeptical, scoffing intelligence and the quiet faith and traditional sentiment of Harding both favor him. Only half facetiously, Trollope calls Arabin at the end an "ornament of the age." The point is that the Barchester Victorian society has produced in him a man who can adapt to the world and still maintain high ideals.

Late in the novel, Arabin complains to Eleanor: " 'It is the bane of my existence that on important subjects I acquire no fixed opinion. I think, and think, and go on thinking; and yet my thoughts are ever running in different directions.' "[34] Arabin, Trollope, and the Victorians may have felt this state of mind to be a burden to them—*certainty* may be more comfortable than *uncertainty*—but it expresses again one of the glories of the age: the free play of the spirit of inquiry and that "disinterested intelligence." We ought to under-

---

[33] Chap. XXXVIII, pp. 369–372.
[34] Chap. XLVIII, p. 470.

stand Arabin's statement in the context of the Barchester world and its background. Outwardly he lives a quiet life of clerical conformity. He seems to be a relatively tranquil member of a stable, solid institution, and yet his mind compulsively ranges everywhere looking for truth. In that seemingly stable Victorian England of the fifties, men like Darwin, Marx, and Mill were also thinking and looking for truth, though their thoughts were "running in different directions." From behind the façade of conformity—out of all the silliness, the squabbling, and the rich diversity of Barchester and nineteenth-century England—ornaments of intelligence could emerge.

But Arabin, though crucial, is only one character, and the novel is the comedy of a whole society. The title, *Barchester Towers*, symbolizes the double thrust of Trollope's human comedy. He wanted his readers to get a detached view of this world, to look down on it—from a tower, as it were—and see honestly its failings, its realities, its hypocrisies, its ridiculousness, as well as its promise. From the detached point of view of comedy, or from a tower, people sometimes look very small. Such a view helps dispel man's pride and his tendency to overestimate his own size and importance. But cathedral towers not only look down, they point upward too, and they represent men's aspirations for moral purpose and meaning in life. The Barchester towers, the expression of human idealism, give visible continuity to the whole changing Barchester scene. Trollope meant to show that as long as the citizens of Barchester and the Victorians recognized the moral as well as the physical reality of these towers and, as best they could, tried to build their society around them, they could, despite their worldly folly, sustain and increase the value of their lives.

VII

The Church in Trollope sometimes resembles a bureaucracy of the Higher Agency. The age of bureaucracy had dawned in the fifties, and before writing *Doctor Thorne*, he interrupted his chronicle of Barsetshire to deal, in *The Three Clerks*, with the great new center of power, the Civil Service. Dickens had just published his brilliant satire of the Circumlocution Office in *Little Dorrit*. His view of bureaucracy reveals the angry state of mind of a man who has stood in line too long and who has been shunted from window to window too many times. But Trollope was himself a shrewd bureaucrat who understood that in an industrializing society with a growing population, a bureaucracy, with all its faults, is necessary. Moreover, the Victorian bureaucracy was changing the world. In *The Three Clerks* the everyday business of government goes on; decisions are made about mining regulations, public works, navigation, industrial reports, and promotions. Trollope points out that all these mundane affairs with their ramifications largely determine the nature of the whole society. Whether one man or another will get rich, whether key jobs will be open to all comers, where and how the landscape of the country will change—these are the kinds of far-reaching questions which he shows the Civil Service deciding. Somehow men must make peace with bureaucracy.

In *The Three Clerks* and in nearly all the rest of his novels which follow, commercialism threatens to corrupt Trollope's world. The change from an agricultural to an industrial economy and the increasing momentum of the capitalistic system put a price on more and more things. Money gradually comes to seem more real than the old immaterial entities such as soul, integrity, love, and duty. In a thousand ways Trollope's characters are tempted—literally—to sell out. Much of *The Three Clerks* concerns the bribing of a public official. A swindler buys off a young inspector of mines with mining stock and tells him the power of money.

"Of course the possession of these shares can have no possible effect on your report. But when men like you and me become of any note in the world, others . . . like to know that we are embarked in the same speculation with themselves. Why are members of Parliament asked to be directors, and vice-governors, and presidents, and guardians, of all the joint-stock societies that are now set agoing? Not because of their capital, for they generally have none; not for their votes. . . . It is because the names of men of note are worth money. Men of note understand this, and enjoy the fat of the land accordingly. I want to see you among the number."[35]

The Three Clerks itself degenerates because of Trollope's confused intentions and his inconsistency, but the great sin of his age, which he identifies here, the habit of equating human worth and cash value, bothers him for the rest of his career.

VIII

Money is the spur which moves the world in *Doctor Thorne* (1857–1858). Trollope imagines how the mushrooming economy and bitter commercial competition affect the rural society in Barsetshire. It has developed, among other things, an assortment of *nouveaux riches* and a laissez faire marriage market. The richest man in the county is now the crude railroad-builder, Scatcherd, who made his money by pleasing the bureaucrats who award government contracts. The tone of British country life was definitely changing.

In the opening pages, Trollope describes the Barset countryside in idyllic terms as a place where the fine old ways still prevail. Greshamsbury, the home of the Gresham family, is a "fine old English Gentleman's seat," and in writing about it he shows, as he did with Ullathorne, the love of tradition and the distrust of modern tendencies: "The old symbols remained, and may such symbols long remain among us; they are still lovely and fit to be loved. They tell us of the true and manly feelings of other times; and to him who can read aright, they explain more fully, more truly than

---

[35] *The Three Clerks*, chap. IX, p. 101.

any written history can do, how Englishmen have become what they are. England is not yet a commercial country in the sense in which that epithet is used for her; and let us still hope that she will not soon become so. She might as well be called feudal England, or chivalrous England."[36] What follows makes this passage highly ironical. And the irony, whether intentional or not, shows again the mentality of Trollope and the age split between an emotional longing for what was passing and an awareness of what was actually happening. Squire Gresham has grown poor, and the most important statement in the chapter is not the wistful love of "feudal England," but a comment by one of Gresham's old tenants: " 'Things be altered at Greshamsbury . . . altered sadly.' "

Commercial values come to dominate both the Greshams and their aristocratic relatives and neighbors, the De Courcys. The preservation of their rank depends on whether they can get the money to maintain their estates. In Barsetshire a new gap opens up between wealth and rank. The two do not necessarily go together any more; even the haughtiest people, like Lady Arabella Gresham and Countess de Courcy, desperately chasing after fat incomes for their children in the marriage market, kowtow shamelessly to wealthy parvenus.

Doctor Thorne, with Sir Roger Scatcherd and his son, Martha Dunstable, Augustus Moffat, and Mary Thorne, is one of the broadest studies of *the parvenu* in Victorian literature. Sir Roger, the former workingman, and his son Louis are gradually absorbing the Gresham property; Miss Dunstable, the homely daughter of a patent-medicine quack, shines in society as England's most eligible maiden; Mr. Moffat, a tailor's son, sits in Parliament and scorns the old landed gentry; and finally, the bastard heroine, Mary Thorne, weds Frank Gresham and saves the family property and status. All of them reflect the broad movement of English

---

[36] *Doctor Thorne* (London, 1926), chap. I, p. 11.

society and the problems which the new social mobility causes.

Sir Roger Scatcherd may be, as one critic says, the sort of character who is "out of place"[37] in Barsetshire, but that is just the point. Whether he fits in or not, he, the "new man," with his money made in industrial capitalism, is a reality in Barset and England, and Barsetshire needs his fortune and some of his raw vitality if it is to continue to prosper. Scatcherd himself, despite his fortune, dies an alcoholic. Trollope knew that competition could isolate a man and make him hopelessly lonely. Scatcherd has slashed his way to the top, but all his money and all his old habits from his days of economic battling make him distrust everyone. Cut off from other men and without cultural education or taste, he never can enjoy his money. To Dr. Thorne he says, " 'When a man has made 300,000 pounds, there's nothing left for him but to die.' " This blusteringly capable money-maker shows how the brawling vigor of late-nineteenth-century capitalism could lead to spiritual alienation and disillusionment with materialism.

But Trollope makes comedy out of the money-grubbing ethics in *Doctor Thorne*. Another parvenu, Miss Dunstable the delightful heiress, reacts with comic detachment and humor to the various sordid schemes to marry her for her money. When, for instance, one of her "instructors in fashion" tells her that her curls are not the proper style, she replies, prophetically, " 'They'll always pass muster . . . when they are done up with bank-notes.' " With frankness and good sense she educates Frank Gresham and makes him see the obscenity of transferring commercial ethics to personal relationships: "Sell yourself for money! . . . For shame, Mr. Gresham! For shame.' "

Moffat, the parvenu protégé of the Duke of Omnium, both represents a mercenary morality in himself and comments on

---

[37] Bradford Booth, *Anthony Trollope* (Bloomington, 1958), p. 45.

the way it affects and transforms society. Ruthlessly he
throws over his high-born fiancée, Augusta Gresham, to try
for Martha Dunstable's two-hundred thousand pounds. In a
comic and enlightening scene, he proposes to her on the
grounds of economic and class interests—oddly mixing ultra-
capitalist values and Marxist-like class solidarity. He begins
by making "common cause":

> The aristocracy, said Mr. Moffat, were not a people to al-
> low the light of their countenance to shine without looking
> for a *quid pro quo*, for some compensating value. In all their
> intercourse with the Dunstables and Moffats, they would
> expect payment. It was for the Dunstables and Moffats to
> see that, at any rate they did not pay more for the article
> they got than its market value. The way in which she . . . and
> he . . . would be required to pay would be by taking each
> of them some poor scion of the aristocracy in marriage; and
> thus expending their hard-earned wealth in procuring high-
> priced pleasures for some well-born pauper. Against this,
> peculiar caution was to be used . . . people so circumstanced
> should marry themselves. . . .
> "It is quite delightful to watch these people [the aristoc-
> racy] . . . now they accuse us of being tuft-hunters . . . that
> is what the world said of persons of our class. Now it seems
> to me that the toadying is all on the other side. The Countess
> does toady you, and so do the young ladies."[38]

Odious as he is, Moffat speaks true. Trollope shows the
De Courcys and Greshams accepting the worst values of the
nouveau riche. When Frank Gresham tells his aunt, the
Countess De Courcy, that he is going back to college, she
remarks, " 'Oh! you are to go to Cambridge again are you?
Well . . . very little is ever gained now by a university connection.' " There is little to choose between the De Courcy
precepts and the obsessions of the greedy Louis Scatcherd,
who boasts that his estate cost him "22,419 pounds, 4 shill-
ings and 8 pence." A perverted money madness infects all

---

[38] *Doctor Thorne*, chap. xviii, pp. 226–229.

social levels in this book. There is an ominous moral rot spreading in Barsetshire more detestable than anything Trollope had imagined in *The Warden* or *Barchester Towers*.[39]

IX

Despite all the debasing effects of the Victorian race for cash, however, Trollope still sees money playing an important part in his comic vision. In *Doctor Thorne*, Mary Thorne inherits her uncle Scatcherd's wealth, marries Frank Gresham, and preserves the basic social order and virtues of Barsetshire life. From a realistic point of view there is too much of Cinderella about the book. Everything works out too neatly. Nevertheless, Trollope believed in the broad pattern of his story. In 1858 he still saw the possibilities for the new riches of capitalism in England to strengthen the whole society. The more money that people have, the less they have to worry, and the more they can devote themselves to their public duties. The influx of industrial wealth, with all the dangers that it brought, might eventually lead to an improved moral and physical well-being of the entire commonwealth—provided men could fight down the money passion. The moral core of the novel lies in a conversation between Dr. Thorne and Mary, his niece and ward, when Scatcherd is tempting them with wealth:

"After all," said he, "money is a fine thing."
"Very fine, when it is well come by," she answered, "that is, without detriment to the heart or soul."
"I should be a happier man if you were provided for as is Miss Oriel. Suppose I could give you up to a rich man who would be able to insure you against all wants?"
"Insure me against all wants! Oh, that would be a man. That would be selling me, wouldn't it, uncle? Yes, selling

---

[39] In 1857, just before he wrote *Doctor Thorne*, Trollope, in *The Struggles of Brown, Jones, and Robinson* (New York: G. Munro, 1882), satirized the commercial spirit of the times and, in comic fashion, previewed the horrors of modern advertising.

me; and the price you would receive would be freedom from future apprehension as regards me. It would be a cowardly sale for you to make; and then, as to me—me the victim. No, uncle; you must bear the misery of having to provide for me—bonnets and all. We are in the same boat, and you shan't turn me overboard."

"But if I were to die, what would you do then?"

"And if I were to die, what would you do? People must be bound together. They must depend on each other."[40]

People must be joined together by something more than the cash nexus.

Dr. Thorne himself epitomizes Trollope's optimistic hope for man in this period, and this may explain why he named the book after a character who hardly figures at all in the basic plot. The changing world that Thorne lives in still allows him, like Arabin and Harding, to keep the sanctity of his individual conscience and also to serve the best interests of his whole society. His work as a physician practicing medicine in the latest mid-nineteenth-century fashion, against ignorant prejudice, wins him respect and independence, while he helps others.

In each of these early novels, Trollope describes the interplay of profession and character and notes the new opportunities of the middle classes to achieve dignity, usefulness, and self-sufficiency in work. And, especially in *Doctor Thorne*, he measures a man's worth by how well he lives up to the ideals of his profession. Although Thorne comes from good stock, he breaks with his family over a matter of conscience and has, Trollope says, "nothing but his profession" to help him get along in life. In a sense, then, he too is a "new man," but he clings to the ideals of the past—particularly the ideals of Christian morality and communal responsibilities. He follows modern methods and adapts to the changing patterns of nineteenth-century life, but he holds on to the traditional belief that a man has a double obligation

---

[40] *Doctor Thorne,* chap. XI, p. 140.

to maintain the health of both his own conscience and the whole community in which he lives. He tries to fit all the new and almost revolutionary facts of life in Barset into the traditional social structure with as little friction as possible. Trollope's own inclination was to try to meet the new realities—industrialism, class mobility, and the need for new skills—while still keeping a framework of the old ideals. Thorne, in himself and in his influence on those around him, successfully blends the new with the old. As doctor, he is both healer and teacher.

Thorne, along with Harding and Arabin in Barsetshire, is able to change with the world and still retain—even strengthen—a moral self. In characters like Mrs. Proudie, Tom Towers, and Moffat we see how ridiculous and frightening Trollope's changing world can be. But his vision is primarily of a society that, with all its follies and problems, has the capacity to absorb change and to profit from it. The ways of compromise and reconciliation remain open. We have in Barset a sweeping human comedy of change.

4
Early Hopes Blighted:
The Threat of
Moving Time

After *Doctor Thorne* Trollope seems much less confident about his world. His comic flair remains, but his vision of life grows darker than it has been since *The Macdermots of Ballycloran*. Life, as he now unfolds it for his most interesting characters, becomes a difficult and sometimes bitter affair, and he is much more concerned with various forms of human failure. In his next four books, *The Bertrams, Castle Richmond, Framley Parsonage*, and *Orley Farm*, the changing world often brings anguish and disillusionment. At just about the same time as Dickens, Trollope takes up in earnest the Victorian theme of "great expectations."[1] He imagines many characters in these books who start out with great advantages—wealth, talent, beauty, or high social rank—then discover that new circumstances frustrate or bewilder them and, for a time at least, blight their lives. As they grow older, experience, the humiliating teacher, upsets their cherished plans and opinions, and the moral problems of change become more perplexing than they were even for Mr. Harding. Trollope in these novels explores the ways that time and the world crush the hopes of the young and the dogmatic beliefs of the old.

---

[1] *Great Expectations* was published in 1860.

By the end of the fifties, the rising expectations of the English had inevitably brought disappointments. Periods of disillusion follow periods of national optimism, and Trollope's writing from 1858 to 1861 was directly and indirectly influenced by the more somber intellectual spirit of the time.[2] There is much greater doubt in his mind about the possibilities for making satisfactory moral adjustments to the new world, much greater fear of the moral corruption arising from change than there was in *Barchester Towers* or *Doctor Thorne*. The dangers of the commercial ethic in his world have always been clear, but now he shows how materialism can spoil the lives not just of the weak or the mediocre, but of the finest people. In these years when he himself had finally reached great success both as an author and as an influential civil servant, his characters find that worldly success is empty. When he keeps insisting that reality can never match expectations, that the world in one way or another breaks or diminishes the spirit of most people, we sense a personal note. Living in time means for Trollope that sooner or later people have to realize that imagination deceives and that they must reconcile themselves to getting less out of life than they hoped for.

I

In the very first chapter of *The Bertrams* (1858) Trollope announces he is going to write about the morally destructive influences on his time of the "money-making activity" and the wild spirit of competition which, he says, leads his countrymen to believe that "success is the only test of merit." He no longer sees money as an agent for possible good, as he does in *Doctor Thorne*. Commercialism corrupts the whole world of this novel and causes the alienation of its hero, George Bertram.

---

[2] See, e.g., *The Fortnightly*, Jan. 1862, p. 81: "The great characteristic danger of our days is the growth of this ignoble littleness of character and spirit."

The Stebbins have called *The Bertrams* "the most modern in tone"[3] of all Trollope's novels, possibly because Bertram is one of the earliest "sensitive young men" in English fiction. We have become familiar with stories of intellectuals with delicate consciences who feel out of place in the dynamic materialistic new age, but Bertram's story is one of the first about a misunderstood, alienated young man in a "realistic" English novel. When the book opens, the world is all before him. He has taken a double-first at Oxford, and he has a very rich uncle and a beautiful fiancée. He is, however, an idealist who prefers honesty and a clear conscience to success, and all the mercenary characters around him cannot comprehend such an utterly strange person. For most of the story he remains isolated, unable to communicate with anyone.

One of the great problems for Bertram is that, with all his promise and high hopes, he cannot find work which satisfies his idealistic bent. All his natural inclination is toward the Church because he strongly believes in religious reform and wants to serve others. But Victorian materialism gradually destroys his religious faith. Trollope was writing this book in 1858, the year before the publication of *The Origin of Species*, when the materialistic sciences were beginning to call all in doubt. Early in the novel George discusses Christian dogma and shows the effect which science was having: " 'About the resurrection of the body . . . it is impossible. . . . Your body . . . will turn itself, through the prolific chemistry of nature, into various gasses by which other bodies will be formed. With which body will you see Christ . . . ? For, of course, every atom of your body changes.' "[4] Bertram, the most moral person in the book, even writes a book, later, *The Fallacy of Early Church History*, debunking religion.

Trollope himself was obviously concerned about the im-

---

[3] Richard and Lucy Stebbins, *The Trollopes: The Chronicle of a Writing Family* (New York, 1945), p. 160.

[4] *The Bertrams* (London: John Lane, The Bodley Head, 1905), chap. xxvi, pp. 476–477.

pact of materialism on religion and the religious impulse. His thinking was changed from the time of *Barchester Towers* and Dean Arabin, whom Bertram resembles. He seems to doubt whether the Church and the modern world can be reconciled and whether a young man can find any satisfactory institutional outlet for idealism. From this time on, whenever Trollope writes about the Church and church-men, he tends to imagine failures.

Trollope was getting at major modern dilemmas about doubt and belief, and his statement about George—"He was angry with himself for not believing, and angry with others that they did believe—says much the same thing as do Yeats's lines, "The best lack all conviction, while the worst/Are full of passionate intensity." Bertram finds nothing to believe in, nothing to hold sacred or to work wholeheartedly for except his personal integrity. And in the end, when Trollope turns him into a drab conformist, and a lawyer, the profession which he had previously rejected out of conscience, his fail-ure is complete.

Bertram's fiancée, Caroline Waddington, betrays him and marries his best friend. She begins with beauty, charm, and a cool intelligence, but the commercialism in herself and her society poisons her existence. Like many intellectual women, she demands everything from life and gets very little. She marries the wrong man and becomes miserable when she sees her own faults magnified in her husband. She knows that she sold herself in marriage like a whore to the highest bidder. Yet Trollope sympathizes with her. She, like George, is in over her head, living in a world where the capitalistic impulse has run wild.

George's rich uncle, whose money makes everyone act and react, embodies the capitalistic spirit in the novel. He is efficient, powerful, and wealthy, but he lacks pity, com-munal feeling, idealism, and ultimate purpose. He is the controlling force of the book, and George, Caroline, and oth-ers, though they may temporarily delude themselves, never stop spinning around the axis of his money. But even *he* finds that "the iron of his wealth" divides people and chills their affections and brings him no joy.

The Bertrams has excellent moments when it evokes the terrifying power of materialism to isolate human beings from one another and shows time blasting the illusions of the young. Lamentably, Trollope dissipates the potential of the book. It succeeds only intermittently because of its illogical subplots, its discrepancies in tone and character, and its tedious prolixity. But a character like George Bertram and the dominant pessimism in the novel mark an important point in Trollope's career. The question of why many of the best people fail—the question that he raises explicitly here—would continue to worry him in the years to come.

II

Failure and deprivation loom large in his next book, *Castle Richmond* (1860). The most interesting characters are starved for love, and Ireland, where the novel is set during the ghastly famine of 1846–1848, is starved for food. Thoughts of Ireland always seem to have reminded Trollope that men's hopes have never been able to eradicate physical and psychological hunger. What stands out in this uneven novel are the descriptions of the famine, and a strange, warped, love quadrangle featuring Countess Desmond, an attractive widow, her daughter Clara, her adolescent son Patrick, and Owen Fitzgerald, a romantic Irishman.

The quadrangle is interesting because it shows Trollope sensing intuitively that a combination of commercialism in personal relationships and passing time would cause psychological perversion in people. Lady Desmond had married a debauched, half-dead earl for his money and title when she was young. He soon died, leaving her frustrated without love. Fitzgerald loves the daughter, Clara, and they are engaged, but the countess breaks up the match because she wants to marry Owen herself. She is, however, too old for him. Time, *tempus edax rerum*, as Trollope says, eats away at her beauty, and she finds out that her daughter has become a more appealing woman than she. The girl, meanwhile, falls in love with someone else. Owen will not have the mother and can not have the daughter. Past follies, Lady Desmond learns, are irrevocable.

Patrick, growing up without a father, develops a passionate fondness for Fitzgerald. Trollope describes a homosexual relationship between the two young men in the chapter, "How the Earl Was Won." Patrick's habit of imagining himself to be in his sister's place, his effeminacy, his romantic feelings, and his desire to touch Owen, together with Owen's tendency to see the boy as a surrogate for Clara make the inversion unmistakable:

He squeezed Owen's arm with a strong boyish love.

There was an expression about his [Owen's] face which the young earl thought that he had never seen the like . . . a gleam in his eye . . . so bright; and a smile . . . so sweet. . . . How can she not love him, said he to himself.

"I [Owen] . . . love her . . . indeed there is nothing else that I do love—except you Desmond."

"I think you are the dearest, finest, best fellow that ever lived," said Fitzgerald, pressing him with his arm.

"Owen!" said the boy again . . . and throwing himself on Fitzgerald's breast, he burst out into a passion of tears.

"By heaven! there is not another man so worthy of a girl in all the world. . . . By heaven! if I were her, I know whom I should love," said the brother.[5]

At the end of the novel Patrick and Owen go off together.

Trollope knew the qualities in his civilization which would spread perversions of all sorts. Lady Desmond's perverted values cause the latent homosexuality here. Her materialism

---

[5] *Castle Richmond* (London: John Lane, The Bodley Head, 1906), chap. xxxvi, pp. 614–630.

and ambition have deprived both of them of the love they need. That the one does not have a father and the other does not marry the girl he loves is her fault. Lonely people whose need for affection has been denied will react in twisted and desperate ways. Time ineluctably brings home the consequences of past actions, and perverted morality produces perverted behavior.

The starvation for love exists against the background of starving Irish peasants. When the famine first becomes widespread, the priggish hero, Herbert, spouts ideas on how to avoid the disaster. He serves on committees, gives cocksure advice, establishes goals, and exhorts people to work hard. But finally, in the best chapter in the novel, "The Last Stage," he comes to understand the horror of the calamity and his helplessness to cope with it. Taking shelter from the rain, he enters a peasant cottage where a young woman is slowly starving to death. He sees a baby lying near the woman on the ground, and when he goes over to look at it, he finds that the baby is dead. All his grandiose schemes for Ireland end in the hopeless gesture of covering the little corpse with a silk handkerchief, and he learns the reality of suffering. Silk and starvation together show something terribly appalling about the conditions of life which Trollope felt men must face up to. He spoiled the integrity of the novel and nearly ruined it by sometimes trying, as a guilt-ridden Englishman, to explain away and make light of the famine. But in the end, all complacency fades away, and what ineradicably remains is the sheer ghastliness of death by hunger.

III

Framley Parsonage (1859–1860), though not as dark as *The Bertrams* or *Castle Richmond,* is tinged with melancholy and disillusionment. Trollope wrote his fourth Barset novel in a mood of resignation to a very imperfect world, and the pattern which unites its sprawling plot is the bending of human will to the limitations of reality. Personal ambition and a longing for social stability motivate most of the characters in this huge panorama of privileged-class mid-Victorian life, but Trollope sees futility in these drives.

Social harmony and happiness inevitably disappear when these characters begin to think of other people as objects to use rather than as human beings with souls. In 1859, just before Trollope began *Framley Parsonage*, Samuel Smiles's *Self-Help* appeared. Trollope thought the doctrine of the times that one must at all costs better oneself could and would lead to pointless competition and social-climbing. Really bettering oneself means, in this book, giving up egotistical pride and ambition, asking little of the world, accepting one's moral responsibilities to others, and learning to value integrity and freedom in oneself and others. Trollope shows us not only that the ambitions and expectations of his characters cannot be fulfilled, but that they usually are not worth fulfilling. At one point a character, after throwing a fashionable party for Very Important People, says, " 'The game is not worth the candle.' " That could be the title of the novel; Trollope's people have to find out how senseless and harmful is the particular game they have been playing in hopes of winning or keeping something.

Nevertheless, one of his special qualities in *Framley Parsonage* and other novels is to love and respect most of his characters even when he imagines them behaving badly. Trollope means it when he says, "Ambition is a great vice . . . if the ambition of the man be with reference to his own advancement, and not to the advancement of others," and the action proves how destructive the game of ambition can be. But he knows that "Adam's fall," as he says, makes us all play the game. Much of what his people do is morally wrong, and yet he values them highly because he understands that people are so much more than what they do in a given time span. He insists that a good person will often act badly—something which happens much more rarely in fiction than one might think—and that human character is so rich, so full of conflicting impulses, that an individual's specific action will often contradict the balance of his whole life.

Let us take, for example, Lady Lufton, who, as the enemy of true love in the novel, snobbishly tries to prevent her son, Lord Lufton, from marrying Lucy Robarts:

> She liked cheerful, quiet, well-to-do people, who loved their Church, their country, and their Queen, and who were not too anxious to make a noise in the world. She desired that all the farmers round her should be able to pay their rents without trouble, that all the old women should have warm flannel petticoats, that the working men should be saved from rheumatism by healthy food and dry houses, that they should all be obedient to their pastors and masters —temporal as well as spiritual. That was her idea of loving her country. She desired also that the copses should be full of pheasants, the stubble-field of partridges, and the gorse covers of foxes; in that way, also, she loved her country.[6]

It is impossible not to see during the whole course of the story both Trollope's amused affection for her and his sympathetic understanding of her views, though she causes others a good deal of pain. If we compare her with Jane Austen's Lady Catherine de Bourgh in *Pride and Prejudice*, who plays exactly the same hostile role in the plot as Lady Lufton, we can see the range of Trollope's sympathetic tolerance for his characters. He usually avoided caricature and black-and-white characterization because he thought they violated the truth. Lady Lufton has a kind of lifelike autonomy and freedom about her that Lady Catherine does not have, and in this illusion of autonomy that Trollope very often creates for his characters, he conveys something of inestimable value in a novelist: an awareness of others—an awareness that a great variety of other people besides author and reader exist and live lives that *matter*.

Trollope finds Lady Lufton and her longing for a nice,

---

[6] *Framley Parsonage* (London, 1961), chap. II, p. 15.

neat, stable little order in Framley and Barsetshire significant. He sees that her capsulated vision of life is appealing,
but that it is a typical pipe dream. Her effort to match her
son with Griselda Grantly in order to strengthen her family
prestige and the conservative cause in the community even
taints her with the social ambition which she despises in
others. Time passes, and a younger generation matures and
goes its own way, as she finds out when her son, Lord Lufton, and her protégé, Mark Robarts, defy her. The breakdown of provincialism and the intrusion of the accelerated
pace of nineteenth-century life into Barsetshire are irresistible. Lady Lufton cannot shut the worldly influences of London and of the ambitious "Chaldicotes" set of people out of
her life and out of Framley. She has to receive the education
of age and make a truce with a world which upsets the status
quo and limits her power to impose her moral and social
standards on the community.

Trollope's belief in the organic nature of the English community is best revealed in the downfall of Sowerby, the
owner of Chaldicotes, whose fault is that he does not realize
how deeply his life is intertwined with the whole social
fabric in the novel. When he fails to maintain his social
position, goes bankrupt, and loses his land, it affects all sorts
of characters in both London and Barsetshire. And his fate
is tied to the eventual fate of the countryside as a whole.
Sowerby's own selfish irresponsibility helps ruin him, but
Trollope also saw that economic pressures of his times were
inevitably changing rural England and destroying natural
beauty. He describes the Chaldicotes estate:

There is an old forest, not altogether belonging to the property, but attached to it, called the Chase of Chaldicotes. A
portion of this forest comes up close behind the mansion,
and of itself gives a character and celebrity to the place. . . .
In former times it was a great forest stretching half across
the country, almost as far as Silverbridge; and there are bits
of it, here and there, still to be seen at intervals throughout

the whole distance; but the larger remaining portion, con-
sisting of aged hollow oaks, centuries old, and widespread
withered beeches, stands in the two parishes of Chaldicotes
and Uffley. People still come from afar to see the oaks of
Chaldicotes, and to hear their feet rustle among the thick
autumn leaves. But they will soon come no longer. The giants
of past ages are to give way to wheat and turnips; a ruthless
Chancellor of the Exchequer, disregarding old associations
and rural beauty, requires money returns from the lands;
and the Chase of Chaldicotes is to vanish from the earth's
surface.[7]

The loveliness of the land, the whole rural way of life, and
the traditional country gentry are doomed to pass away because men like Sowerby do not have the strength or the will
to give up self-indulgence and protect the country. Trollope
imagines him after he has lost his entire property and inheritance:

Of all the inanimate things of the world this wood of Chaldicotes was the dearest to him. . . . He would watch the
decay of the old trees and the progress of the young, and
make pictures in his eyes of every turn in the wood. He
would mark the colour of a bit of road as it dipped into a
dell, and then, passing through a watercourse, rose brown,
rough, irregular, and beautiful against the bank on the other
side. And then he would sit and think of his old family: how
they had roamed there time out of mind in those Chaldicotes
woods, father and son and grandson in regular succession,
each giving them over, without blemish or decrease, to his
successor. So he would sit . . . and, thinking of these things,
wished that he had never been born.[8]

He has a sense of beauty and tradition, but he does not have
the character to preserve them and resist the ugliness in his
world. In Sowerby, Trollope is talking about one of the important failures of the last two centuries, man's lack of moral
responsibility for his physical environment.

---

[7] Chap. III, pp. 21–22.
[8] Chap. XXXVII, pp. 404–405.

The central figure in this study of failed ambitions is Lady Lufton's young vicar at Framley, Mark Robarts. Intelligent and well-meaning, he begins with every possible advantage —a good wife, a kind patroness, and an excellent living. And yet by the end of the novel he has—temporarily—betrayed his calling, compromised his good name, and lost his self-respect. Because he has been lucky and spoiled early in life, he thinks of himself as "different from other persons, more fitted by nature for intimacy with great persons." A clergyman, he nevertheless adapts the slogans of economic competition; he decides that "he had to look to rise in the world, as other men did," and that "he could not *afford* not to know" various influential people, including the Duke of Omnium, Smith the politician, and Sowerby, who gets him almost hopelessly in debt. Robarts is basically good, despite his naïveté and callow conceit. He can learn from his humiliation that he is not better than less fortunate people, but Trollope begins realizing in him the immense potential in his world to corrupt good people in Barset as well as in London.

The corrupting process goes to work on one of the most interesting characters, Martha Dunstable, the parvenu heiress. One of the triumphs of Trollope's comic art, she continually ridicules the greed, pomposity, and shallow pretensions of the smart set in the book. When Mrs. Proudie tries to impress English society by giving a "conversazione," Martha bursts in:

" 'And so this is a conversazione, is it? . . . Well, I declare it's very nice. It means conversation, don't it, Mrs. Proudie?'

" 'Ha, ha, ha! Miss Dunstable, there is nobody like you, I declare.'

" 'Well, but don't it? and tea and cake? and then, when we're tired of talking, we go away, isn't that it!' " [9] In *Doctor Thorne*, she exists as a blithe spirit, combining wit, sense, and a good heart to live with a kind of graceful and airy

---

[9] Chap. XVII, pp. 188–189.

freedom, enjoying high society, but keeping clear of its sordid aspects. In *Framley Parsonage*, however, she becomes more hardened and cynical. Trollope, in an oddly moving way, shows the sparkling but callous upper-class world gradually forcing her to hide her natural warmth and generosity and throw up a protective wall of sarcastic irony around herself in order not to be hurt: "She was living now very much with people on whom kindness, generosity, and openheartedness were thrown away. She was clever also, and could be sarcastic; and she found that those qualities told better in the world around her than generosity and an open heart. And so she went on from month to month and year to year, not progressing in a good spirit as she might have done."[10]

The worst of it is that Martha knows that her character is deteriorating, that she cannot escape the immoral influence of the glittering *haut monde* as she had hoped. She has also to face up to the fact that her wealth prevents her from ever experiencing the kind of romantic love that was supposed to be the dream of Victorian maidens:

"All this money which my father put together, and which has been growing like grass under May showers, has turned me into an abortion. I am not the giantess eight feet high, or the dwarf that stands in the man's hands . . . . But I am the unmarried woman with—half a dozen millions of money—as I believe some people think. Under such circumstances have I a fair chance of getting my own sweet bit of grass to nibble, like any ordinary animal with one head? I never was very beautiful, and I am not more so now than I was fifteen years ago."[11]

Time threatens her with loneliness, and she later chooses to take sedate old Doctor Thorne in a marriage of friendship and trust. In Thorne, she gets affection, decency, and morality, but she gives up passion and excitement. His reaction

---

[10] *Ibid.*, pp. 189–190.
[11] Chap. XXXVIII, p. 411.

when he reads her acceptance of his proposal says it all in
a typically Trollopian way: " 'And so I am going to marry
the richest woman in England,' said Dr. Thorne to himself
as he sat down that day to his mutton-chop." Trollope wants
to make it very clear with that mutton-chop that her hopes
for both a glamorous life and a good moral life are irreconcil-
able. This attitude may be predictably middle-class—
especially Victorian middle-class—but there is very little to
suggest that it is not true.

One of the best things about *Framley Parsonage* is the
way Trollope presents the dehumanizing effects of social-
climbing. The Grantlys, the Proudies, Robarts, Miss Dunstable, and most of the rest—even Ludy Lufton—come, at
some time or other, to perceive other people as specific quan-
tities of walking social prestige and ranks, rather than as
human beings. Neither the formidable Duke of Omnium
nor the much-sought-after young Lord Dumbello has any
definite personality; both are blank. Trollope's point is that
in this rank-conscious world they exist only as titles, not as
people.

But he goes further and insists that looking at others as
social commodities dehumanizes the beholder in turn. The
status-mad Griselda Grantly catches Lord Dumbello for a
husband, but she herself turns into a cold, beautifully sculp-
tured monster. Nothing brings home the passing of time in
Barsetshire more sharply or discouragingly than the short
conversation before her marriage between Griselda and her
grandfather, Mr. Harding. They are literally beings from
different ages who can no more communicate with each other than could Cotton Mather and a Hollywood starlet:

"Grizzy, my dear," he said to her—he always called her
Grizzy, but the endearment of the appellation had never been
appreciated by the young lady—"come and kiss me, and let
me congratulate you on your great promotion. I do so very
heartily."

"Thank you, grandpa," she said, touching his forehead
with her lips, thus being, as it were, very sparing with her

kiss. But those lips now were august and reserved for nobler foreheads than that of an old cathedral hack. . . . She kissed him, therefore, sparingly, and resolved that her words with him should be few.

"You are going to be a great lady, Grizzy," said he.

"Umph!" said she.

What was she to say when so addressed?

"And I hope you will be happy—and make others happy."

"I hope I shall," said she.

"But always think most about the latter, my dear. Think about the happiness of those around you, and your own will come without thinking. You understand that; do you not?"

"Oh, yes, I understand," she said.

"And Grizzy—I believe it is quite as easy for a rich countess to be as happy, as for a dairymaid—" Griselda gave her head a little chuck which was produced by two different operations of her mind. The first was a reflection that her grandpa was robbing her of her rank. She was to be a rich marchioness. And the second was a feeling of anger at the old man for comparing her lot to that of a dairymaid. . . . "Being a countess—that fact alone will not make you happy."

"Lord Dumbello at present is only a viscount," said Griselda. "There is no earl's title in the family."

"Oh! I did not know," said Mr. Harding, relinquishing his granddaughter's hand; and after that, he troubled her with no further advice.[12]

Trollope is definitely worried about moral degeneration in his time. Though he seems resigned here to the futility of giving moral advice, one cannot read this passage without sensing a change from the moral optimism of *The Warden*.

Almost as vacuous as social-climbing is the political-climbing that goes on in the novel. For the first time Trollope treats the upper reaches of the British political world, which he describes here in mildly satirical, mock-epic terms. Politics in the novel is a perpetual game of king-of-the-mountain in which personal ambition rather than ideology provides the incentive. Politicians are very much alike, and

---

[12] Chap. XL, pp. 436–437.

it is foolish to hope for much from them, since their first loyalties are to themselves and to the *game* of politics. He is not
a good conscious political theorist, but he understands the
workings of power better than almost any other English or
American novelist. Disraeli in his novels is much better at
setting down great political issues and problems, but Trollope has no equal in getting at all the trickery, the backbiting, the temporary personal alliances, the secret compacts
with the press, the patronage, the survival-of-the-fittest
mentality, the emphasis on money and connections, which
characterize the party politics and the whole political realm
of the West in modern times. His earnest, if pompous politician, Harold Smith, is comically futile in his attempt to
make an impact on the political system, because he cannot
comprehend or change the political game. Politics, says
Trollope, is men, and if you expect very much of men, as
Smith does, you will be disappointed.

What, more than anything else, gives *Framley Parsonage*
its aura of sorrow and defeated idealism is Trollope's great
character, Josiah Crawley. Not until *The Last Chronicle of
Barset* would he realize the tragic possibilities of this man,
but even here, in the relatively small role that he gives Crawley, he shows how life can warp the spirit of a potential
saint. The young, dedicated man had married a good woman
and decided to serve God and other men selflessly: "They
two had gone forth determined to fight bravely together, to
disregard the world and the world's ways, looking only to
God and to each other for their comfort. . . . In such a manner they would live, so poorly and so decently, working out
their work, not with their hands but with their hearts." The
result after fifteen years is this: "It had been a weary life
and a fearful struggle, made up of duties ill-requited and
not always satisfactorily performed, of love and poverty, of
increasing cares, of sickness, debt, and death."[13] Poverty has
shamed and embittered him and destroyed his faith in him-

---

[13] Chap. XIV, p. 156.

self and, at times, in God. His early dream of himself as a poor man of God, serving his flock and living happily with a quiet spirit, turns into a hoaxing mirage.

The problems of Crawley's failure, a we shall see later, led Trollope into his most profound study of despair. Here Crawley seems to pose very well the terrible moral dilemma that the Victorians were facing: Worldliness and materialistic ambitions did not lead to contentment—they understood that; but unworldliness, altruistic intentions, and strict morality might very easily lead to misery. Life, in *Framley Parsonage*, is essentially a disillusioning process, and the more you ask from it—whether you ask for worldly success or spiritual peace—the more disillusioning it is.

When Trollope wrote this novel, he was almost fifty and beginning to feel the discouraging psychological effects of age. One seemingly incidental and innocuous passage at the end of the novel sums up, I think, his state of mind at this time. He winds up the bland love story of Lufton and Lucy Robarts in this unconventional way:

I will not say that the happiness of marriage is like the Dead Sea fruit—an apple which, when eaten, turns to bitter ashes in the mouth. Such pretended sarcasm would be false. Nevertheless, is it not the fact that the freshest, fairest blush of the flower has been snatched and has passed away, when the ceremony at the altar has been performed. . . . There is an aroma of love, an undefinable delicacy of flavor, which escapes and is gone before the church portal is left, vanishing with the maiden name, and incompatible with the solid comfort appertaining to the rank of wife. To love one's own spouse, and to be loved by her, is the ordinary lot of man, and is a duty exacted under penalties. . . . No; when the husband walks back from the altar, he has already swallowed the choicest dainties of his banquet. The beef and pudding of married life are then in store for him;—or perhaps only the bread and cheese. Let him take care lest hardly a crust remain—. . . .[14]

---

[14] Chap. XLVIII, p. 522.

Beneath these chatty sentiments, there is a kind of stoic resignation to the fact that time degrades whatever one idealizes. *Framley Parsonage* is essentially a skeptical book, and it implies that nothing can live up to one's expectations. Disappointment is the eventual lot of man. But Trollope, unlike Crawley, does not wail about it; these simply are the facts of life, and one can only try to make the best of a disillusioning world. One may live reasonably well if one does not overestimate oneself or hope too much.

IV

His next novel, *Orley Farm* (1860-1861), is one of his best. It has the same kind of scope as *Framley*, but it has more emotional force and a clearer focus. Its two main characters, Sir Peregrine Orme and Lady Mason, have a greater psychological intensity than anyone in *Framley Parsonage*. Like that novel, *Orley Farm* describes the painful education of people who come to feel and understand the terrible inconstancy of the world. Out of a series of important discoveries which the characters make about themselves and their world, and out of their selfishness and their equivocal moral actions, comes the vision of human experience which we might expect from Trollope: Life gives people instincts and ideals which keep them from living in harmony with each other; they have to compromise principles and abandon much of what is dearest to them in order to get along. Men necessarily live in a fallen state.

Lady Mason and Sir Peregrine Orme, her seventy-year-old protector and—for a short time—fiancé, dominate the novel. Other characters may be important and interesting, but they all, in one way or another, help to reflect, intensify, or explain the acquisitive drive that, twenty years before the story begins, led Lady Mason to steal for her son. They all prove the inadequacy of Sir Peregrine's impossibly high ideals and moral standards.

Lady Mason's downfall results from essentially the same kind of act as her original crime. Having acquired the property for her son by a seemingly successful fraud apparently buried in the past, she legally reclaims the land for him at his coming of age, taking it away from a tenant and giving it to her son Lucius for a second time. This act stirs up the enmity which finally exposes her. Trollope carefully makes clear that her illegal commitment to Lucius's interests is not something over and done with; it has somehow to be continually renewed. A mistaken decision in the past impinges on her freedom of action in the present.

The real crisis in Lady Mason's story comes in her confession to Sir Peregrine Orme who, at the time, is engaged to marry her. When she tells Orme that she forged the will, she renounces all her worldly hopes and, in a sense, those of her son also. Trollope makes it clear that had she not confessed, she would have had Orme's honorable name and his power, and no one need ever have known of her crime. His great generosity, however, begets generosity in her, and she becomes, for the first time, an honest and moral human being. Her acknowledgement of her guilt is the exact opposite of her original sin. Before, she had deliberately disobeyed the wishes of an old man—her husband—in order to further the material interests of her son and herself; here, she disregards the wishes of an old man—Orme—for his own good, even though she knows she is throwing over all her worldly hopes. Robert Adams, a perceptive critic of *Orley Farm*, disparages the confessional scene and calls it psychologically weak,[15] but I find its psychology both convincing and intricate. Lady Mason cheated old Mason, a man who, though nominally her husband, was actually more of a father to her, since he was forty-five years older than she. Now, years later, having become intimate with Sir Peregrine, another kind and protective father-figure, she naturally tends to show her

---

[15] See Robert Martin Adams, "*Orley Farm* and Real Fiction," *Nineteenth-Century Fiction* (June 1953), pp. 27–42. I am indebted to this illuminating article for its analysis of commercialism in *Orley Farm*. I disagree, however, with Mr. Adams's claim that the book's "center of interest . . . is commercial man" (p. 33).

guilt feelings and tries to make amends. The loyal kindness of Orme shames Lady Mason and persuades her to face her own guilt: "She had intended still to keep her terrible secret to herself. . . . But he had overcome her by his generosity; and in her fixed resolve that he should not be dragged down into this abyss of misery the sudden determination to tell the truth at least to him had come upon her."[16] In confessing, she finds out from Orme's confused and horrified reaction how her crime appears objectively to others, and this releases the flood of contrition and masochistic feeling which swamps her. Trollope's discussion of Lady Mason's guilt is weak and contradictory because he automatically falls back on a rigid code of morality which hardly applies to her case. But his *image* of her is brilliant because it conveys so clearly her will to suffer and, metaphorically, the state of her being for the rest of the novel:

Slowly and very silently she made her way up to her room. . . . It was as yet early in the morning, and the servant had not been in the chamber. There was no fire there although it was still mid-winter . . . soon the bitter air pierced her through and through, and she shivered with the cold as she sat there. Presently the girls did come, and . . . offered to light the fire, but she declared that she was not cold. Her teeth were shaking in her head, but any suffering was better than the suffering of being seen.

She did not lie down, or cover herself . . . nor did she move from her place for more than an hour. By degrees she became used to the cold. She was numbed, and, as it were, half dead in all her limbs, but she had ceased to shake as she sat there. . . .[17]

No English novelist before Trollope, and very few since, have described as extensively the ordinary, unsensational, but widely prevalent forms of masochism which so many people, filled with real or imagined guilt, indulge in. Mas-

---

[16] *Orley Farm* (London, 1963), "double volume" (see Author's Note, p. viii), chap. xlv, p. 43 (II).

[17] *Ibid.*, pp. 49–50 (II).

ochistic behavior continually shows up in his work, from the
case of Feemy in *The Macdermots of Ballycloran* to that of
Henry in *Cousin Henry*. Lady Mason is a prime example.
In all her talk about her own vile depravity, in her servile
way of abasing herself to everyone after her confession,
Trollope makes us see the horrible pain that apparently
normal men and women can inflict upon themselves in their
obsessive craving to atone for their sins.

What needs most of all to be stressed about Lady Mason's
story is its parallel with the Christian doctrine of the Fall of
Man, the original story of early hopes blighted. Original
sin, eventual confession, recognition of guilt, remorse, sorrow, resignation to pain, and the hope of future salvation—
the typically Christian pattern of man's experience—form
crucial parts of Lady Mason's experience. Her original sin
is remote—not even within the time span of the novel; but,
in the same way that, according to Christianity, original sin
is an inescapable part of man's life right from the time of
his birth, her sin dominates her existence. A good but deeply
flawed woman, she stands out in Trollope's vision of life
here—a vision in which struggling humanity lives with the
trappings and consequences of its own selfishness.

For Sir Peregrine Orme, the discovery of Lady Mason's
crime means that he must reevaluate the whole ethical outlook of a lifetime. In fact, after she tells him about her
forgery, the real suspense of the story lies in what his attitude toward her will finally be, and Trollope immediately
switches from her psychology to his. "What was he to do?
How was he to help her? And how was he to be rid of her?
How was he to save his daughter from further contact with
a woman such as this? And how was he to bid his daughter
behave to this woman as one woman should behave to another in her misery? Then too he had learned to love her.
. . ."[18] In the first place, he has extremely inflexible notions

---

[18] *Ibid.*, p. 46 (II).

about personal morality: A person is either good or bad, an action is either right or wrong, and an honest man can easily tell the difference between good and bad people, between right and wrong actions; moreover, there must be no compromise with wickedness. For much of the novel, Trollope makes Sir Peregrine the acme of Victorian moral rigidity. He believes in that lovely Victorian myth of "the pure and good woman" which puts females on towering pedestals of superhuman virtue, with angels flitting about their heads. What ought he to think when he learns that this handsome and admirable woman whom he loves has committed a felony? He finds gradually that the impact of Lady Mason's sin and retribution deepens his capacity for pity, for love, and for grief. It is not so much the actual content of the words which he comes at last to speak about her that makes them so moving; it is rather what these words tell about him and the way they bring home the quiet, but remarkable transformation of his moral consciousness:

" 'I have forgiven her altogether'."[19]

" 'Are we not all sinners?' "[20]

" 'Had she not chosen it herself, she could now have demanded from me a home. Why should I not give it to her now?' "[21]

" 'I was harsh to her . . . cruelly harsh'."[22]

" 'Were I alone in the world I would still beg you to go back with me. . . . I am not alone. . . . But . . . I have learned to love you too well'."[23] He now feels the universality of sin and weakness and the sinner's need for mercy, and he finds to his amazement that a lapse in virtue can make the sinner more, rather than less, lovable.

---

[19] Chap. LXXIX, p. 396 (II).
[20] *Ibid.*
[21] *Ibid.*, p. 397 (II).
[22] *Ibid.*, p. 398 (II).
[23] *Ibid.*, p. 402 (II).

The moral conventions of his beloved daughter-in-law, Mrs. Orme, and the social laws of the world prevent him from ever marrying Lady Mason and condemn him to utter misery for the rest of his life. He realizes that they are the same conventions and laws which he had always before accepted without question. He obeys them still out of duty to his family, but because he finds that life without Lady Mason is empty, he finally understands how morbid rigid convention can be and how much pain it can inflict. Orme can no longer believe in that influential strain of neo-Calvinism which divided people into the virtuous and the wicked.

Trollope, in this old character, imagines with great sensitivity a crisis of the Victorian conscience as it comes to realize what a price it pays for the security of a fixed moral code, how much that moral code—no matter how admirable in itself—inhibits the freedom of the individual to act independently and to be his own judge of human character and circumstance. Only the best novelists have been able to make a change in and development of character seem credible, and Trollope does this with Sir Peregrine. The change in Orme's moral consciousness expresses the unique experience of one who finds that impersonal patterns cannot be imposed on life; it also expresses the common experience of the Victorians who found it difficult to reconcile their ideal of general conformity to fixed and particular moral standards with the equally strong ideal of the sanctity of the individual conscience. And beyond that, the change in Orme touches on the experience of all men living in an unpredictable world that shatters their pet ideas and opinions and forces them to learn unexpected lessons every day.

V

Like old Orme, young Lucius Mason has to change his ideas and give up his idealistic assumptions. Lucius believes in the righteousness of any person or cause in which he puts his faith, but, like most moralists, he has little love or sympathy for others, since they usually do not live up to his ideals. When Trollope created this coldly unattractive but high-minded character with his intolerance for the weaknesses of others, he was getting at another large Victorian problem: the extremely high moral standards which they thought necessary for a good life could sometimes make humanity seem despicable and life seem worthless to them because people obviously could not maintain these standards. One often sees in Thackeray, Dickens, and later in Trollope himself, for example, something which approaches a hatred of humanity for its sheer incapacity to live morally. Even the secret and smug hope of moral superiority—which must surely be one of the most common hopes of men—fades when Mason learns that only by fraud does he own Orley Farm.

Orley Farm is, among other things, a marvelous study of youth and age. Youth's frightful intolerance and tyrannical moral evangelism, its helpless ignorance of life, its freshness, its idealism, its egotism and arrogance, its intelligent insight, its brash confidence, its vulnerability, and its resiliency all stand out in the characterizations of Lucius, the young lawyer Felix Graham, and old Orme's grandson, young Peregrine. But Trollope, as Robert Adams says, is above all "the poet of middle-aged experience." He is one of the most skillful of all novelists in expressing the sense of loss and regret, the narrowing of possibilities, the dispelling of illusions, the knowledge that time and emotion can no longer be wasted, the resignation to the existence of evil, the surprisingly intense passion, and the feeling of obligation to the young which come to people as they age. In passage after passage dealing with Sir Peregrine, Lady Mason, her lawyer and friend, Mr. Furnival, and Mrs. Furnival, he excels in making us see all these consequences of growing older. Lady Mason remarks, for example, of her son, " 'It seems to me that I care more for his soul than for my own.' "

And Sir Peregrine, when he loses her, has nothing left to do but wait "patiently, as he said, till death should come to him."

In the chapters dealing with the Furnivals, Trollope manages to get down wonderfully the atmosphere of quiet desperation in an old marriage gone sour and to convey the feelings of both husband and wife. Furnival married a poor girl for love and then, supported by her, worked fiercely as a lawyer for thirty years; but when he at last becomes rich and successful, he finds himself tied to an ignorant, jealous old woman whom he no longer loves. She is miserable because he neglects her, and he is miserable because he knows he will never be free of her. Neither one, however, is really to blame for their failing marriage; the only villains are time and change, those implacable enemies of love's young dream.

It had come now—all of which they had dreamed, and more than all they had dared hope. But what good was it? Was he happy? No; he was fretful, bilious, and worn with toil which was hard to him because he ate and drank too much; he was ill at ease in public; . . . and he was sick in his conscience—she was sure it must be so: he could not thus neglect her, his loving constant wife, without some pangs of remorse. And was she happy? She might have revelled in silks and satins, if silks and satins would have done her old heart good. . . . Not but what she could have been ecstatic about a full skirt on a smart body if he would have cared to look at it. In truth she was still soft and young enough within, though stout, and solid, and somewhat aged without.[24]

Age does wither and custom does stale people in Trollope.

But aside from time, the usual cause of imperfection and

---

[24] Chap. XI, p. 109 (I). Trollope's portrait of Furnival and his story of Orme's love for a younger woman coincide with his first meetings and intimacy with Kate Field whom he seems to have come to love in more than a fatherly way. See, e.g., Anthony Trollope, *Letters*, ed. Bradford Booth (London, 1951), pp. 116–118.

sin in *Orley Farm* is commercialism. Trollope carefully gives Lady Mason a family background in trade: "Her own parents had risen in the world,—had risen from retail to wholesale, and considered themselves . . . to be good representatives of the commercial energy and prosperity of Great Britain. But a fall had come upon them,—as a fall does come very often to our excellent commercial representatives." Her marriage is a business affair: "He [Sir Joseph Mason] who settled her parents' financial affairs took to his bosom as his portion of the assets of the estate, young Mary Johnson, and made her wife and mistress of Orley Farm."[25] Marrying on a *quid pro quo* basis, Lady Mason reacted according to the only ethic she knew—the commercial ethic —when she learned that her husband meant to cheat her. Ironically, Lady Mason's enemies in the case, Attorney Dockwrath and Joseph Mason, her stepson, are men to whom all life is also business. Trollope, satirizing a certain bourgeois mentality, says that Mason's idea of morality is "paying your tradesmen regularly," and he gives Dockwrath one of the more significant remarks in the book when he has him say, " 'In this enterprising country all men are more or less commercial.' "

Trollope also uses the commercial spirit of his age as a source of comedy and satire in *Orley Farm*. In Mr. Moulder, the gourmandizing food-and-beverage merchant, and Mr. Kantwise, a seller of collapsible tables and chairs, he creates two of the funniest traveling salesmen in fiction. Both Kantwise, who sees everyone he meets as a potential customer for his sleazy metallic furniture ("It's the real Louey Catorse," said Mr. Kantwise), and Moulder, a grotesque, obese glutton, help characterize the atmosphere of shoddy commercialism in which Lady Mason lives. Certainly Moulder, a kind of walking appetite who prides himself on being "commercial," embodies the excesses of a materialistic cul-

---

[25] *Orley Farm*, chap. II, p. 13 (I).

ture. Trollope imagines Christmas Day at the Moulders', and uses this scene to satirize the belly-worshipping greed that permeates affluent societies. Moulder, on this holy day, makes the table his altar and a turkey his savior:

"It weighed twenty-four pounds, for I put it on the scales myself, and old Gibbetts let me have it for a guinea. The price marked on it was five-and twenty, for I saw it. He's had it hanging for a fortnight, and I've been to see it wiped down with vinegar regular every morning. And now, my boys, it's done to a turn. I've been in the kitchen most of the time myself, and either I or Mrs. M. has never left it for a single moment."

"How did you manage about divine service?" said Kantwise, and then when he had spoken, closed his eyes and sucked his lips.

Mr. Moulder looked at him for a minute, and then said, "Gammon."

For the next three or four minutes Moulder did not speak a word. The turkey was on his mind, with the stuffing, the gravy, the liver, the breast, the wings, and the legs. He stood up to carve it, and while he was at work he looked at it as though his two eyes were hardly sufficient.[26]

Like Dickens, Trollope uses the act of eating and how people look upon it to define not only the nature of particular characters but also various moral tones in his world. Food to Victorian novelists is like sex to modern writers.

Part of the world of commerce in the novel is the Law. Most of the lawyers sell their services to clients regardless of their own views about the merits of the case. Worrying about legal standards, Felix Graham does not understand how lawyers like Chaffanbrass and Furnival can subordinate honesty for gain and reputation. Yet Trollope presents, on the whole in *Orley Farm*, a fair and illuminating picture of the legal system. Law and legal morality merely prove that men live in a fallen state; they do not cause the fall. When

---

[26] Chap. XXIV, p. 241 (I).

we compare the treatment of the legal system in *Bleak House* with that in *Orley Farm*, we find that Trollope's view is not only fairer than Dickens's, it is truer. Dickens sees an imperfect and corrupt institution destroying the moral fiber of man. Trollope sees the imperfect nature of man necessarily having to create the legal institution in order to bring some stability into life. He knows perfectly well that as a device of man it will often work unjustly, but for him the legal profession—like any work—is a consequence of man's fall.

Graham attacks attorneys for separating personal and professional ethics and also for emphasizing victory in a trial rather than truth. His criticism makes sense theoretically, but when we turn to Lady Mason's case, we see that it would be unjust for her to be convicted and sent to jail. But that is exactly what would have happened had Graham had charge of her defense. He finds himself assisting her at her trial, yet he knows she is guilty. Should he do his duty by his client or should he tell the truth? The question paralyzes him, and he does nothing. We have here the bugbear of every moralist: the conflict of two loyalties, each of which is based on important ethical ideals. Perfect justice can not possibly be obtained, and moral choices in the flawed world of *Orley Farm* often prove to be the difficult choices between greater and lesser wrongs. Trollope does not say that Felix is wrong (as a matter of fact, he often uses Graham as a mouthpiece for his own sentiments), but he does show that, right or wrong, Felix does not really aid the cause of higher justice and morality here.

The moral ambiguity in Graham's clash with the ways of the world—that is, the failure to resolve the ethical questions raised by the clash—is typical of the novel. Trollope often leaves it to the reader to pass moral judgments on the characters and action. Sir Peregrine's daughter-in-law, Mrs. Orme, for example, plays a major part in the plot. She prevents Sir Peregrine from marrying Lady Mason after he has forgiven her and found out just how much she means to him. Almost without protest, Orme and Lady Mason accept her decision. Is Mrs. Orme's act moral or not? One might conclude either that she acts selfishly or that she takes the unpleasant responsibility of upholding reasonable moral standards in the family. Trollope himself does not even analyze the question. What he does is to make a reader see the human tendency to throw a cloak of morality around self-interest, to become oblivious to the connection between what one thinks is right and what will benefit one. The irony here is that Mrs. Orme, like Lady Mason, has her own son's interest at heart before everything else. Trollope imagines what people *will do* under pressure from a changing world, not what they ought to do.

When Trollope falls back on easy black-and-white morality—for example, when he shrilly attacks lawyers or castigates Lady Mason as a terrible sinner—his writing becomes strident and shallow. But usually the force of his narrative directly contradicts these moments when his marvelous power to distinguish what *is* true from what *ought* to be true failed him. The whole drift of the book and the accumulation of experience in it stress moral complexity and deny the possibility of easy solutions for ethical problems. Trollope denies one of the fondest hopes of the Victorians, the possibility of establishing a workable and fixed moral code which would improve human behavior and also spare people the agony of making their own moral decisions.

Among the great and lasting moral questions raised in *Orley Farm* are these: To what degree is it proper to compromise the truth in order to achieve a desirable end? How far ought forgiveness of sin to extend here on earth? What are the limits of one's proper duty and loyalty to one's children? Does idealism bring about more harm than good? Is righteousness a mask for cruelty and ego gratification? Trollope does not provide answers to these problems—time would eventually prove specific answers wrong or dated anyway.

The valuable thing is that he shows these questions arising naturally in particular lives and insists that ethical considerations are always concrete and always important.

Trollope's moral ambiguity can be annoying when it prevents him from understanding and imagining as fully as he might a character such as Mrs. Orme. But at other times it reinforces his impressive interpretation of life in which he points out how dangerous and difficult it is to pass moral judgment on people and how individual lives resist schematizations into moral patterns. It also reflects the extreme insecurity and uncertainty which lay beneath the outward conformity in the Victorian age.

His interpretation of life as he presents it in *Orley Farm* has a coherence which his other books of this period often lack. Almost everything in the book tends to create the image of a lapsed world in which pain, sin, and confusion necessarily exist. And experience, with its unpredictability, teaches people that they cannot dominate this world nor impose their wills upon it for long. Time and a mutable world bring Lady Mason and Peregrine Orme new wisdom and sorrow, and their experience, unique as it is, expresses the human condition as Trollope saw it in these years of his own success. People and societies can never entirely escape from their tainted pasts, nor can they avoid the disappointment which inevitably comes as the future becomes the present. In Trollope as in the novels of Anthony Powell, all must dance to the music of time.

5
Love and the Victorians: Thorns Among the Roses

Love blooms or fades in all of Trollope's novels, and in the group of books following *Orley Farm* it becomes his main interest. In most of his earlier novels, love relationships tend to be conventionally stereotyped or irrelevant. In *The Three Clerks, Doctor Thorne,* and *Barchester Towers* he accepted an idealized Victorian version of love as the purifying and redeeming element in life and used it as a "pledge to the future" to create a sense of fulfillment and hope at the end: there is little serious concern in his world with the unhappy realities of love. Even *The Bertrams,* with its unhappy love affair, has an illogical happy ending. But beginning with *The Small House at Allington,* he examines incessantly the complexities of love, romance, and marriage.

Trollope became possessed by the whole schizoid nature of love among the Victorians. In 1862, while he worked on *The Small House,* Meredith's *Modern Love* and the final version of Coventry Patmore's *Angel in the House* both appeared. Patmore celebrates the literal Victorian belief in the holiness and unity of love and marriage; Meredith does just the opposite and stresses the sheer hell of married life. The age idealized home and family, the loving Biedermeier queen of domesticity, the eternally devoted lover, the eternally faithful beloved, but it had to contend with such

realities as maiden aunts, fortune hunters, prostitutes, materialistic merger-marriages, and lifetime separations of husbands and wives. The sixties brought new frankness and
objectivity about love, sex, and women to Britain, and
changing attitudes about relationships between the sexes
developed. Even so, the forces of Bowdlerism, sexual repression, and semireligious sanctification of love flourished as
never before.[1] Trollope, in this period, managed to get down
the confusion and conflict about love which worried Victorian souls. He knew that a love ideal existed and that
basically it sprang from a deep yearning for personal stability. Though ideas about it might be shifting, it consciously
or unconsciously affected almost every better-class Victorian.

Briefly, the dogma of idealistic love insisted: that true love
between man and woman culminating in marriage is a
sacred source of all civilized feeling; that this *true* love is
spiritual and eternal rather than physical and perishable;
that once a person loves another, he is bound to love faithfully for as long as he lives whether or not his love is re-
quited; that to marry without true spiritual love is a terrible
sin; that one can have only a single true love; that women
are naturally pure, angelic creatures unless corrupted by
men; that women are less physical, less slaves to their bodies
than men, therefore they are morally "higher beings"; that
men ought to respect the delicacy and the moral superiority
of females; that life without love is incomplete; that the
state of loving is mysterious and God-ordained—love is above
and beyond rational analysis. This may be oversimplified, but
something very like it was well established, understood, and
set down in various forms by the sixties. The love faith had
the same sort of direct and indirect influence on the Victorians that any significant contemporary religion has on
people. They might hate it, reject it, disbelieve it, or sub-
scribe to it, but they all had somehow to deal with it.

---

[1] See Walter E. Houghton, *The Victorian Frame of Mind
1830–1870* (London, 1957), pp. 341–393.

Trollope, like his age, was torn. He sharply defined and tried to uphold the love myths, but he categorically described the breakdown of the love ideal. In *The Small House at Allington, Rachel Ray, Can You Forgive Her?, Miss Mackenzie,* and *The Claverings,* he gets at the perils of love—the run-of-the-mill, yet heartbreaking difficulties of love and marriage. The horrors of unrequited love, the mental tortures of marriage, the cruelties that men and women inflict on each other, the obstacles that society puts in the way of young lovers—all these things contradict romanticized notions that self-deceiving readers might have about love's ideal love bliss. Love can become a terrible curse in Trollope, "this agony of flesh," in Meredith's words. And yet almost fanatically he wanted to believe that it was a blessing, that Patmore was right when he called love the "sole mortal thing of worth immortal." Tension between the love ideal and the real love behavior of people shaped his fiction as it shaped nineteenth-century life and as it in curious ways still shapes twentieth-century life.

I

The Small House at Allington (1862–1863) is about the disturbing sterility of love in his world. Either the characters cannot live up to the love ideal, or, if they do, they get hurt. Nearly all of them are unsuccessful lovers, unhappy and childless husbands and wives, old maids, bachelors, or widows. The world here seems sick and ominously barren, despite the superficially comfortable Barsetshire life and the comedy of London bureaucracy. Trollope begins and ends with sterile, thwarted love. The first chapter concerns Squire Dale who "had fallen in love with a lady who obstinately refused his hand, and on her account he had remained single." In the last chapter Lily Dale and John Eames both vow to stay single after failing to marry their loves. Trollope purposely creates a pattern of infertility in a stagnant and impotent society.

Lily Dale, the heroine, tells us a great deal about the
strengths and weaknesses of the Victorians, about their
ideals, their psychology, and their passions. Early in the
book, she seems to be extremely attractive. For the first time
Trollope imagined a lovely, virtuous young girl who has the
lively wit and the pride of his antiheroines, but, like them,
can make mistakes. She has what so many women in Victorian fiction lack, intelligence and the ability to articulate
emotion. When she falls in love with Adolphus Crosbie, she
is genuinely charming. Trollope neither patronizes nor idealizes these two, and their behavior develops naturally out of
their own individuality rather than from a conventional
image of romance. At first wary of Crosbie and his faults,
she gaily treats him with mocking irony, but gradually her
defenses against him lapse, and when he kisses her she displays the depth of her feeling and cries helplessly to him,
" 'Oh, my love! My love! My love!' "[2] The exact words are
very important: it is actually *her love* she loves rather than
Crosbie the man. Just before this he tells her that she longs
to love, and she replies, " 'Oh yes. *I would be nothing without that.* . . . It is a delight to love you; to know that I may
love *you*.' "[3] Loving makes her *something*, gives her identity,
and she delights in perceiving her own love. Without taking
a superior tone, Trollope shows that Lily loves an illusion of
Crosbie that exists only in her own mind, not the character
which we see.

Skillfully he renders the real Crosbie's own puzzled state
of mind once he wins Lily. He mulls over those typical
questions which men generally ask themselves when they
become sure of their women: Now that I have her, is she
really worth giving up my freedom for?, and Couldn't I do
better? Trollope is careful not to make him a villain even
when he breaks his engagement. He is simply a weak, con-

[2] *The Small House at Allington* (London, 1950), "double
volume" (see Author's Note, p. viii), chap. ix, p. 123 (I).

[3] *Ibid.*, p. 122 (I), italics mine.

fused man, well-meaning but lacking the capacity to love
deeply. Lily's idolatry of him is understandable, but even in
love, idolatry causes harm. Trollope may gush about love in
bad sentimental passages, but his assessment of Crosbie and
Lily's love affair is tough and realistic.

We get an idea of why the Victorians idealized love as they
did when we compare Lily with Jane Austen's Emma. Both
are brilliant, imaginative girls living in rather cloying circumstances, and both are slightly bored and rebellious.
Their societies constrict them and give them little to do;
each asserts her will through romantic illusion. But Emma
learns that illusions prevent self-knowledge and endanger
herself as well as others. She must learn to merge her being
with her society and take her proper place in that society.
Emma's wise and moral knight, Knightly, teaches her that
happiness and fulfillment depend on living up to social
standards and finding harmony between her personality,
her needs, and the social structure in which she lives. The
moral center and the social ideals of her world *do* coincide,
and her love for Knightly is ultimately a rational emotion.
Reason and conscience can show her the error of her impulses and actions. In the relatively well regulated social
order in which she can take some security for granted, she
finally sees illusions for what they are.

Lily Dale lives more precariously. She has no fixed place
in society. The society itself is changing and so are its standards and ideals. The characters are unsure about their
values, and none of them serves as a center of intelligence
and morality. Trollope deliberately makes her social position ambiguous: she is a poor girl from a good family, well
educated, with uncertain expectations. People try to curb
her strong personality, but for what reason she hardly knows.
She is expected to be passive and to accept whatever comes
along. Her love for the ideal Crosbie whom she imagines
allows her to create an active self in a society which no
longer can be counted on to provide a sense of identity. Her

stubborn, unhappy love counteracts her fear of nothingness. When Crosbie jilts her, she will not stop loving him because to do so would be to betray the separate identity that her love provides her. She cannot renounce her love because it is she as lover that she loves, not Crosbie. Her illusion becomes her very being. At the end, she tells her mother almost proudly, " 'He [Crosbie] has changed, but I have not.' "[4] By not changing, she proves her will stronger than those around her.

Trollope perceived that love could fill two needs. It could give the illusion of something permanent in oneself beyond the reach of time and change, and it could give one a feeling of distinction in an unstable society. Love in *Emma* is a force for integration in the world; in *The Small House* it is an idealistic means of escape from a disappointing world.

In his shaping imagination, if not in his conscious mind, Trollope understood the morbidly destructive side of the love ideal. Lily's character deteriorates because her romanticized love for Crosbie saps her capacity for affection. After he marries someone else, her masochistic devotion to the sacredness of her love make her family and friends suffer. She turns into a demanding, difficult spinster. The trouble is that Trollope sometimes tries to wring out pathos and sympathy for her as a love saint of the faithful heart. He *tells* us how admirable her loyalty to Crosbie is while he *shows* how perverse and selfish it becomes. He was right to describe sympathetically the intricate motivation which could make a spinster, but wrong to ask sympathy for a self-indulgent sentimentality that debases a human soul.

II

The wounded-fawn, bleeding-heart behavior of Lily and the other unrequited lovers in the novel is ultimately frivolous. Trollope says as much when he compares Lily to a

---

[4] Chap. LVII, p. 383 (II).

lower-class London girl, Amelia Roper. Class and economics
had a lot to do with the idealistic code of love, as we shall
see. Like Lily, Amelia is jilted. John Eames gets carried away
and promises to marry her, but then, remembering his *true
love* for Lily, he welshes. Amelia loves him, but when he
drops her, instead of pining away like Lily, she lures his best
friend into marriage. The lower classes could not afford to
idealize love. Just before her wedding, she tells John: " 'It's
all trash and nonsense and foolery; I know that: It's all very
well for young ladies as can sit in drawing-rooms all their
lives, but when a woman has to make her way in the world
it's all foolery. And such a hard way too to make as mine.
. . . Not that I'm going to complain. I never minded hard
work, and as for company, I can put up with anybody. . . .
it's all over now and I wish you good-bye.' "[5] In the early
part of the book, Trollope tends to patronize Amelia as a
rather insensitive girl, but in the end he gives her a kind of
dignified courage and a knowledge about the hardship of
reality which the idle, self-pitying Lily never has. Lily can
choose to remain single because her uncle agrees to support
her, but Amelia's poverty means she must marry or be exploited.

The Small House at Allington lets a good many cats out
of the bag of nineteenth-century love worship. If one followed the code, one automatically proved oneself genteel—
exalted over those people who married out of economic
necessity. One literally had "class." Also the faithfulness of
loving young ladies had an economic motive behind it, as
we see when Lily promises to wait indefinitely for the struggling Crosbie. It gave a man time to establish his financial
and class standing before he had to support a family. And
the comic scenes in the disreputable London boarding house
where John Eames lives show how men could pass the time
while remaining "true" to the girls they left behind. Since

---

[5] Chap. LIX, pp. 404–405 (II).

the eternal-love business did not apply to the lower classes, there were plenty of girls, like Amelia and the amorous Mrs. Lupex, with whom bachelors could console themselves. The Victorians attempted to spiritualize love, but the flesh naturally always demands its own.

Still, whatever worldliness actually lay behind the love code, they themselves never doubted that love was the greatest force opposing crass, soul-withering materialism. The love ideal condemned the barter-marriage system for making commodities out of people. Since time immemorial the upper classes had married in order to bolster economic and social status, but this offended the idealism of the Victorian middle classes. Either it made love and marriage mundane, or it divorced one from the other. Merger-marriage was literally sacrilegious. When Crosbie drops Lily to marry Lady Alexandrina De Courcy for her title and her connections, he behaves blasphemously.Trollope nevertheless has sympathy for him and through him shows how insistently the nineteenth-century success-ethic pressured the middle classes into using marriage to get ahead. Poor Crosbie ends up as a rather touching, miserably married victim in the clash of two mighty Victorian faiths—the worship of success and the worship of love.

Materialistic self-interest perverts and kills romantic love in the novel, leaving people either isolated or trapped in hellish marriages, and Trollope's irony keeps pointing up the shriveled spirit of romance. Crosbie, feeling guilty about leaving Lily for Alexandrina's rank, tries to boost his morale by comparing himself to "those sundry heroes of romance, . . . Lothario, Don Juan, and Lovelace."[6] And the feeble Victorian heir to these caddish and dashing lovers, the one would-be passionate adulterer in the book, is the dull young Plantagenet Palliser.

The whole magnificent Palliser series of novels begins

---

[6] Chap. XXV, p. 339 (I).

with the short episode of his flirtation with Griselda, Lady Dumbello. Trollope realized that not only was love behavior shaped by society, but that in turn it helped form the whole character of his world and had far-reaching effects on social and political life. It is important to see that he invented Palliser, the future Prime Minister, just when he was writing this damning critique of Victorian love practices. Later he makes him a fascinating image of humanity, but here he calls him "a thin-minded, plodding respectable man, willing to devote all his youth to work."[7] A government expert buried in statistics, and a proper Victorian with a repressed libido, Palliser is love-starved, and twenty minutes of innocuous conversation with Griselda convinces him that he is mad about her. But the whole thing stays in his mind. He is too timid to tell her how he feels, and finally, very much afraid of the free emotional life which seems to lead toward sin, he pleases his elders by meekly letting himself be married off to a wealthy heiress.

During this silly infatuation Palliser displays a deeply repressed nature that sometimes bursts out with flashes of irrationality. He is dissatisfied with conventional propriety, yet believes this is a wicked impulse in him which ought to be checked. He fears passion and fails to communicate his strong emotions or arouse feeling in others. He tends to be passive and unworldly and to lack daring. These weaknesses are exactly the same ones which hurt him later on, not only as husband and father, but also as a politician. The private experiences of love and the cultural attitudes toward love could be crucial in forming the psychology of a public leader and thus crucial in political history. Moreover, Palliser's flaws are also faults which the ruling classes revealed in the second half of the century—probably they were the major weaknesses of the Victorian age.

What distinguishes *The Small House* as fiction is Trollope's powerful analysis of a society that goes sterile and warps

---

[7] Chap. XXIII, p. 319 (I).

some of its best people. To harden love into a selfish, private dogma, as Lily and others do, to make it an otherworldly ideal which has nothing to do with another person or the realities of life, is to be on the side of infertility and—finally —death. But Crosbie and those who deny love, making people into objects to be used for gain, also side with death because they literally dehumanize people.

In two short, seemingly incidental conversations, Trollope's intention and effect of creating a perverted atmosphere of infertility come clear: As the aristocratic but stupid George De Courcy starts to bed, his wife says seductively, " 'George —if I have a baby, and if he should be a boy, and if—,' " but he immediately cuts her short, " 'Oh, nonsense . . . I'm going to sleep.' "[8] Later, Crosbie's wife Alexandrina, talking with her sister, complains about her marriage. The sister says, " 'Perhaps you'll have a baby, you know.' 'Psha!' ejaculated Lady Alexandrina; 'I don't want a baby and I don't suppose I shall have one.' "[9] Like love in Blake's poem "The Sick Rose," love in *The Small House* is wormish, dark, life-destroying, and barren. It is directed toward ideals or things, not human beings. It does not reproduce.

III

Trollope understood how love could become a self-contained, fanatical drive for psychological and material security. People, in trying dogmatically to live up to the love code and avoid the risk and emotional pain of change, could cut themselves off from others and miss the rich fecundity of life. Yet his next book, *Rachel Ray* (1863), shows love as the liberating force which allows his society to adapt itself to change and to build.

He sets his story in a small village called Baselhurst and makes it a microcosm of Victorian England. The most power-

---

[8] *Ibid.*, p. 329 (I).
[9] Chap. XLVIII, p. 245 (II).

ful, most active townspeople are religious neo-Puritans. Rachel Ray grows up in a stifling environment dominated by an Evangelical group that regards "all the outer world . . . as wicked and dangerous." Trollope hated Evangelicalism as much as it was in him to hate anything human, and he saw love as a potential influence to counteract its life-despising mentality.

Of course the Evangelical spirit helped form the Victorian love code. One sees the tie between the love religion and Evangelical Protestantism in Lily Dale, whose love expresses itself in holy faith rather than in earthly works. It becomes a state of mind rather than a tangible relationship with another. Trollope, however, thought that real love ought to open up a person to the wonder and goodness of the world and expand the awareness of life's possibilities, as he imagined it doing for Rachel Ray. He believed in love as a religion, but this religious feeling was very practical and earthly.

Luke Rowan, a pragmatic, optimistic young man falls in love with Rachel and makes her fall in love with him. The community blocks their way, but they finally marry. That is basically all there is to the plot. Once the two pledge their love early in the story, they become ciphers of faithfulness, and real conflict disappears. Nevertheless, the novel is charming. Baselhurst has all the familiar traits of the actual Victorian scene. Changes of all kinds are going on, old-timers get crotchety and fearful, young men like Luke Rowan bring to town modern business methods which worry the established businessmen, religious factions wage ecclesiastical war, a London Jew comes down to contest the town's seat in Parliament, and all the while the strong Evangelical set views the world with alarm and tries with some success to mold people into a strict, narrow, moral pattern.

In Trollope's view, love is what makes it possible to build a decent life in such conditions. It tempers Rowan's aggressive ambition with concern for others and breaks down Rachel's distrust of humanity. It cracks those religious, mind-forged manacles of the Victorians. Romantic love has the same kind of revolutionary, earth-shaking impact on the individual soul in *Rachel Ray* as sexual love has in Orwell's *1984*. Each has the power to liberate human emotions from the puritanical fear of other people and the dull conformity which breeds contempt for the world. In an early chapter, Rachel Ray goes walking one evening with Luke Rowan. Her pious Evangelical sister, Dorothea, also goes out. A magnificent sunset fills the Baselhurst sky, but Dorothea, busy condemning Rachel in her thoughts for being out alone with a man, does not even notice. Obsessively afraid of love, she is blind to beauty. Just a few yards away, however, Rowan has been pointing out the sunset to Rachel, and she, beginning to fall in love with him, feels for the first time the glory and immensity of life:

> In the few moments that they stood there gazing it might almost have been believed that some portentous miracle had happened, so deep and dark, and yet so bright, were the hues of the horizon. It seemed as though the lands below the hill were bathed in blood. . . .
> She looked down into the flood of light beneath her, with a full consciousness that every moment that she lingered there was a new sin; with full consciousness too that the beauty of those fading colours seen thus in his presence possessed a charm, a sense of soft delight, which she had never known before.

Later she muses:

> But he bade her look into the clouds for new worlds, and she seemed to feel that there was a hidden meaning in his words. As she looked out into the coming darkness, a mystery crept over her, a sense of something wonderful that was out there, away—of something so full of mystery that she could not tell whether she was thinking of hidden distances of the horizon, or of the distances of her own future life, which were still further off and more closely hidden. She found herself trembling, sighing, almost sobbing.[10]

---

[10] *Rachel Ray* (London, 1924), chap. IV, pp. 38–42.

The fusing of image and idea makes this a lovely and moving passage, the kind of thing to keep in mind when we hear that Trollope is "pedestrian." Its almost Lawrentian lyrical intensity reminds us that, after all, Trollope and the Victorians were right: love is a religious force and does have an irrational, magical effect on people. The paean to love in the novel is finally convincing because we see a person coming alive to discover and enjoy herself, her lover, and the whole physical world.

IV

Like most idylls, *Rachel Ray* ends in a happy marriage, and the impetus which makes nineteenth-century novels end so regularly with "ideal" marriages must be taken seriously. It is more than just an archetypal literary formula manifesting itself; it expresses the strongest wishes of a particular age and people. The Victorians were profoundly moved by the idea of happy marriage as the crowning glory of existence. The idea had the power of vital myth. The joining of sympathetic lovers kept reaffirming the faith that, in a time of radical individualism, secure happiness and fulfillment could be found in a personal relationship—that communion, love, and understanding were still to be had in spite of all the new and old forces of alienation. A happy union at the close of all those books captured the nineteenth-century imagination, not just because it had the appeal of "the life force," but because it seemed to promise that an end to loneliness, a full appreciation of oneself by another, and freedom of self-expression—this was especially important for women —were distinct possibilities in life.

But the particulars of heaven-on-earth will not bear closer scrutiny than heaven-in-the-sky and, in fact, surprisingly few Victorian novels, or any other novels for that matter, deal with marriage in much detail or at all well. Marriages in fiction—particularly nineteenth-century fiction—almost always seem artificial and static. They tend to follow rigidly preconceived patterns: they are comic (the Caudles, the Proudies), or irrevocably doomed to misunderstanding (the Shandys, the Bennets), or unhappiness (the Casaubons, the Lydgates, the Osmonds), or—less often—ideal (the Meagles, the Darnays). They lack the contingencies of real marriages with their continuing processes of change and readjustment.

Trollope, in the most interesting part of *Can You Forgive Her?* (1863–1864), begins rather than ends with marriage. He takes up where he had left off in *The Small House at Allington*, with Plantagenet Palliser and his new wife, Lady Glencora. His treatment of married life in this and the other Palliser novels is one of the finest in fiction.[11] He had a cast of mind which rebelled against the absolute way in which people speak and write about marriages: "She made a bad marriage," "He made a good marriage," "They made an ideal couple," "They were mismatched," and so forth. For Trollope this kind of talk only falsifies that most intricate of human relationships, a relationship which varies from day to day and year to year. In his autobiography he calls the Pallisers his best characters, and he says significantly, "It was my study that these people, as they grew in years, should encounter the changes which come upon us all." He wanted to get away from easy judgments and conventional attitudes toward marriage and to bring out the infinite complexity and the kinetic quality of the Pallisers' relationship.

Unfortunately the beautifully conceived story of their early life together is surrounded and partially spoiled by the longer Alice Vavasor part of the book. Trollope's weakness of inconsistency is never more damaging than in *Can You Forgive Her?* He simply failed to resolve and integrate the shallow-minded, idealistic notions of nineteenth-century love and marriage which he set down in the Vavasor–John Grey scenes with his sophisticated interpretation of the Pallisers.

---

[11] See Arthur Mizener, "Anthony Trollope: The Palliser Novels," in *From Jane Austen to Joseph Conrad*, ed. Robert C. Rathburn and Martin Steinmann (Minneapolis, 1958), for an illuminating, always interesting study to which my reading of the Palliser novels is much indebted.

Both parts of the book assault conventions of the love code, both deal with triangles, and both are concerned with feminine guilt. Trollope begins well, imagining that a woman may have extreme difficulty in *knowing* whether she is in love or not and therefore may make stupid mistakes about men before she knows whom she wants to marry and why. Alice Vavasor jilts her upright fiancé, John Grey, because she thinks he is too good for her, then gets engaged to her wicked cousin, but at last decides that she loves John and marries him. But eventually Trollope realized that something was going wrong and that these characters who were going to show the inadequacies of convention and proprieties were themselves turning into wooden stereotypes; after two hundred pages or so he introduces the Pallisers.

Glencora's marriage leads to conflict of two ideals, both of which the Victorians knew ought to be sacred: true love and marital fidelity. She was made to marry Palliser for social and economic reasons, although she loved Burgo Fitzgerald. She is very young, and for a time she wants to run off with the irresponsible Fitzgerald because, with her head full of Victorian romance, she knows that she still loves him and she feels that she has just as much reason to be true to him as to her husband. Trollope's nerve failed him in creating Alice, but he had more courage with Glencora. He imagined a young, likable, intelligent, married woman loving a charming rogue of her own free will without his deceiving her. This was something new in the English novel. He wanted to show how dangerous the glorification of love could be. He sympathizes with her in her merger-marriage, but he also makes it perfectly clear that had she had her way and married Fitzgerald, the man whom she loves and who loves her, her life would have turned out to be disastrous.

Nineteenth-century novelists were obsessed by the souls, the psychology, and the changing roles of leisure-class women. Such brilliant creations as Emma Woodhouse, Di Vernon, Emma Bovary, Becky Sharp, Dorothea Brooke,

Anna Karenina, and Isabel Archer all show their authors' concern with woman's rebellion against convention, her conscious quest for individuality, and the effects on society. Glencora Palliser is one of the greatest of these nineteenth-century women in European fiction. In her, Trollope expresses carefully and fully, not only the frustration, flightiness, passion, and courage of a single high-spirited Victorian woman in all her complexity, but also a kind of universal feminine plight. She continually has to fight for her independence, insisting that her personal feelings be considered and that she be treated as *herself, Glencora,* a unique individual, and not as some conventional woman or wife. She has to keep battling the idea that she ought to curb her personality, that she ought to be genteel rather than honest and make herself conform to an abstract pattern of ideal feminine behavior.

The love ideal asserted that girls could be, and often were, angelic creatures. Over and over in Victorian literature you find the words "pure" and "angel" used to describe women, and the mystical belief in feminine purity helped make love holy. Trollope shrewdly says that a society which kept inculcating the belief that women ought to be pure—that purity is somehow a normal feminine condition like wearing dresses—would cause a strong sense of guilt in women who were wise enough to know just how impure they were and how impossible it was to live up to the angel-in-the-house ideal. Glencora finds herself so far below this ideal and so full of passion, emotion, and defiance that she comes to think of herself as hopelessly lost anyway, with very little to lose by completely defying all decorum. " 'Do you know,' " she says, when her husband has taken her abroad so that Burgo Fitzgerald cannot tempt her to run off, " 'there are moments when I almost make up my mind to go headlong to the devil, —when I think it is the best thing to be done.' "[12] Her guilt

---

[12] *Can You Forgive Her?* (London, 1953), "double volume" (see Author's Note, p. viii), chap. LXVIII, p. 354 (II).

only makes her more reckless. Why try to be perfect when you know you are irreparably wicked? Trollope describes the desperate quality of her mind as she realizes that she can never possibly live up to Victorian moral expectations: "Whatever way she might go, she was lost. . . . She did not count herself for much, what though she were ruined?"[13] Glencora keeps running up against the walls of propriety. People tell her that she must not do things like waltzing, joking, or gambling, because they are unbecoming to a woman. But gradually we see that this nineteenth-century propriety is a form of tyranny dictating that women accept their lot as members of an oppressed second sex. An example shows the kind of circumscribed world in which Glencora must live; a man converses with Alice about how she spends her time: " 'Do you hunt?' 'No.' 'Do you shoot?' 'No; I don't shoot.' 'Do you ride?' 'No; I wish I did . . .' 'Do you drive?' 'No; I don't drive either.' 'Then what do you do?' 'I sit at home, and—' 'Mend your stockings?' "[14]

With more leisure and more education for women, they naturally came to resent a cloying atmosphere in which they seemed to be molded for decoration like so many hollow-headed figurines. Glencora's difficulties in loving her husband, her impulsiveness and her querulousness, are various reactions against the stifling of her individual liberty. When you limit freedom, you also limit the capacity to love. Glencora's frustrated spontaneity and her longing to be free are moving. One evening in Switzerland where Palliser has brought her to keep her away from Fitzgerald, Glencora and her party sit above a river:

Suddenly, there shot down before them in the swift running stream the heads of many swimmers in the river, and with the swimmers came boats carrying their clothes. They went by almost like a glance of light upon the waters, so

---

[13] Chap. LVIII, p. 22 (II).
[14] Chap. XXIII, p. 291–293 (I).

rapid was the course of the current. There was the shout of the voices,—the quick passage of the boats,—the uprising, some half a dozen times, of the men's hands above the surface; and then they were gone down the river, out of sight— like morsels of wood thrown into a cataract, which are borne away instantly.

"Oh how I wish I could do that!" said Lady Glencora.

"It seems to be very dangerous," said Mr. Palliser. "I don't know how they can stop themselves."

"Why should they want to stop themselves?" said Lady Glencora. "Think how cool the water must be; and how beautiful to be carried along so quickly; to go on, and on, and on! I suppose we couldn't try it?"

. . . As no encouragement was given to this proposition, Lady Glencora did not repeat it.[15]

Trollope did not sympathize openly with the feminist movement that was gathering steam just when he was writing this novel (1864), but he understood the feminine need for action, emotional outlet, and an end of intense repression.

Glencora is one of the few women ever created by a male novelist who has a fully developed, conscious sense of humor. She uses her wit subversively to puncture her husband's maddening reserve and shock the officious companions whom he forces on her. But a poignant, almost desperate quality about her humor makes it seem like a plea for the integrity of her being. She needs dignity and personal respect, and when she makes fun of Palliser for noting the number of eggs consumed daily in Paris or shows plainly how bored she is at having to listen to him explain economics and the National Treasury, she in effect fights against having her interests dictated for her by her husband. In mocking him she attacks that common male belief that certain matters are important just because a *man* says so.

Despite their sentimentality about women and love, the Victorians exploited both. Trollope brings out the vulner-

---

[15] Chap. LXIX, p. 371 (II).

ability of Glencora by comparing her to a pathetic prostitute. Side by side with the crinoline world of feminine propriety and hearts-and-flowers love there existed another world of sordidness. Trollope, however, knew they were really just parts of the same world. Two women in the novel show love for Burgo Fitzgerald: Glencora and a whore who appears twice. Each time the whore accosts Burgo just when he is thinking about the way that Glencora was sold into marriage. Both women have been victimized and used as objects, and each responds to Fitzgerald because without condescending he treats them with affection. Here is the second meeting of Burgo and the girl:

". . . You are so handsome! I remember you gave me supper one night when I was starving. I ain't hungry now. Will you give me a kiss?"—"I'll give you a shilling, and that's better," said Burgo. "But give me a kiss too," said the girl. He gave her first the kiss, and then the shilling, and after that left her and passed on. . . . "I wonder whether anything really ails him?" thought the girl. "He said he was wretched before. Shouldn't I like to be good to such a one as him!"[16]

Immediately after this, he goes to Glencora and nearly persuades her to go off with him. She resists but tells Alice,

"I am not such a fool as to mistake what I should be if I left my husband and went to live with that man as his mistress. . . . But why have I been brought to such a pass as this? And as for female purity! Ah! What was their idea of purity when they forced me to marry a man for whom they knew I never cared? . . . How;—when he [Fitzgerald] kissed me, and I could hardly restrain myself from giving him back his kiss tenfold, could I respect myself? But it is all sin. I sin towards my husband feigning that I love him; and I sin in loving that other man, who should have been my husband."[17]

By arranging the book so that we have to compare the re-

---

[16] Chap. LXVI, p. 324 (II).
[17] Chap LXVII, pp. 343–344 (II).

actions of these two, Trollope points up the fact that women are women. In some ways they are all alike, and yet each is a unique creature which a complex range of emotions and an unpredictability which belies the conventional image of the passive Biedermeier love-goddess and the stereotypes of the "good" or "bad," the "virtuous" or the "fallen" woman. Both the "high" woman and the "low" woman need affection as well as money, have active physical yearnings for the man, behave in surprising ways; and both have been prostituted.

If Trollope were given to simple moral generalities, then by all rights the Palliser marriage would be miserable, since it was based on businesslike convenience instead of love. Prostitution took many forms in Victorian England, and for Trollope it meant the corruption and failure of love. But he always likes to show how life upsets generalizations, even his own, and of course the Palliser marriage is wonderful— wonderful in the sense that it shows Glencora and Palliser finding surprising new depths and qualities in their own beings, and wonderful in the sense that it fills one with awe at the capacities for courage and kindness that couples show in the ordinary process of marriage. One really has to read this part of *Can You Forgive Her?* to see the delicate mastery of which Trollope was capable. He brings home the bafflement and the quiet shock of the newly wedded couple as they probe more and more deeply into each other's character and slowly discover there odd idiosyncrasies, unsuspected emotional intensity, uncongenial temperament, strange ambitions and faults, and—astonishingly—unselfish devotion to one another. A crisis comes when after a quarrel Glencora frankly tells Palliser that he does not love her and that she does not love him. Trollope describes his reaction when he is alone:

Then something of an idea of love came across his heart, and he acknowledged to himself that he had married without loving or without requiring love. Much of all this had

been his own fault. Indeed, had not the whole of it come
from his own wrongdoing? . . . But now,—now he loved her.
He felt that he could not bear to part with her, even if there
were no question of public scandal, or of disgrace. He had
been torn inwardly by that assertion that she loved another
man. She had got at his heart-strings at last. There are men
who may love their wives, though they never can have been
in love before their marriage.[18]

But a short passage from this section cannot really show its
quality. One needs to see how these superbly imagined characters develop and interact over a long time and many pages.
Trollope conveys the anguished efforts to adjust and compromise, the soul-searching, the hurt, the clash of personalities, the impatience, the pride, the inability to communicate,
the wishful daydreams, the misinterpretations of motives
and action, the working at cross-purposes, of these two admirable and well-intentioned young people. Their strained
relationship makes us understand more fully the enormous
difficulties inherent in marriage. To make life tolerable, Glencora must give up Fitzgerald for good and Plantagenet must
give up his appointment to the cabinet to be with his wife
for a time. Each must sacrifice what has been dearest to
him. Marriages, Trollope shows, are not to be idealized; they
are made on earth, not in heaven.

V

One of the specific troubles of the Palliser marriage is that
Glencora does not get pregnant. The reason why Hawthorne,
James, and Tolstoy so much admired Trollope was that they
knew he had that rare ability to make a reader sense the importance which commonplace experiences have for the
people who live them. No other English novelist before him
had thought of describing realistically the chagrin and the
sense of guilt that a passionate but apparently sterile young
woman might feel at not bearing a child or the way that her

---

[18] Chap. LIX, p. 243 (II).

barrenness might affect her psychology and actions. Trollope could take this sort of ordinary problem and, without vulgarizing or falsifying it, turn it into distinguished fiction. He communicates the emotional interest and significance that such a dilemma has in real life only for those immediately concerned with them.

Glencora, full of inner self-reproach, outwardly displays the neurotic bitchiness and guilt which post-Freudians might expect of a woman beginning to think of herself as a sexual failure. The theme of sterility again was running in Trollope's mind. Not until Plantagenet learns to accept his wife's passionate nature and give himself up to her for a time can their marriage be fertile. Palliser and the ruling classes *need* the fire and heart of a Glencora if they are not to stagnate. Her pregnancy and the birth of an heir keeps them together, gives them respect for each other, and turns their relationship into something promising for the future.

Trollope was, however, breaking a main axiom of the love code by making sex between the Pallisers a happy thing. When their child is conceived Glencora still loves Burgo, not her husband. A woman who loved one man supposedly could not stand to be touched by another; she ought, as Alice implies, to detest the very thought of "caresses from a man that she did not truly love," whether he was her husband or not. But Glencora has no such idealistic scruples. Sex with her husband is a force for good and helps love develop; Trollope does not see it as a degrading instinct in this part of the book.

Despite the great chapters dealing with the Pallisers, *Can You Forgive Her?* is a maddeningly contradictory novel. In the terribly repressed character, Alice Vavasor, he seems to sympathize with the fear and distaste of the Victorians for sex. At one point he upholds the code and calls "that wondrous aroma of precious delicacy" the "greatest treasure of womanhood." But we know from this and other novels that not "delicacy" but honesty, warmth, generosity, real pas-

sion, charm, wit, and common sense were the qualities he
most valued in women. He thought that he ought to prefer
Alice over Glencora according to the angel-in-the-house
dogma, and he says that tedious Alice has the finer nature of
the two. Glencora, however, is an exuberant, touching,
though often foolish human being, and Alice is a hard-
hearted, boring prude. A whole shift in the male idea of what
a woman ought to be seems to happen in the novel. Alice,
the self-righteous, conscientious, passive, sexless "good" girl,
cannot compete with the impulsive and many-sided Glencora. Alice the "Victorian" fades into obscurity next to
Glencora, who seems very much like that intractable, often
unsatisfied, and always intriguing creature, "modern woman."

Nevertheless, the sexlessness of a squeamish Alice Vavasor
obviously produced conscious sympathy in the Victorian
middle classes. Why did they want so much to dislike sex?
In *Miss Mackenzie* (1864), an odd scene takes place in which
a man sees the bare flesh of his future wife's arm one night
when she talks to him in her dressing-gown. He mistakenly
thinks that she is trying to lure him with her sex appeal and
is deeply shocked. What caused this almost pathological
fear of the body that Trollope reflects here? One of the major reasons had to do with the matter of class and status. The
body and sex and their associations with animality and the
more brutish physical life of the lower classes scared many
of the Victorians somewhere in the depths of their insecure
bourgeois psyches. By rejecting "animality" and suppressing sex, they could prove that they were different from all
those countless dirty people at the bottom of society. They
tried to repress the animal in themselves because that animal
linked them to a hard world that was too close and too
threatening—it reminded them of an existence they would
rather forget. Collectively the Victorian middle class was
nouveau riche, and parvenus as a rule try to repress whatever reminds them of their earlier unpleasant life.

The bare-flesh scene also shows that in an age of individualism and commercialism men felt very literally, though perhaps unconsciously, that their wives were "private property."
No one but the owner must "use" this property, and it must
come to him in an unsullied state, like a fine piece of merchandise. A woman's "purity"—often a euphemism for vir-
ginity—was a very important possession for a man.

Sex, with its power to upset individual and social stability,
is of course one of the most unpredictably volatile of forces.
In a time of bewildering change and insecurity the Victorians tried to minimize its power to disrupt lives. The placid
passivity of so many Victorian heroines became a positive
virtue in a time of change. There were also conscious idealistic motives for sexual repression. In the spirit of St. Paul
this evangelical age really did have a yearning for "higher
things." By denying the flesh as much as possible they hoped
to free human energy which they could then use to attain
spiritual goals. It takes a certain gallantry to battle physiology
and carnal desires as the Victorians did, and we ought to
remember after all that sex to them was like fattening foods
to a hungry dieter.

The trouble comes when contempt for the flesh leads to
contempt for humanity and to the kind of sterility that we
see in *The Small House* and the other books of this period.
To underplay the physical connection between people can
lead to alienation. Trollope felt that the spiritualizing of love
and the distrust of the body were causing people to "get out
of touch" with each other. In *Miss Mackenzie* he insists that
his world can not do without earthy human love and pride
in the flesh. He begins with a thirty-six-year-old repressed
spinster. Her life seems drab and wasted, but suddenly she
finds herself with a little money and independence. In a
subtly restrained, but marvelously candid scene showing a
particular combination of insight and delicacy possibly beyond the range of any other Victorian novelist, Trollope

imagines Miss Mackenzie first realizing her womanliness, her sexuality, and her need for love:

She got up and looked at herself in the mirror. She moved up her hair from off her ears, knowing where she would find a few that were grey, and shaking her head, as though owning to herself that she was old; but as her fingers ran almost involuntarily across her locks, her touch told her that they were soft and silken; and she looked into her own eyes, and saw that they were bright; and her hand touched the outline of her cheek, and she knew that something of the fresh bloom of youth was still there; and her lips parted, and there were her white teeth; . . . She pulled her scarf tighter across her own bosom, feeling her own form and then she leaned forward and kissed herself in the glass.[19]

In effect, she renounces celibacy; and though this passage appears early in the book, its decisiveness and emotional force make all the rest of the story anticlimactic. The drama of the novel lies in this private victory of life over Victorian repression and bodily shame. The effort to suppress sensual pleasure, that is, the pride and joy of seeing and touching flesh that Miss Mackenzie shows, cost the individual psyche and society too much for it to continue indefinitely.

VI

Trollope fills *The Claverings* (1864) with implications about the cost of idealizing love and women and gives us candid insights into all sorts of exotic Victorian courting and mating habits. Again he tried to uphold the Biedermeier love ideal, but he describes so clearly the mental strains that the ideal imposes and the twisted psychological and social motives behind it that he makes the disintegration of the love

---

[19] *Miss Mackenzie* (London, 1924), chap. IX, pp. 110–111. George Eliot may well have had this passage in mind when, at the beginning of *Daniel Deronda*, she portrays Gwendolen Harleth kissing her image in the mirror.

code seem inevitable. The plot presents neatly what must have been a common dilemma for Victorian men; Harry Clavering has to choose between two women whom he loves —Julia Ongar, an alluring, passionate young widow who married a perverted husband for money and knows about sex and sin, and Florence Burton, one of those passive, nondescript virgins. Trollope grasps the conflict between kinds of love that disturbed and sometimes destroyed the Victorians.

The important thing is that he recognizes that it *is* possible for a sympathetic young man to love two women—two *types* of femininity—at the same time. In fact he sees the *necessity* of having two images of Woman. One senses in Harry's story the growing tension created by contradictory longings within the idealistic framework of Victorian society. Men wanted docile, safe, predictable women whom they could take for granted while they went about making their careers and—more than incidentally—building an empire and a modern civilization. They needed stable domestic havens set apart from the competition of the individualistic age, and women in whom they could institutionalize their cultural ideals. But goodness and tranquillity were not enough for them; the pressures of an increasingly organized civilization seemed to squeeze spontaneity and freedom out of their lives, leaving a good many libidos longing for sex, wildness, and mystery in women. Freud's dictum that the subject matter of a repressed image or thought can make its way into the consciousness on the condition that it be denied holds true for the Victorian novelists; they were always projecting their own unconscious tendencies and wishes on "villainesses" whom they obviously empathize with and even love—see, for example, Dickens's Miss Wade, Thackeray's Becky Sharp, Collins's Miss Quirt, and Meredith's Mrs. Mount, as well as Julia Ongar.

With nineteenth-century sentimentalization of love and women came the sinister tendencies toward perversion and various forms of sexual obsession which infected the privileged classes. Except for Swinburne, who finished the brilliant novel *Love's Cross-Currents* in 1863, Trollope was about the only outstanding novelist of the time to treat these matters frankly. In *The Claverings* Julia tells Harry about her marriage to the obviously sadomasochistic Lord Ongar. Among other things Ongar started rumors for his own pleasure that Julia cuckolded him, and he even arranged to let his best friend make love to her. When she refused to go along, Ongar set out to destroy her reputation before he died.

Semiofficial praise and sanctification for women helped bring about a latent sadistic male desire to mistreat and debase them. Sooner or later idolatry calls forth iconoclasm, and we see this in the Ongar marriage and the less sensational relationship between Hugh Clavering and Julia's sister Hermione. Sir Hugh, bitter because his wife can bear him only one sickly child who dies, treats her with calculated cruelty and rationalizes his behavior: "He thought of his own home. What had his wife done for him that he should put himself out of his way to do much for her? She had brought him no money. She had added nothing either by her wit, beauty, or rank to his position in the world. She had given him no heir. What had he received from her that he should endure her commonplace conversation and her washed-out dowdy prettiness."[20] There is a kind of generalized hostility behind this statement protesting that Sweet Victorian Woman is not the treasure that she is supposed to be. Trollope brings out the connection between Hugh's belief that a woman ought naturally to live beyond all possible reproach, and his deliberate effort to humiliate his wife and make her suffer. Sadistic behavior of men toward women troubled Victorian writers, though they often disguised the

[20] *The Claverings* (London, 1924), chap. xxxv, pp. 373–374.

subject by setting it back in some distant past. For instance, men treat women with great cruelty in Browning's *The Ring and The Book*, Tennyson's *Idylls of the King*, and Arnold's *Tristram and Iseult*. Trollope, however, wanted his readers to see perverse male cruelty in a contemporary context.

The doctrine of women's moral superiority was bound to cause deep resentment. Julia, hearing that her rival for Harry is an "angel," replies that, whatever they may profess, "men are not always fond of perfection. The angel may be too angelic for this world."[21] Eventually everybody hates a model of deportment. Trollope was getting bored with the little blobs of feminine purity that passed for heroines in novels, and he could barely bother to draw one in *The Claverings*. Florence Burton, the good girl whom Harry finally marries, never becomes much more than a saccharine outline and hardly appears. She wins him because of her brother's wife, Cecelia Burton, a fascinatingly complex little champion of feminine wholesomeness and moral influence.

Cecelia, the most interesting character in the book, makes clear many of the reasons why the Victorians idealized love. At first superficially, she seems to be the very pattern of a happy Biedermeier queen of cozy hearth and home. Unmistakably, however, Trollope shows her carrying on a vicarious love affair with Harry Clavering. From the beginning they flirt with one another. Compulsively, Cecelia determines that nothing shall keep him from marrying her inert sister-in-law. Trollope ironically makes Cecelia, who idealizes the passive purity of Florence and detests the emotion and candor of Julia Ongar, use her overwhelming will power and her sex appeal to bring Harry into the family and deposit him in Flo's sexless lap. Cecelia decides, "He was good-looking and pleasant . . . and was altogether too valuable as a lover to be lost"[22]—valuable to herself as well as Florence. And yet at

---

[21] Chap. XXXVII, p. 391.
[22] *Ibid.*, p. 386.

the end all seems innocent. Trollope shows how Cecelia carefully stays ignorant of her own deepest motives and tells herself that she can be proud of bringing about a marriage of "true love."

In this whole strange affair, we get an idea of how the love code functioned to prevent adultery among the more affluent Victorians. Cecelia lives a life full of leisure with plenty of time for romantic daydreams. She has few outlets for emotional energy beyond intense personal relationships, and she lives in a big house with many rooms and thick doors. Her privacy is taken for granted as her intimate meetings with Harry show. He attracts her strongly, and nothing keeps them from an outright affair except her devotion to the fixed ideals of love and marriage. The Victorian efforts to disembody love took place in a social context filled with sexual temptation and opportunity.

The sublimation of the sex drive implicit in the love code provided for domestic tranquillity and social order, but it had certain other more positive rewards for women. Cecelia can enjoy Harry's company indefinitely with a good conscience. She can comfortably fulfill the wishes of her psychic life, as, for example, when she projects her own ideal self-image on Florence and then mates Harry to the surrogate self. She can revel in the surety of her own moral superiority. Julia shocks her and proves her "sinfulness" by confessing that she loved Harry even while her husband was alive. Cecelia smugly knows that *she* would never say such a "terrible" thing, and Trollope's irony points out the joy of glorying in one's own goodness and of shutting out the knowledge of one's immoral impulses.

Women could use the love ideal as an actual weapon to obtain power over men. Cecelia thinks about Harry: "Ah how sweet it would be to receive that wicked sheep back again into the sheepfold and then to dock him a little of his wandering powers, to fix him with some pleasant clog, to tie him down as a prudent domestic sheep should be tied, and make him the pride of the flock."[23] By imagining such a thought in her mind, Trollope gets down both the feminist will to tame and control men through the love code and his own resentment against the emasculating force of his society. Cecelia also shows how the love ideal appealed to the democratic instincts of the middle class. It asserted that love, not material interest, should be the basis of marriage. She wails to Harry about his duty to marry the poor Florence rather than the rich and aristocratic Julia. Love could be the social equalizer. The person who married for money, no matter how wealthy and high he might end up, was unquestionably beneath the person who married for love. Cecelia knows that she and Florence are "better" than a countess, Julia, because they faithfully obey the love ideal.

So the Victorian heart had its own good reasons for following a love code. But in order to believe in it one had willfully to distort life and repress the truth of one's whole being. The cost became too much to bear. Repression demands more repression until it creates obsession, and obsession eventually breaks loose. This rule holds true for cultures as well as individuals. Twentieth-century preoccupation with sex, for example, results from the kind of nineteenth-century repression of sexuality we see in Cecelia and Lily Dale. The difference between a Lady Chatterley and a Cecelia or a Glencora Palliser is merely that Lady Chatterley no longer represses the impulses which they all share.

Trollope, in trying to uphold the love ideal in *The Claverings*, shows why it was becoming insupportable. The book ends in shallow dishonesty. He sacrifices the truth of his art to maintain a simple, pretty notion of love, and he makes all moral and emotional problems disappear. Harry's dilemma fades away when Cecelia and his mother urge him to marry Florence. In the last pages he just forgets that he had loved Julia for years and never gives her a second thought. Trol-

---

[23] *Ibid.*

lope wrenches the logic of the whole novel out of shape, denies all the complexity of relationships that he had carefully set up, to fit a simplistic scheme. But instinctively he *does* follow the logic of his better judgment: in the supposedly happy ending, he reduces Harry from a likable, complex figure to a mushy, babbling yes-man. The love religion prevails, but it utterly diminishes the man. Trollope communicates this even if he tried to keep from admitting it to himself.

He knew that love makes the world go around, but that the Victorians, like all people in love with love, wanted it to make their world stop. True love, for many of them, meant unchanging love, something fixed and sure, a faith of the heart that the mind could cling to in a time of flux. A compulsive wish to impose pattern on experience helped to form and bolster nineteenth-century love myths. Like Lily Dale, one could try to will through love a permanent condition and an identity which nothing could change. Since mere physical attraction cannot be sustained, love had to be made spiritual. The playing down of sex helped make love seem less earthly and more ideal and, thus, immutable.

Yet for Trollope what is immutable and static is not human. When he is really serious about describing and celebrating love, he insists on the importance of its *physicalness*. Rowan's touch of Rachel, Glencora's pregnancy, Miss Mackenzie's discovery of her attractiveness—these come as epiphanies of the possibilities of love, and they have to do with the transient flesh as well as the spirit. He believed in and perpetuated the love faith, but he thought that love ought to be humanized, not idealized. Idealized love often means an egotistical act of self-assertion in which one loves a projection of oneself that one creates in another person, not a union of two people. Both Lily Dale and Glencora have found "ideal" loves, but they have no real conception of Crosbie or Fitzgerald, the men they supposedly love. The Pallisers show that wedded love cannot be ideal; if you do not begin to see and know the other person and give up ideals, it cannot even exist. Trollope expresses the Victorian wish to make marriage a part of ideal love, but in every marriage that he imagines he proves the vanity of that wish. Marriage cannot be an ideal; it is a process of two people continually relating to each other, and it keeps changing.

In certain moods he hated the self-deception of his society and could become cynical. In *The Claverings*, he invents a Madame Gordeloup, a European intriguer and an earlier comic version of James's Madame Merle, to satirize English idealization of love: "Love is very pretty at seventeen, when the imagination is telling a parcel of lies, and when life is one dream . . . what you call love, booing and cooing with rhymes about de moon, is to go back to pap and panade . . . if a woman wants a house and de something to live on, let her marry a husband; or if a man wants to have children let him marry a wife."[24] Of course he did not believe in this sort of matter-of-fact utilitarian thinking (the whole love religion of the period, including Trollope's own celebration of love, was partly a reaction against utilitarianism), but he wanted to criticize the Victorian tendency to see love as an escape from the world.

His own ambivalent, sometimes confused, fascination with the subject of love keeps his books of these years from having the consistent integrity of great novels, but it results nevertheless in great characters and great passages. There is an uncertainty of tone in each of these books which comes from trying to sustain a dying myth of love. Still, his anatomy of love is one of the finest in nineteenth-century fiction, and it gives us a new intimacy with the Victorians and the heritage which we take from them. The clumsy, painful efforts of the Pallisers to integrate love and marriage and keep alive their ability to love, the menace of the sterile love be-

---

[24] Chap. XVIII, p. 188.

havior in *The Small House at Allington*, which turns people into things or ideas, Miss Mackenzie's strangely moving delight in her flesh, the revelation of the world's wonderful fecundity which Rachel Ray senses when she falls in love, Lily Dale's longings for permanent identity and surety through love, Cecelia's sexual sublimation—matters like these touch and shape our lives.

6

The Allegory of Change:
Patterns of a World
In Transition

Before the Victorian era, time and change had generally been regarded as earthly properties in an eternal order; in the nineteenth century a reversal gradually took place, and people in mass sensed that the idea of eternal order was itself a product of historical forces existing in time and subject to change. Hans Meyerhoff, in *Time in Literature*, discusses this shift, and one passage in particular bears significantly on Trollope:

. . . attempts at postulating a dimension of eternity or a world beyond came to be questioned and obscured as a result of the new and wonderful dimensions opening up before mankind in *this* world and a part of the astonishing pattern of changes in human history. Time thus came to be experienced more and more as constant change and to be enclosed with the dimension of human life and history in this changing world. The concept of eternity was still retained within the religious outlook, but this outlook increasingly lost its force, function, and significance when placed within the context of the actual human and historical situation. It became a "belief" to which lip service was still paid, but to which there was little correspondence in terms of the reality of the human situation.[1]

---

[1] Hans Meyerhoff, *Time in Literature* (Berkeley and Los Angeles, 1960), p. 90.

Trollope imagined this soul-shaking transition as the private experience of his characters in his books of 1865 and 1866, years just preceding the passage of the 1867 Reform Bill when the Victorians seemed especially concerned with change. Social and psychological reasons combined to make him invent narratives and people which would convey more emphatically than ever before the comprehensive movement of his life and times in allegories of change.[2]

What happens to a society and to its individual members when traditional religious habits of thought become anachronistic and "eternal truths" turn out to be relative? Will resulting changes be good or bad? What are the large patterns of such change? How do people shape them and how do they affect people? These questions and others like them always moved Trollope and compelled him to answer hypothetically in his fiction. They directly control and give form to *The Belton Estate, Nina Balatka,* and most especially to *The Last Chronicle of Barset,* which communicates his sense of passing time and social transition in the most powerful, sustained, and sweeping terms he had yet found.

I have said that for Trollope, as for his era, change was a Janus. By the mid-sixties he saw the two faces in his mind's eye as his own and his dead father's. He was now over fifty —about the same age as his father had been when, with the miserable boy Anthony living with him and watching, the father moved into the depths of suffering and failure. Trollope's prestige as a writer and public servant was at its height; for him the pattern of change had been from despised, unlucky, ugly duckling to popular and successful Victorian swan. But he had seen his father change from a promising and talented lawyer to an incompetent, penniless, mad old man, and it became necessary for him to allegorize *that* pattern of experience as well as his own. He had always

---

[2] See Jerome Buckley, *The Triumph of Time* (Cambridge, Mass., 1966), for an important study of the Victorian concepts of time, history, and progress.

identified strongly with his father because his mother had seemingly abandoned both of them in a crucial and painful time of life, leaving them to share their misery. He had now to find images, characters, plots, and large metaphors which would express his inner preoccupation with change and the kinds of effects it had on his father and himself.

During his last years, the father worked obsessively on something called the *Encyclopaedia Ecclesiastica,* which was to be a ten-volume history of all Christian denominations. With his life falling apart, he tried to find permanence and meaning in a kind of eccentric vocation to the eternal Church: he would explain the whole history of its structure and its terminology. It was a pathetic, worthless project that he never finished, but it had lasting effects on the son. Anthony saw that it was all pointlessly irrelevant to the realities of their world; the old man was hopelessly lost in the past, out of date, with no idea of what was important about religion in the nineteenth century. The volumes he did complete, Trollope says, were "buried in the midst of that huge pile of futile literature the building up of which has broken so many hearts."[3] The example made him wary of getting bogged down in the past with an outmoded subject matter. Yet, from the father, the son seems to have got his own strange vocation to explain the significance of the people in the Church and the changing status of religion. His novels, especially the novels of this period, culminating in *The Last Chronicle of Barset* with the apotheosis of his father as the Reverend Josiah Crawley, are filled with the religious history of the age. They seem somehow to be the son's vindication and completion of the *Encyclopaedia Ecclesiastica.*

I

The Belton Estate (1865) is a human comedy and a love story, like its predecessors, but it is also Trollope's optimistic allegory of the progress of the Victorian spirit, an allegory

---

[3] Anthony Trollope, *An Autobiography* (London, 1953), chap. I, p. 12.

of what Humphry House has called "religion in a state of
transition from supernatural belief to humanism."[4] Clara
Amedroz, a girl in whom Trollope nicely personifies a collective Victorian consciousness, moves from the constricting,
pessimistic world of her symbolically named Aunt Winterfield, a rigidly intolerant, Calvinistic woman, to the promising world of her lover and—finally—husband, Will Belton.
In order to love and to live a full happy life she has to break
free of the insidiously gloomy Winterfield teachings that
have become part of her. Mrs. Winterfield, with her Puritan-
ism and mindless religiosity, represents much the same kind
of thing that Dickens attacked through Mrs. Clennam in
Little Dorrit and that Arnold would call Hebraism in *Culture and Anarchy*. Here is Trollope first describing her:

No woman ever lived, perhaps, with more conscientious
ideas of her duty as a woman than Mrs. Winterfield of Prospect Place, Perivale. She was an excellent lady—unselfish,
given to self-restraint, generous, pious, looking to find in her
religion a safe path through life—a path as safe as the fact
of Adam's fall would allow her feet to find. She was a woman
fearing much for others, but fearing also much for herself,
striving to maintain her house in godliness, hating sin, and
struggling with the weakness of her humanity so that she
might not allow herself to hate the sinners. But her hatred
for the sin she found herself bound at all times to pronounce
—to show it by some act at all seasons. To fight the devil was
her work—was the appointed work of every living soul, if
only living souls could be made to acknowledge the necessity of the task . . . Life at Perivale was a very serious thing.
. . . There was a look of woe about her which seemed ever
to be telling of her own sorrows in this world and of the sorrows of others in the world to come. . . . Such as she was,
she made life very serious to those who were called upon to
dwell with her.[5]

Characteristically he is fairer to the repressive nineteenth-

[4] Humphry House, *The Dickens World* (London, 1941), p.
132.
[5] *The Belton Estate* (London, 1923), chap. I, pp. 10–11.

century Evangelical spirit than either Dickens or Arnold. Mrs. Winterfield raises Clara when her inept father ruins himself. Old Amedroz personifies those irresponsible qualities which the Victorians attributed to the upper classes in the wicked Regency and pre-Victorian days. Before Victorian times there was very little reason for people of the Winterfield faith to trust in the goodness of the world. The Puritan, Nonconformist, and Evangelical strains of British religion thrived and grew among the poor, who had a very hard time of it. How could the world be good when it was ruled by a wicked dissolute aristocracy? It was obviously bad, and what mattered was to take care of one's own fate and to build a moral aristocracy for God. Pleasure was an invention of the devil that led you to squander time, money, and health; if you made pleasure and the pursuit of happiness the end of life, you simply insured that you and your descendants would remain low and without capital. Not until the nineteenth century did large numbers of these people move into the privileged classes and begin to take over the world. Trollope understands the Winterfield background and even intimates that the strict Winterfield regime was necessary to make a decent future possible for Clara (much as theorists maintain that Protestant discipline was necessary to create the abundance of capitalism or that Evangelical discipline was needed to train the managers of the British Empire). Nevertheless, times have changed and Mrs. Winterfield is wrong. People must understand that they live in a world that is good. What they need is a progressive, humanistic faith that embraces life with all its beauty and potential, not a crabbed creed that teaches distrust and contempt. They need liberalism and spiritual liberation: "But if she [Mrs. Winterfield] was right—right as to herself and others,—then why has the world been made so pleasant? Why is the fruit of the earth so sweet; and the trees,—why are they so green; and the mountains so full of glory? Why are women so lovely? and why is it that the activity of man's mind

is the only sure forerunner of man's progress?"[6] He kills Mrs.
Winterfield off as he would later kill Mrs. Proudie off in *The
Last Chronicle* because he wanted to see the end of soul
tyranny by those who dreaded pleasure. Religious belief like
everything else must change and not be allowed to petrify
in old bitter dogmas of fear.

Clara has a difficult time shaking off the Winterfield doc-
trines and learning about tolerance and love in the world. A
turning point comes when she decides, in the face of puritanical criticism, to remain friends with a good woman who
had once lived for three years as a man's mistress. More important is the traumatic scene in which the power of physical love touches her for the first time. Full of neo-Calvinist
ideas about the sinfulness of natural emotion, Clara decides
dutifully to marry the suitor whom her aunt chose for her,
rather than Will Belton whom she likes. But Belton will not
be put off:

He gazed upon her for some few seconds, remaining quite
motionless, and then opening his arms, he surrounded her
with his embrace, and pressing her with all his strength close
to his bosom, kissed her forehead and her cheeks, and her
lips, and her eyes. His will was so masterful and his strength
so great and his motion so quick, that she was powerless to
escape from him until he relaxed his hold. . . . She stood for
a moment trembling, with her hands clenched, and with a
look of scorn upon her lips . . . and then she threw herself
on a sofa, and, burying her face sobbed aloud, while her body
was shaking as with convulsions.[7]

This is her baptism into a world of physical and emotional
love, and after this incident she overcomes Winterfield shame
and recognizes her love for Will Belton. He, like Rowan in
Rachel Ray, stands for pragmatic, liberally progressive forces
in Victorian life, and Clara belongs to him at the end.

---

[6] Chap. VII, p. 89.
[7] Chap. XXII, p. 293.

Broadly, *The Belton Estate* suggests the whole buoyant progressive side of any age in transition, with its strong faith that the future will be better than the past. It is one of Trollope's most optimistic, least nostalgic books. The changes he records are almost all for the better, and what he describes as passing deserves to pass. Clara Amedroz's pattern of experience follows Trollope's own. Like her, he moved from despondency to hope, from loneliness to community, from callowness to maturity, from ignorance to sophistication, from the depressing Winterfield atmosphere of his youth to the hearty Belton world of his middle age. The world opened up for him just as it opens up for Clara.

II

The charm of *The Belton Estate* lies in Trollope's skill in conveying realistically Clara's discovery of the everyday joys of the world. But her growing faith in the goodness of life depends ultimately on a change in the religious outlook of the century. Orthodox religions set up walls between people, walls that Trollope thought ought to come tumbling down.

His odd little novel *Nina Balatka* (1865) makes this point even more strongly than *The Belton Estate*. In it, he batters at the highest religious barrier of all in nineteenth-century European society, the one separating Jew and Christian. Anton Trendelssohn, a Jew out of the Prague ghetto, and Nina Balatka, a Catholic, fall in love, fight free of the religious prejudices of their elders, and marry. The story is promising, but Trollope's talent was not for thesis novels, and his performance is flat and second-rate. Knowing, and probably caring, little about people in Prague, he could only sketchily imagine his characters and their actions. The exception is Trendelssohn, in whom Trollope lets us see a *man* rather than a Jewish stereotype, something rare in Victorian fiction. Bradford Booth praises this "psychological portrait" and says: "Trollope develops in Anton the disabling experience of

ghetto segregation and persecution. Anton has a number of
regrettable character traits: he is stubborn, haughty, suspicious, but he is honest, sincere, and honorable. In him Trollope traces the disintegration of European ghetto society and
the emergence of a more self-reliant Jewish individualist who
can escape environmental neuroses."[8] His own needs and
wishes and his affection for Nina come to mean more to him
than traditions of his religion or the customs of his family.
His freedom of choice is not limited at the end by his Jew-
ishness. As religion lost some of its mystical aura, Trollope
hoped it would lose its alienating effects. He hits hard at the
self-righteous bigotry of Nina's relatives, whose mean, narrow religion makes for hatred instead of love between people. It allows them to despise Trendelssohn because he is a
Jew. Creeds which do not lead to humane behavior are worn
out. The last sentence of the novel symbolizes the change
Trollope sees as the world becomes more secularized and
people leave behind old religious shibboleths: "Early in the
following year, while the ground was yet bound with frost,
and the great plains of Bohemia were still covered with
snow, a Jew and his wife took their leave of Prague, and
started for one of the great cities of the West."[9] The age of
assimilation is upon us.

III

In these two relatively simple books, the ebbing of religious intensity seems a positive good. Not so in *The Last
Chronicle of Barset* (1866), where the spectre of a utilitarian
age sapping man's religious impulse saddens Trollope. The
large and unifying theme of this great panoramic novel is the

---

[8] Bradford Booth, *Anthony Trollope* (Bloomington, 1958), pp.
30–31.
[9] *Nina Balatka* (London, 1951), chap. XVI, p. 191. See Edgar
Rosenberg, *From Shylock to Svengali* (Stanford, 1960), p. 281.
Mr. Rosenberg quotes this ending in his short, penetrating discussion of *Nina Balatka*.

relentless secularization of the world. Inevitably secularization brings tragic loss for some as spiritual and moral
passion disappears. On the last page Trollope, diffidently
apologizing to pious types in his audience who took offense
at his Barsetshire clerics, explains ironically: "Had I written
an epic about clergymen, I would have taken St. Paul as my
model; but describing, as I have endeavored to do, such
clergymen as I see around me, I could not venture to be
transcendental." Transcendentalism is dead for him, and as
a matter of fact, to prove it he *did* write an epic featuring
a modern St. Paul, the Reverend Josiah Crawley. Crawley,
alienated and hating his materialistic society, moves miserably through the novel like some sort of breathing anach-
ronism from apostolic times. In a world where money talks,
he knows a primitive language of the spirit, and he cannot
cope with the changed conditions of the age:

There was nothing so bitter to the man as the derogation
from the *spiritual grandeur* of his position as priest among
men, which came as one necessary result from his poverty.
St. Paul could go forth without money in his purse or shoes
to his feet or two suits to his back, and his poverty never
stood in the way of his preaching, or hindered the veneration
of the faithful. St. Paul, indeed, was called upon to bear
stripes, was flung into prison, encountered terrible dangers.
But Mr. Crawley,—so he told himself,—could have encountered all that without flinching. The stripes and scorn of the
unfaithful would have been nothing to him, if only the faithful would have believed in him, poor as he was, as they
would have believed in him had he been rich![10]

Pauline thinking and Pauline "grandeur" have little place
in a society which patronizes Crawley for being poor and
persecutes him for being a bad accountant. He is accused of
stealing a twenty-pound check, and when he cannot satisfactorily explain how he got it, he and his family are nearly

---

[10] *The Last Chronicle of Barset* (London, 1958), "double
volume" (see Author's Note, p. viii), chap. XII, p. 118 (I).

destroyed. Trollope thought he erred in making the plot turn on Crawley's uncertainty about where the check came from, but symbolically the godly man's failure to understand and keep track of the currency of the age works perfectly.

A few years after *The Last Chronicle*, George Eliot, about to deal with many of the same problems, would write in her prelude to *Middlemarch* of "the ardently willing soul" that finds "no epic life wherein there was a constant unfolding of far-resonant action"; of "spiritual grandeur ill-matched with the meanness of opportunity." These phrases exactly describe Crawley. A potential apostle with the capacity to lead a Church Militant and help mold the conscience of his country, he finds himself without the means to uphold Christian dignity and relegated to obscurity—until he is accused of theft. In a secular age, the day of the religious visionary is done. Thinking of both his dead father and the drift of the times, Trollope made Crawley an ironic center for his world in transition. Crawley is a would-be tragic martyr-hero in a melioristic, rational world that no longer really believes in tragedy or heroes. He is an aloof eccentric in a world run largely by committees, bureaucrats, and middlemen; a fanatic in a world that needs and honors social cooperation, conformity, and convention; a scholar in a world that increasingly finds traditional scholarship and the past irrelevant. He illuminates the price and the anguish of change.

The *Last Chronicle of Barset*, like *Vanity Fair*, *Great Expectations*, and *Middlemarch*, is one of those monuments of the Victorian age. Around Crawley, Trollope constructed a massive, many-layered narrative that was his most ambitious attempt to tell his countrymen where they had been, where they were, and where they were going. It is terribly long, even for Trollope; he has been accused of padding the novel disgracefully. According to some critics, the scores of old characters from other Barset novels plus many new ones, the long subplots, the London scenes with their farce and satire, detract from the moving *Crawley Agonistes* part of the book.

But he knew what he was doing. He wanted to put Crawley
into context. After reading *The Last Chronicle* one feels the
immense density of its world and the deepening *interrelated-
ness* of modern life. The length and variety of the novel helps
reinforce Trollope's important perception: Crawley must
live in a world whose sheer bulk and range tend to swallow
up the drama of private suffering and make the dignity and
stature of the single human being less visible. The novel with
its huge population is in a way *about* the growing importance
of society and the waning importance—relatively speaking—
of the individual soul. That is what makes it a hard and
fatalistic book.

Both the first and last chronicles of Barset turn on a crisis
in a clergyman's life, but Crawley's world is much less provincial than Harding's, much broader, much harsher, much
more confused. Not directly, but indirectly, Crawley's dilemma touches many more people than Harding's. Life is a
more public affair. The way Crawley is treated helps set a
tone toward religion which permeates the whole nation. In
the same way, the manners of London *nouveaux riches* or
London bureaucrats affect Crawley's status, though they may
never have heard of him. To understand what is happening
to Crawley and what it means, we need to know what is happening to all sorts of people in Barsetshire and the rest of
England.

Seymour Betsky notes that, in the Barset novels, "There is
a continual movement from the comparative stability of a
rural order . . . into the profoundly disturbing rhythms of the
world of London."[11] These "rhythms" are the secular rhythms
of a utilitarian culture which obliterates regional differences
and minimizes man's spiritual nature. In *The Last Chronicle*, they engulf Barsetshire and change it so that it loses its
specialness. Trollope, as we saw, created in Barset a place
where a tenuous harmony could be preserved between

---

[11] Seymour Betsky, "Society in Thackeray and Trollope," *From
Dickens to Hardy* (London, 1958), p. 160.

worldliness and idealism. The ecclesiastical makeup of the
Barset society in the earlier novels symbolizes the will and
the hope of men, no matter how imperfect, to live up to
accepted spiritual ideals and to organize earthly life in a way
that is pleasing to God. But the Barchester towers that
pointed the way to higher things before, for Harding, Arabin, Mark Robarts, and others, seem to have dwindled out
of sight in *The Last Chronicle*. Barsetshire is no longer a
distinct and vital community of religious individualism, nor
a significant locus of moral conscience in the Victorian world.
It is a mere adjunct to a sprawling secular society. The Barsetshire idealists, Harding, Crawley, Mrs. Proudie, and Arabin, either die or are tamed. The title itself announces that
the old individualistic Barset way of life is finished and has
no future.

By the end of *The Last Chronicle*, Crawley's idealism, his
sense of personal mission to carry out the divine will and do
his duty to God, and his "romantic agony" all seem obsolete.
He has no trouble justifying himself to his God: "He was not
guilty before God. . . . He knew that well enough. . . . In
spite of his aberrations of intellect, if there were any such,
his ministrations in his parish were good. Had he not
preached fervently and well,—preaching the true gospel?
Had he not been very diligent among his people, striving
with all his might to lessen the ignorance of the ignorant,
and to gild with godliness the learning of the instructed?
Had he not been patient, enduring?. . . . Who had been tried
as he had been tried, and had gone through such fire with less
loss of intellectual power than he had done?"[12] Yet the collective pull of society and what it believes is so strong that
Crawley comes to doubt his own senses and to accept the
idea that he took the check when he was out of his mind.
What matters in the changing Barsetshire world is not a
man's relation to God or to himself, but his relation to other
men. People have to fit in if they are to get along, and get-

---

[12] *The Last Chronicle*, chap. LXI, p. 219 (II).

ting along smoothly in the world is everything. When Crawley decides to resign on principle, a colleague, speaking with
the common-sense voice of the world, says scathingly, " 'And
you will turn your wife into the poorhouse for an ideal' "
Someone at the close remarks that Crawley has been
a real hero, but his lawyer scoffs: " 'I don't know about being
a hero. I never quite knew what makes a hero, if it isn't
having three or four girls dying in love for you at once. But
to find a man who was going to let everything in the world
go against him, because he believed another fellow better
than himself!. . . . It's not natural; and the world wouldn't
go on if there were many like that.' "13

To the representative Victorian of the world, the hero and
the saint are queer, outmoded figures. Crawley despises that
world, but he also cannot ignore it or help envying those who
do well in it, and his own weakness makes him particularly
bitter: "It was the fault of this man that he was imbued too
strongly with self-consciousness. He could do a great thing
or two. He could keep up his courage in positions which
would wash all courage out of most men. He could tell the
truth though truth should ruin him. He could sacrifice all that
he had to duty. . . . But . . . when accepting with an effort
of meekness the small payment made by the world to him,
in return for his great works, he could not forget the great
payments made to others for small work."14 Even for a man
of faith, the power of the world seems everywhere and the
power of God hardly apparent at all, not even in his own
soul. Crawley's agony, like that of Hopkins in his sonnets
of despair, is rooted in the historical disappearance of God.15

But the outside pressures on Crawley even deny him the
right to give way to despair. His wife calls his indulgence in
grief "of all luxuries the most pernicious." Despair is wrong

---

13 Chap. LXXIV, p. 354 (II).
14 Chap. LXI, p. 220 (II).
15 See J. Hillis Miller, *The Disappearance of God* (Cambridge,
Mass., 1963).

for Crawley, not because it insults God and shows a weak faith, but because it really means a renunciation of the world, that is, a renunciation of the *only* reality, and thus—by definition—it is insanity. Crawley has a tragic sense of life; he believes in a malevolent fate which may torture a man's whole life, and he believes in the inevitability of suffering. But people like his wife and family, his daughter's lover, Major Grantly, and Mr. Toogood, his lawyer—the people who control the world of the book at the end—do not allow him tragedy. They believe in *the* popular dogma of modern times, *progress and change for the better in the world.* When Crawley pours out "with joyous rapture, his appreciation of the glory and the pathos and the humanity . . . of the awful tragedy . . . of Oedipus,"[16] his family humors him as they would some half-witted old man who was mad about an antiquated hobby.

Trollope sets up a marvelous contrast between the idealistic Crawley and Toogood, the practical London lawyer who clears him. Shrewd, active, and successful, Toogood, like a canny early-day Rotarian, moves through the world, making himself pleasant to people, taking life as it comes without brooding about it, but always working to make himself and his family rich and comfortable. He tells Crawley the essence of religion: " 'The best way to be thankful is to use the goods the gods provide you.' "[17] He is the man whom the world honors while it despises Crawley.

Trollope sees the materialistic credo of Toogood winning everywhere. Just give Crawley a good living at the end and presumably he will live happily ever after. The broken hopes of his whole life, the disintegration of his mind, can be cured by a tranquil future of material comfort. Provide for a man's material needs and you solve his problems. These are the assumptions of the new utilitarian Barset society and to some extent of Trollope himself, as he runs away at the end from

---

[16] *The Last Chronicle*, chap. xvii, p. 179 (I).
[17] Chap. XXXII, p. 326 (I).

the logic of the book. To give him his due, he is extremely shaky about Crawley's final happiness, devoting just one sentence in the conclusion: "Mr. and Mrs. Crawley became very quiet at St. Ewold's and, *as I think, contented.*"[18] Hesitantly he adopts the point of view of the tragedy deniers in the novel to please the tragedy deniers who made up his audience.

Nevertheless, despite Trollope's failure to "go all the way" with Crawley, he creates one of the most genuine tragic figures in nineteenth-century English fiction. When Nietzsche, defining the nature of tragic experience, said, "There are few pains so grievous as to have seen, divined, or experienced how an exceptional man has missed his way and deteriorated," he might have been describing Crawley. The essence of tragedy is, after all, not an unhappy ending or even death, but the wasted potential of a man's life and unjustified and unjustifiable suffering. Crawley stands out as a striking figure who symbolizes that recurring tragedy of human waste, the great man whose talents are mismatched with his times.

Crawley stands between two worlds, "One dead, the other powerless to be born." With brilliant intuition Trollope lets us see the religious impulse in Crawley groping to find an outlet in revolutionary ideology. In his parish live the workers who have moved into Barsetshire, transforming "rolling broad English acres" into "brick-built tenements." Barset is being industrialized, and Crawley comes to identify with the poor laborers who have suddenly appeared:

There had sprung up a colony of brickmakers. . . . They had come thither from unknown regions, as labourers of that class do come when they are needed. . . . They were all in appearance and manners nearer akin to the race of navvies than to ordinary rural labourers. They had a bad name in the country; . . . The farmers hated them, and consequently they hated the farmers. They . . . were vilified by the small old-established tradesmen around them. . . .

---

[18] Chap. LXXXIV, p. 448 (II), italics mine.

Mr. Crawley, ever since coming into Hogglestock, had been very busy among these brickmakers, and by no means without success. Indeed the farmers had quarrelled with him because the brickmakers had so crowded the parish church, as to leave but scant room for decent people. . . . But Mr. Crawley had done his best to make the brickmakers welcome at the church, scandalizing the farmers by causing them to sit or stand in any portion of the church which was hitherto unappropriated. He had been constant in his personal visits to them, and had felt himself to be more a St. Paul with them than with any other of his neighbors around him.[19]

He feels the injustice of the workers' lot and compares his unfair life to theirs in the brickfield. At one point he ponders on why people think he is guilty: "And I'm a poor man,—the poorest in all Hogglestock; and, therefore, of course, it is stealing. Of course I am a thief. Yes, of course I am a thief. When did not the world believe the worst of the poor?"[20] Crawley despises the bourgeois world and has a true revolutionary hatred of special privilege and middle-class genteel convention. He thinks like a rebel as he goes to confront Bishop Proudie:

He took great glory from the thought that he would go before the bishop with dirty boots,—with boots necessarily dirty,—with rusty pantaloons, that he would be hot and mud-stained with his walk [shades of sweat-drenched socialist realism!] hungry, and an object to be wondered at by all who should see him, because of the misfortunes which had been unworthily heaped on his head; . . . And yet he would take the bishop in his grasp and crush him,—crush him,—crush him! . . .
Then he stalked on, clutching and crushing in his hand the bishop, and the bishop's wife, and the whole diocese,— and all the Church of England. Dirty shoes indeed! Whose was the fault that there were in the church so many feet

---

[19] Chap. XII, p. 120 (I).
[20] *Ibid.*, p. 124 (I).

soiled by unmerited poverty, and so many hands soiled by undeserved wealth?[21]

Later on, the religious impulse would transform itself into social concern, and politics would usurp the place of theology in the minds of many idealists, but Trollope cannot yet imagine the grievances of Crawley and the workers in political terms. Crawley's agony and lack of fulfillment are in part the dilemma of the troubled Victorian conscience still putting faith in a dying ideal of heavenly justice and unable to formulate effectively its desire and instincts for political justice.

IV

The workers and tenements in Barset show one pattern of change, but nothing brings home the passing of old modes more powerfully than the deaths of Mrs. Proudie and Mr. Harding. Mrs. Proudie, of course, has domineered in Barchester as a great comic personification of Evangelical rigidity. But very suddenly in *The Last Chronicle* Trollope changes her into a pathetic woman with emotional depth and then kills her off. Why? Trollope said he did it because he heard two clergymen at his club denouncing her. But, as Frank O'Connor says, his pretense that he got rid of her because of a chance remark is simply an example of his fatuous and evasive attitude toward his own work: "Trollope fails to tell us what he could have done, if the two clergymen had not spoken. Of course, intuitively, if not intellectually, he had already known that Mrs. Proudie had to die. . . ."[22] Like her antagonist Crawley, Mrs. Proudie is always mouthing the word "duty," which to the Victorians meant the inner light to right conduct coming ultimately from God and not depending on the approval of others. When people doubt that her moral tyranny is really God-ordained and reject it,

---

[21] Chap. XVII, p. 180 (I).
[22] Frank O'Connor, *The Mirror in the Roadway* (New York, 1956), pp. 174–175.

she begins doubting herself and listening to the voice of the world. The spirit of Proudieism dies when introspection lets a person see that ideas of duty and righteousness are bound up with selfish motives and when self-esteem comes to depend on the opinion of others. Bishop Proudie finally rebels against his wife because he can no longer stand to be humiliated by her in front of Crawley and the rest of Barsetshire. What they think of him comes to mean more to him than her absolute ideals of duty and conduct. O'Connor cites Trollope's easy and logical—yet daring—development of the Proudies and his deepening of Mrs. Proudie's character as proof of his mastery. Notice what the changes in Mrs. Proudie's psychology just before she dies tell us about the shifting patterns of Victorian perception and moral thought:

Of her own struggles after personal dominion, she was herself unconscious; and no doubt they gave her, *when recognized and acknowledged by herself*, many stabs to her inner self, of which no single being in the world knew anything. . . .

Mrs. Proudie was in this like other women,—that she would fain have been loved had it been possible. She had always meant to serve him [her husband]. She was conscious of that; conscious also in a way that, although she was clever, yet she had failed. At the bottom of her heart she knew that she had been a bad wife. And yet she had meant to be a pattern wife! She had meant to be a good Christian; but she had so exercised her Christianity that not a soul in the world loved her *or would endure her presence if it could be avoided!* She had sufficient insight to the minds and feelings of those around her to be aware of this.[23]

A dying Mrs. Proudie questioning herself, full of guilt, worrying about the fact that others do not love her, means that secularism has destroyed forever the old Evangelical world of Proudie absolutes.

---

[23] *The Last Chronicle*, chap. LXVI, pp. 274–281 (II), italics mine.

Harding's passing is much sadder than Mrs. Proudie's, and
it is done with consummate artistry. When he goes, the virtue
of powerlessness seems to die out of the world. If we think
of the generally bad connotation which the word "meek" has
now, and then remember its connotation in the phrase "the
meek shall inherit the earth," we can get an idea of what the
death of Harding means and what Trollope was trying to get
across. Through the last quiet days of Harding's old age runs
a subdued elegiac strain, not just for the man, but for Christian meekness and modesty. Trollope felt that the fascination
and identification with power and the drive *for* power in the
modern world were killing the ideal of innocence, and he was
right. We find few characters like Harding or Dickens's
simpleminded, innocent Mr. Dick in the fiction of the last
hundred years because we tend either not to believe in or
not to respect innocence. Harding's special qualities in *The
Last Chronicle*—his gentleness, his positive will *not* to control others, his serenity, his *harmlessness*—have not been
much honored in our era—much to our shame, for they are
the qualities which make life in the world bearable.

In one deft remark about the wife of a Harding grandson,
Trollope can point out the shallowness of a new age which
cannot appreciate Harding's exquisite nature and finds him
a quaint provincial relic: "Lady Anne . . . was always pro-
digiously civil to him, speaking to him very loud, as though
he were deaf because he was old, and bringing him cheap
presents from London of which he did not take much heed."[24]
City patronizes country, youth patronizes age, worldliness
patronizes innocence; and the Harding wisdom—a holy wisdom of limiting desire—is lost.

After Harding dies, Archdeacon Grantly eulogizes him:

"He lacked guile, and he feared God,—and a man who
does both will never go far astray. I don't think he ever
coveted aught in his life,—except a new case for his violon-

---

[24] Chap. LXXVIII, p. 392 (II).

cello and somebody to listen to him when he played it."
[How fitting that Trollope should have made Harding a
lover and performer of music—of all man's pastimes, surely
the most innocent!] The archdeacon got up and walked
about the room in his enthusiasm; and, perhaps, as he walked
some thoughts as to the sterner ambition of his own life
passed through his mind. What things had he coveted? Had
he lacked guile? He told himself that he had feared God,—
but he was not sure that he was telling himself true even
in that.[25]

Grantly is the one old character who lives and flourishes at
the end of the novel. He is basically a secular man—as Crawley says, he is "of the earth, earthy," and so he fits into the
changing scene.

Trollope is a master at stating large themes and meanings
through symbolic juxtaposition. In a quiet family scene early
in the novel, Grantly serves Harding a last bottle of 1820
port. Harding then reminisces, and in an almost Proustian
way the wine calls up for him the easy-going time of his
youth and the relaxed lives people used to lead: " 'Dear,
dear; how well I remember your father giving the order for
it. There were two pipes, and somebody said it was heady
wine. "If the prebendaries and rectors can't drink it," said
your father, "then the curates will.' " By the end of the
passage the wine comes to symbolize the world of the past
and Harding's style of life itself: " 'It has lasted my time,' "
he had said, and when Trollope concludes by saying, "Mr.
Harding drank the last glass of the 1820 port,"[26] we seem to
be at the end of an era.

A few pages later, he first introduces us into the flashy
and hard world of Dobbs Broughton, a crass parvenu finan-
cier in London. At dinner Broughton brags to his guest. " 'Old
Ramsby, who keeps as good a stock of stuff as any wine
merchant in London, gave me a hint, three or four years

---

[25] Chap. LXXXI, pp. 421–422 (II).
[26] Chap. XXII, p. 224 (I).

ago, that he'd a lot of tidy Bordeaux. It's '47, you know. He had ninety dozen, and I took it all . . . . I only gave one hundred and four for it then; it's worth a hundred and twenty now.' "[27] Like Harding, Broughton defines himself and the world he moves in when he talks about the wine. But his is plentiful, and Harding's is used up.

V

Trollope had two good and specific reasons for including the contrapuntal London scenes having to do with the Broughtons, the cut-throat businesswoman Mrs. Van Siever and her daughter Clara, the painter Conrad Dalrymple, and Madalina Demolines; he wanted to show the dynamic, amoral urban world of runaway materialism and wild speculation that was changing Barsetshire and the face of England and making idealism passé, and he wanted to show the spiritual emptiness and the rootlessness of this world. Dobbs Broughton, the speculator who ends up a suicide, is a mere sketch of the sort of thing Trollope would do later in *The Way We Live Now* and *The Prime Minister*, but with the others his social satire succeeds brilliantly. Through them he slashes away at the venality, the crass philistinism, and the ugliness of the city milieu in a manner that both corroborates and complements Dickens's Podsnappery. Here, for example, is a dinner-party conversation about Mrs. Van Siever, a *nouveau riche* arbiter of taste, between Dalrymple and her daughter: " 'It is merely the fact that her sympathies are with ugly things rather than with pretty things . . . and she likes to have everything dark, and plain, and solid.' 'If everyone were like your mother, how would artists live?' 'There would be none.' "[28] But in this London of cold facts, hard cash, ledgers, and selfishness, life gets boring. People try

---

[27] Chap. XXIV, pp. 256–257 (I).
[28] *Ibid.*, p. 255 (I).

flirtation, sex, art, sham romance—anything that might help
fill the spiritual vacuum. Madalina neurotically imagines in-
trigue, Maria Broughton—tired of her dull husband—dithers
over her titillating unconsummated little affair with an *artist*,
Clara rebels against her utilitarian bourgeois upbringing
by posing for pictures, Dalrymple tries to live up to the
role of Artist as Romantic Hero—they all float around looking for something to fill their faithless lives. Dalrymple is
the most interesting of these characters. "Society" is thrilled
by him and gives him the honor that it withholds from
Crawley the Christian minister. Trollope senses the middle
classes turning to the artist for vicarious *frisson* and for
idealistic values both in his art *and* his life. Yet Dalrymple,
like Broughton, is himself an opportunist: "Dalrymple,"
Trollope says, "whom the rich English world was beginning
to pet and pelt with gilt sugar-plums, and who seemed to
take very kindly to petting and gilt sugar-plums . . . There
was also ever some story told in Dalrymple's picture over and
above the story of the portraiture. This countess was drawn
as a fairy with wings, that countess as a goddess with a
helmet. The thing took for awhile and Conrad Dalrymple
was picking up his gilt sugar-plums with considerable
rapidity."[29]

Bradford Booth calls this London section "discordant—a
bit of vulgarity brushing the sheen of the sublime,"[30] but of
course that is exactly Trollope's point. He is like those old
masters that Auden talks about in "Musée des Beaux Arts"
who were "never wrong" about suffering. It is part of his
interpretation of life that Crawley's agony takes place in a
world full of vulgar materialism, triviality, arid souls, chaotic
emotions, and small people. These people are changing the
tenor of life, and Crawley belongs to the old order. Dalrymple, for instance, uses the past for profit, flattering his
customers by painting them as classical or legendary figures.

---

[29] *Ibid.*, p. 243 (I).
[30] *Anthony Trollope*, p. 58.

But Crawley identifies emotionally with the past; when he is in the depths of misery he has his daughter read to him,

—a passage out of a Greek poem, in which are described the troubles and agonies of a blind giant. No giant would have been more powerful,—only that he was blind, and could not see to avenge himself on those who had injured him. "The same story is always coming up," he said, stopping the girl in her reading. "We have it in various versions, because it is true to life.

> Ask for this great deliverer now, and find him
> Eyeless in Gaza, at the mill with the slaves.

It is the same story. Great power reduced to impotence, great glory to misery, by the hand of Fate,—Necessity, as the Greeks called her; the goddess that will not be shunned! At the mill with slaves! People, when they read it, do not appreciate the horror of the picture. Go on, my dear. It may be a question whether Polyphemus had mind enough to suffer; but, from the description of his power I should think that he had. 'At the mill with slaves!' Can any picture be more dreadful than that? Go on, my dear. Of course you remember Milton's Samson Agonistes. Agonistes indeed!" His wife was sitting stitching at the other side of the room; but she heard his words,—heard and understood them; and before Jane could again get herself into the swing of the Greek verse, she was over at her husband's side, with her arms round his neck. "My love!" she said. "My love!"

He turned to her, and smiled as he spoke to her. "These are old thoughts with me. Polyphemus and Belisarius, and Samson and Milton, have always been pets of mine. . . . The impotency, combined with his strength, or rather the impotency with the memory of former strength and former aspiration, is so essentially tragic."[31]

This great passage evokes the emotional lives of both Crawley and his wife, but the context of Crawley's world deepens the passage infinitely and lets us see how inappropriate his

---

[31] *The Last Chronicle*, chap. LXII, pp. 232–233 (II).

response is to the realities of his age. He is "so essentially tragic" because for good or ill the changing world has passed him by, leaving him as useless and irrelevant as a Samson in Threadneedle Street. He is as remote as his heroes from the world of the Grantlys, the Johnny Eameses, the Dalrymples, the Bishop Proudies, and the Toogoods.

VI

For Trollope, *The Last Chronicle of Barset* marked a turning point. Through Crawley, he at last came to an understanding of his father and his father's failure to cope with life. He consciously recognized that a part of himself identified with the father, rebelled against the patterns of transition, which unfairly ruined such men as Crawley. He felt a new malice toward the materialistic course of the world, and that made possible his great period of social satire. Both the outward evidence of his own times and the inward memory of his father proved that power had moved from God and godly men to the world and worldly men. If secularism could free—had freed—people from living under religious guilt and intolerance, it could also lead to mammonism and amorality, small-mindedness and extreme psychological confusion. Trollope was himself a very worldly and practical man, as his autobiography proves, but there was the other side of him that loved sanctity and was ashamed of his own worship of success. That side comes out only in his novels when he draws a Harding, a Crawley, a Barchester Cathedral, or when he excoriates a brutal, money-grubbing society. Frank O'Connor says that Trollope was obsessed by the conflict between worldliness and sanctity, and wonders why he comes down, "again and again on the side of worldliness."[32] More accurately, he tried to find a balance between sanctity and worldliness which avoided the extremes of each, but he finally found that the *world* had come down on the side of

---

[32] *The Mirror in the Roadway*, p. 182.

worldliness. The whole Barsetshire saga was an attempt to locate realistically the place and the possibilities for religious idealism in the age. It was also an act of propitiation to the scorned sanctity and unworldliness of his father. In *The Last Chronicle*, he set down an allegory of change in which sanctity and concern for anything beyond this world become historically obsolete, but he also paid full homage to the tragedy inherent in such change. His *Encyclopaedia Ecclesiastica* was finished.

7
Obsessive Psychology And the Tyranny of Public Opinion

A character in *The Eustace Diamonds* says: " 'They're a queer lot, ain't they—the sort of people one meets about in the world.' " Trollope would have agreed with Eric Hoffer's dictum that "a population undergoing drastic change is a population of misfits."[1] In a changing world people become very compulsive. They worry about where they are going to end up and whether they can adapt themselves to the future. They look around for certainties. They cling to pet theories, goals, dogmas, particular images of self, the comforting past, plans for the future—anything for surety in the swirl of time and events.

The *Last Chronicle of Barset* shows the weakening influence of otherworldly religion. More people were coming to believe that conduct was good or bad, not in God's eyes, but in men's. Trollope thought they were transferring their reverence from God and his supposed dictates to public opinion and worldly prestige. In periods of flux people want and need both order and direction. If they no longer have fixed and predictable expectations or the guidelines of supernatural religion, then public opinion—what Trollope calls "the world"—becomes the new earthly god that ranks and

---

[1] Eric Hoffer, *The Ordeal of Change* (New York, 1964), p. 2.

grades them. A breakdown in idealism usually leads to more, not less, concern about what the neighbors think. Without a firm hierarchy or an absolute religious code, a man's standing comes to be exactly what others think it should be, and he frets about his status. He may even try to lift his own status by manipulating public opinion.

In book after book following *The Last Chronicle*, Trollope wrote about obsessive psychology and the tyranny of public opinion. Over and over he creates characters who worry about what other people think of them, who want to shine in society, and who rush to follow the latest fads and fancies. They try to fit in with influential groups and want to help make and direct public opinion. And he kept imagining other characters (though often they are the same) whom change and outside pressure upset so much that they compulsively latch on to some idea and, in their one-track minds, try to build protective shells against the unpredictability of an unstable world.

The clash of external pressures and internal values becomes more and more difficult to resolve in his fiction. He saw his society in danger of losing its balance. People could easily lose their individual moral standards and even their sense of identity, and drift like flotsam on the currents of public opinion. Or they might close their minds to reality, to community, to history, to everything but inner needs and drives in a desperate effort to preserve a distinct personality. His farewell to Barset meant that he no longer believed clerical ideals could effectively check materialism and comfort those whom the world had disappointed. Barsetshire had been a haven for harmonizing the new and the old, but Barsetshire was gone. The Victorians now had to live in a less idealistic world. London replaces Barchester as the center of Trollope's fiction, Parliament and the fashionable drawing room replace the Cathedral and the bishop's palace as the symbolic centers of power, and politicians (male and female) replace clerics as the central figures in his world.

In politics one ought to understand the opinions of others,

know the times thoroughly, accept gracefully the change-
able nature of affairs, and, without compromising one's integrity, blend personal will and desire into an art of the
possible. The great problem of political life had become for
Trollope the major problem of the age: how to care about
other people, please them, and still make and keep one's own
soul.

I

Phineas Finn (1866–1867) and its sequel *Phineas Redux*
(1870–1871) are political novels of extraordinary range that
deal directly with the problem. Together they frame and
give form to an inquiry into the effects of Victorian public
opinion and obsessions and their relationship to change.
There is nothing much like *Phineas Finn* in English fiction.
It is partly an initiation novel, a la *Tom Jones*, partly an
analysis of the Victorian body politic with its spectrum of
pressure groups, points of view, and axes for grinding, partly
a "society" novel. Like Proust in *Le côté des Guermantes*,
Trollope tried to imagine the psychology and movement of
the national aristocracy, but he is more concerned than
Proust with the ruling class in politics, more interested in
the relationship between social power and political power.

Few other novelists give us such an acute sense of what
it is like to live at the heart of a civilization's power elite.
When novelists write about politics they usually get so
wrapped up in the political issues of their work that they
fail to give their characters the individuality and the convincing private lives that we expect in good fiction. Trollope's characters have great political significance and seem
almost to represent various social constituencies, yet they
usually think and act like people rather than types. No matter how much a man is like other men of his class or how
much he is conditioned by the pressure of the times, he lives
within the limits of his own mind and perceives life individually.

Critics have sometimes said that Trollope is so interested

in the intimacies of personal life and so sketchy about large
political issues and classes other than his own, that *Phineas
Finn* is not really a political novel at all. But this is surely
wrong. He is very clear and very good on the most important
political questions, namely, what politics should do and what
motivates politicians. Trollope always sees life in political
terms—that is, he cares about the health of the polis and cannot imagine the quality of personal life as distinct from the
quality of life in the community. In all his books from *The
Macdermots* to *The Landleaguers* he insists that a really good
life cannot be led in a bad community. Politics ought to be a
process which helps all kinds of people, people with the sort
of diversity that we see in *Phineas Finn* to live bearable lives
—happy lives if possible, though that is sometimes too much
to hope for. On balance, politics should bring real betterment
to people (a tricky thing to judge). Trollope always seems to
be asking the implicit question in the novels, "Are things getting better or not?" Politics, in short, is for him a continuing
process of conciliation, not a program.

Presumably everyone knows that the psychological motives
of politicians and the interplay of personalities make political history. Politics in Trollope often turns out to be what
Fielding called "politricks," a game that men play first and
foremost for their own benefit—to win and aggrandize themselves. When he makes Phineas Finn, his hero, begin a political career out of vain and ambitious motives, he seems to be
saying that the politician, good or bad, is always somehow
a man on the make, acting for self, whether he knows it or
not.

Finn is important both as a character and as a formal center for the novel. He is a catalyst through whom Trollope can
bring together the most important strands of Victorian Establishment life, but like Arabin and Crawley in the Barset
series, he also tests his society. What happens to him and
how he develops tell us about the nature and worth of his
world. Trollope has consciously meant Finn to be "typical"

and neutral, but he has put a good deal of himself into this character. Like Trollope, Finn comes over from Ireland to find success in England, moves into the fashionable world, and still keeps some of the passive detachment of an outsider. And like Trollope, he becomes more and more disillusioned.

In Finn's world, the pressures and demands on one are becoming greater, but the world is still small enough so that one man can feel these pressures and personally know the people who exert or typify them. Social life and political life are intertwined and are often the same thing in the novel. The ruler of the Establishment milieu is public opinion; however, public opinion in Trollope is a complicated and subjective thing. It usually means one's own interpretation of what others think and expect. It may be social convention, the opinions of friends and associates, political consensus, or popular will. In any case, living under its tyranny means caring desperately about it and making it the business of one's life to stand out or stand well in the eyes of others.

Trollope wrote *Phineas Finn* in 1867 when public opinion caused the second Reform Bill to be passed, and everything in the novel takes place against this background of agitation. Finn gets into political clubs, Whiggish salons, and Parliament as a Liberal who will support the general Party policy of reform. According to Mr. Monk, his political mentor, " 'It is becoming more and more apparent every day that all legislation must be carried . . . in obedience to the expressed wish of the people.' "[2] The main reason why it is apparent is that the people threaten to get out of hand. In *Phineas Finn* and his other writing of this period, violence becomes very much a part of Trollope's fictional world. An era of great change brings with it an atmosphere charged with potential violence.

Trollope really does not know a lot about "the people," but he does understand the coercion for change in England

---

[2] *Phineas Finn* (London, 1951), "double volume" (see Author's Note, p. viii), chap. LVIII, pp. 225–226 (II).

and its various effects on *upper-class* people. A rather matter-of-fact passage in the novel gives us an idea of the pent-up, rebellious emotion abroad in its world.

When Phineas got back to London ... he found that there was already a great political commotion in the metropolis. He had known there was to be a gathering of the people in favor of the ballot, and that ... there was to be a procession with a petition. ... Phineas found that the town had been in a state of ferment for three days, that on Wednesday forty or fifty thousand persons had been collected at Primrose Hill, and that the police had been forced to interfere,—and that worse was expected. ...

The petition was to be presented at six o'clock, but the crowd, who had collected to see it carried into Westminster Hall, began to form itself by noon. It was said afterwards that many of the houses in the neighborhood of Palace Yard and the Bridge were filled with soldiers. ... In the course of the evening three or four companies of the Guards in St. James's Park did show themselves and had some rough work to do. ... The police, who were very numerous in Palace Yard, had a hard time of it all afternoon. ... As the evening went on, the mob extended itself to Downing Street and the front of the Treasury Chambers, and before the night was over all the boardings round the new Government offices had been pulled down. The windows also of certain obnoxious members of Parliament were broken. One gentleman who unfortunately was said to have said that the ballot was the resort of cowards, fared very badly;—for his windows were not only broken but his furniture and mirrors were destroyed by the stones that were thrown.[3]

The very understatement of this report shows that this sort of incident and feeling was commonplace in the privileged-class consciousness and did not need stressing. The personal attitudes, actions, and reactions of the privileged-class characters ought to be seen in the context of greater public power and expectations, unleashed social energies, and a less rigid class structure.

---

[3] Chap. XXV, pp. 275–282 (I).

"At this time," says Trollope, "*the world* was talking much about Reform," and Phineas must try to adapt to this world and please the people in it. Advice and pressure come to him from all sides, and since he is both an inexperienced young man and a politician, he must take into account all the influences on him. Barrington Erle, a dedicated party hack, preaches total obedience to the aristocratic Liberal party leaders and "Liberal politics": " 'Convictions! [Erle says] . . . I've had to do with them all, but a fellow with convictions is the worst of all. . . . It ought to be enough for any man, when he begins, to know that he's a Liberal.' "[4] What's good for the moderate Liberal party is good for England, according to Erle and the party chiefs. An ambitious young man will do well for his country and also "have his price," by becoming *an organization man, a loyal party member*. Monk, the idealistic Member of Parliament, teaches Finn loyalty to the cause of reform and devotion to progressive change for the people. Then there are the Radicals like Bunce, and the opinion-makers and demagogues like Turnbull and the yellow-journalist Slide, all of whom want Phineas to be "a people's friend."

But Finn gets conservative and reactionary advice, too. His law teacher, Mr. Low, calls Monk's progressive ideas "claptrap" and tells him to forget the frivolity of politics and public affairs. The truth is that one has to make one's own way before even thinking about the public welfare. Low expresses a conservative view which sees the world as a very hard place and human nature as weak and untrustworthy. The individual can do little for others except to work hard, become successful and see that strict laws are obeyed. A man does well by cultivating his own garden and upholding established order. All else is wishful foolishness. Misery exists because people are lazy: " 'Phineas, my dear fellow, as far as I have yet been able to see the world, men don't begin either very good or very bad. They have gener-

---

[4] Chap. LXVII, pp. 336–337 (II).

ally good aspirations with infirm purposes;—or, as we may
say, strong bodies with weak legs to carry them. Then, because their legs are weak, they drift into idleness and ruin.
During all this drifting they are wretched, and when they
have thoroughly drifted they are still wretched. The agony
of their old disappointment still clings to them.' "[5] Low's
fatalism, with its inherent distrust of political solutions, explains many of the contradictions in Victorian life and much
of the seeming callousness toward the suffering of the lower
classes.

His gloomy, but provocative talk is much different from
the political cynicism of Phineas's fellow Member of Parliament Fitzgibbon, who says, " 'I hate all change.' " Finn tells
him that he favors a government that gets things done for
the people, and Fitzgibbon replies, " 'Doing things, as you
call it, is only bidding for power,—for patronage and pay.
. . . Come down and have a glass of brandy-and-water, and
leave the people alone for the present. The people can take
care of themselves a great deal better than we can take care
of them.' "[6]

About all this Phineas's mercurial friend, Lord Chiltern,
the great reactionary in the novel, says with total disdain, " 'I
know nothing whatever about politics. . . . I never did—and
never shall. . . . It's the meanest trade going I think, and
I'm sure it's the most dishonest.' "[7] This sort of frustration
with politics and social organization becomes extremely important in Finn's and Trollope's world, as we shall see.

One reason for Chiltern's contempt is that political success
depends in large measure on pleasing the Establishment
society. Politics in Trollope often seems frivolous and ama-
teurish—women whispering to powerful politicians on behalf
of handsome, pleasant young men, important political decisions being made at dinner parties, personal likes and dislikes shaping public policy—yet his picture was undoubtedly

---

[5] Chap. V, pp. 54–55 (I).
[6] Chap. III, p. 31 (I).
[7] Chap. VIII, p. 93 (I).

true for the nineteenth century and is much closer to the truth today than official propaganda would have us believe. Any aspiring politico must charm an elite constituency of fashion and power.

Finn's problem is that he is too good at pleasing everybody and making his way up in the government. Trollope purposely makes him a rather bland if ambitious young man who for most of the book does not seem to know his own mind. Doing what other people want and continual compromising tend to blur his identity and to make him seem at times insincere without meaning to be. Fearing for his independence, he finally chooses, not without regrets, to back Irish reform against his party leaders and to resign from the government on principle. He feels that the system has "cabined, cribbed, and confined" his personality and his ideals. Only by defying public opinion can he become a real man instead of a mere "success."

Trollope carefully structures a series of parallels to show the inseparability of public and private life. The time when Phineas is voting against his convictions and pleasing important people in government is just the time when he is flitting from one society woman to another, flirting and making love. When he decides to vote for Ireland, he also decides to marry his poor Irish girl friend and turn down Madame Goesler's cash. In the country house or in Parliament, he is necessarily the same kind of man.

II

The outstanding parallel in the novel is of course between the political world and the feminine world of Society (with a capital S). Society, for Trollope, is the politics of women, and social prestige to them is like political power to men. The ladies' maneuverings, rivalries, alliances, and difficulties resemble those of the men in Parliament. Status-seeking and power-seeking spring out of the same motives and take much the same form.

Like almost all the characters in its world, the great women in *Phineas Finn*—Lady Laura Standish, Madame Goesler, Lady Glencora, and Violet Effingham—are neurotic, defensive, and ambitious. But they are also witty and charmingly passionate, and they give the novel its special glory. They are as full of comic insight and witty satire as any of the *grandes dames* of Meredith, Swinburne, Wilde, or Shaw. Other Victorian novelists seldom match Trollope's ability to write realistically and affectionately about women. He did not fear or resent them as a class, the way so many of his contemporaries did. When he imagined a woman, he saw a person and not a moral or psychological metaphor; and unlike so many writers, he loved the sex and could forgive its faults.

He shows in this novel an understanding of how much a woman is the prisoner of public opinion and how much she has in common with that energetic mob of people looking for an independent place in the sun. One finds sympathy for feminine courage and nerve in the face of institutionalized repression—a repression whose strength comes through in remarks like this one of Laura's: " 'There is no tyranny to a woman like telling her of her duty. Talk of beating a woman! Beating might often be a mercy.' "[8]

Trollope recognizes both the sexuality of his women and the conventional pressure on them to repress it and divert its force into a drive for prestige. When he explains Laura's reasons for making a miserable marriage and suppressing her love for Finn, we see the power of public opinion insidiously perverting her nature:

> She had married Mr. Kennedy because she was afraid that otherwise she might find herself forced to own that she loved that other man who was then a nobody;—almost nobody. It was not Mr. Kennedy's money that had bought her. This woman in regard to money had shown herself to be as generous as the sun. But in marrying Mr. Kennedy she had

---

[8] Chap. LV, p. 194 (II).

maintained herself in her high position, among the first of
her own people,—among the first socially and among the
first politically. But had she married Phineas,—had she become Lady Laura Finn,—there would have been a great
descent. She could not have entertained the leading men of
her party. She would not have been on the level with the
wives and daughters of Cabinet Ministers. She might, indeed
have remained unmarried! But she knew that had she done
so,—had she so resolved,—*that which she called her fancy
would have been too strong for her*. She would not have remained unmarried. At that time it was her fate to be either
Lady Laura Kennedy or Lady Laura Finn.[9]

Kennedy versus Finn, the demands of the inner world versus
the demands of the outer world—how to reconcile the two
(which Laura never succeeds in doing) becomes the great
problem for everyone in the book, including the most interesting of all the women, Madame Max Goesler.

Marie Goesler, an exotic-looking, wealthy Jewish widow
of an Austrian banker, is the Disraeli of aristocratic English
Society in the novel. Along with the affairs of Phineas (Trollope deliberately makes their careers parallel), her climb
to the top of the social ladder and her crisis of conscience
dominate the last part of the novel. She manipulates people
and public opinion like a masterful politician, but she has
self-knowledge and generosity to go with her worldliness.
Trollope's tolerance and imagination allow him to break
through the Victorian stereotypes of *Jewess* and *social climber*.

Madame Max Goesler was a lady who . . . was ambitious
of doing the very uttermost with those advantages which
she possessed. . . . She found herself possessed of money,
certainly; of wit,—as she believed; and of a something in her
personal appearance which, as she plainly told herself, she
might perhaps palm off upon the world as beauty. She was
a woman who did not flatter herself, who did not strongly

[9] *Ibid.*, pp. 193–194 (II), italics mine.

believe in herself, who could even bring herself to wonder that men and women in high position should condescend to note such a one as her. With all her ambition, there was a something of genuine humility about her, . . . And though she prized wealth, and knew that her money was her only rock of strength she could be lavish with it, as though it were dirt.

But she was highly ambitious, and she played her game with great skill and great caution. Her doors were not open to all callers;—were shut even to some who find but few doors closed against them;—were shut occasionally to those whom she most specially wished to see within them. She knew how to allure by denying, and to make the gift rich by delaying it.[10]

Her success in making room at the top shows the power of democratizing forces undermining the class structure—not the least of which is the appeal of frank, cosmopolitan sexiness.

"Public estimation," as Trollope puts it, regards the haughty, remote old Duke of Omnium as the most exalted noble in all English society. In the previous Barset and Palliser novels Trollope surrounds the Duke with an aura of exclusiveness. Now we see him as a kind of earlier British version of one of Proust's Guermantes and an easy mark for the lovely wiles of Marie: "He was sick of fair faces, and fat arms, and free necks. Madame Goesler's eyes sparkled as other eyes did not sparkle, and there was something of the vagueness of mystery in the very blackness and gloss and abundance of her hair,—as though her beauty was the beauty of some world which he had not yet known.' "[11] Through Phineas's eyes we see the Duke snub her when they first meet, and watch her coolly stifle her dislike and go after him in her compulsion to feel herself a woman of some importance in the world. To her he becomes for the moment a title,

---

[10] Chap. LVII, pp. 209–210 (II).
[11] Chap. LX, p. 246 (II).

a symbol of social success rather than a person. Here is a sample of the gaily sophisticated badinage with which she fascinates him:

The Duke and Madame Max Goesler were together again before luncheon, standing on a terrace at the back of the house, looking down on a party who were playing croquet on the lawn.

"Do you never play?" said the Duke.

"Oh yes;—one does everything a little."

"I am sure you would play well. Why do you not play now? I should like to see you with your mallet."

"I am sorry your Grace cannot be gratified. I have played croquet till I am tired of it, and have come to think it is only fit for boys and girls. The great thing is to give them opportunities for flirting, and it does that."

"And do you never flirt, Madame Goesler?"

"Never at croquet, Duke."

"And what with you is the choicest time?"

"That depends on so many things,—and so much on the chosen person. What do you recommend?"

"Ah,—I am so ignorant. I can recommend nothing."

"What do you say to a mountain-top at dawn on a summer day?" asked Madame Max Goesler.

"You make me shiver," said the Duke.

"Or a boat on a lake on a summer evening, or a good lead after the hounds with nobody else within three fields, or the bottom of a salt-mine, or the deck of an ocean steamer, or a military hospital in time of war, or a railway journey from Paris to Marseilles?"

"Madame Max Goesler, you have the most uncomfortable ideas."

"I have no doubt your Grace has tried each of them,— successfully. But perhaps, after all, a comfortable chair over a good fire, in a pretty room beats everything."[12]

Trollope manages to make this sort of thing seem bright and winning and, at the same time, implicitly sad and empty be-

---

[12] Chap. XLVIII, pp. 109–110 (II).

cause her manner is so divorced from her real feelings and her deeper self. He imagines her not as an amoral demirep like Proust's Odette, nor as a single-minded social climber like Madame Verdurin, but as a much more profound and vulnerable woman.

She finds herself torn between her need to impress others and her desire to be better, more honest, and more loving than she has been:

She was ever discontented with herself, telling herself that all that she had done was nothing, or worse than nothing. . . . And what if she caught this old man, and became herself a duchess . . . would that make her life happier; or her hours less tedious. . . .

In acting the raptures of love on behalf of a worn-out duke who at best would scarce believe in her acting, there would not be much delight for her. She had never yet known what it was to have anything of the pleasure of love. She had grown, as she often told herself, to be a hard, cautious, selfish, successful woman, without any interference or assistance from such pleasure. Might there not yet be time left for her to try it without selfishness,—with an absolute devotion of self,—if she could only find the right companion? There was one who might be such a companion [Finn], but the Duke of Omnium was not such a one.

There is a strong sexual impulse behind these last thoughts (which later causes her to propose to Finn), and we immediately get a typical Victorian sublimation: "But to be Duchess of Omnium! After all, success in this world is everything;—is at any rate the only thing the pleasure of which will endure."[13] The last sentence is ironic, but amazingly shrewd in what it implies. Not only does she admonish herself to remember that success outlasts the pleasures of love, she also thinks of success almost in religious terms. Success is what the Victorians were beginning to have instead of

---

[13] Chap. LX, pp. 250–251 (II).

God. The whole passage again shows the tremendous schizoid pressures of Victorian—and modern—life.

Trollope makes the parallel between Madame Max and Phineas explicit when he gives her the exact words that he uses to complain about having to satisfy public opinion: She is, she says, " 'the most cabined, cribbed, and confined creature in the world.' "[14] She renounces the Duke's offer of marriage, as Phineas gives up office and turns down her offer, to prove that she can still make personal, moral choices, and that independent principle and self-esteem can still mean more than prestige. But Trollope, always insisting on the dubiety of his age and of human nature, imagines that no matter how morally right their decisions are, they both know that they will often regret choosing conscience over ambition and public esteem. Madame Max speaks some of the most important words in the book to Finn: " 'Of course decency, morality, and propriety, all made to suit *the eye of the public*, are the things which are really delightful. We all know that, and live accordingly. . . . But . . . I am sure you agree with me that you often envy the improper people,— the Bohemians,—the people who don't trouble themselves about keeping any laws except those for breaking which they would be put into nasty, unpleasant prisons. I envy them. Oh, how I envy them.' "[15] She seems to be caught in what we might call the Victorian squeeze. All of Trollope's writing in these years relates to that "eye of the public" and that longing to break loose, both of which he sees getting stronger.

III

The pressures in this changing world can become intolerable and lead to obsessive, violent behavior. Lord Chiltern, who nearly kills Finn in a duel, is Trollope's first sympathetic

---

[14] Chap. LXXII, p. 389 (II).
[15] *Ibid.*, italics mine.

character who is really dangerous. He hates the modern world with its compromises and its collectivization and re-acts against it violently. He has that kind of primitive an-archic energy which, in a peculiar way, has helped shape modern culture. Like some early-day Lawrentian character, he believes in simplicity, nature, emotion, violence, and hon-esty—what Lawrence might have called "blood." In fact, like Mellors, he devotes his life to hunting game and a wom-an. Chiltern (the name symbolizes his withdrawal from modern life), living in an effete, cloying age, finds his one opportunity for manly adventure in winning Violet Effing-ham away from her other tame suitors. Everything about him connotes sexuality, and pursuit of woman and sex be-comes for him an obsession. Sex is one of the few things left that seems personal. The imagery used to describe him is sometimes startlingly sexual: Violet Effingham says, " 'Your brother, Laura, is dangerous. He is like the bad ice in the parks where they stick up the poles. He has had a pole stuck upon him ever since he was a boy.' "[16] His sexuality and force attract Violet, but she, like others in Trollope's vision, has the problem of balancing desire with her sense of what the public expects of her. She has to try to tame him and punish herself for loving him before she can give way to his force. One sees in almost all of Trollope's women of this period a barely suppressed hysteria that their split yearnings cause.

The changing modern fashions make others compulsive besides Chiltern. Laura's husband, Robert Kennedy, fanati-cally religious in a secular time and a hater of women's rights in a time when woman's role is changing, goes half-mad in his efforts to make his wife conform to ideas of Calvinist propriety. Feeling useless, he has nothing to do but brood about Laura's imagined sins against God and himself. Even Lady Glencora bursts out neurotically when the future title

---

[16] Chap. LII, p. 155 (II).

of her little boy is threatened by the Duke's projected marriage to Marie. In all of this lies Trollope's undertone of worry: Is the changing Victorian society cracking under its stresses and strains?

Phineas Finn, as Trollope says in the autobiography, is only half of a whole novel. Not until after six years and several more books would he finish it with *Phineas Redux*. In the meantime, he suspended judgment on its world and especially the fate of its two "test" figures, Phineas and Madame Goesler, while he went more deeply into the psychological obsessions that he saw infecting the privileged classes: obsessions with sex, class, religion, identity, work, prestige, success, and, above all, change.

IV

Of course all people are ridden with obsessions, but the Victorians tried to make a virtue of them. They honored the concept of "character," and by "character" they meant the distinctive and predictable responses that a man could be expected to make in most circumstances and his willingness, for good or bad, to act unflinchingly upon his idea of duty. In the long, uneven book *He Knew He Was Right* (1867–1868), Trollope shows how the man of firm "character" can shut his eyes and heart to reality with terrifying results. Louis Trevelyan, the man who knows he is right, loses his mind and ruins himself and his wife. Trollope mistrusts the strong individual will because it gets in the way of the accommodation between self and community which must take place in order to make life bearable. The man who knows he is right is wrong and lacks humility. The single human mind is imperfect, and certainty is an illusion. In fact the need for certainty, which Trollope saw everywhere in his society, shows weakness. It means that the individual can no longer handle the contingency of experience and seeks to shut it out. Too much "character" could break his society up in the clash of uncompromising wills.

Trevelyan is obsessed by what he considers the disobedience and sexual infidelity of his wife, Emily, and by the baseness of the modern English world. Trollope amplifies on themes that he had touched on with Chiltern and Robert Kennedy. Trevelyan's psychological deterioration, even smothered as it is by tedious subplots and hundreds of unnecessary pages, is fascinating abnormal psychology. Handsome, intelligent, and rich, he begins with "all the world before him where to choose,"[17] but he chooses to do nothing much at all. Out of the boredom of too much leisure and too little responsibility, he and his wife quarrel. He cannot stand Emily's independence. He detests his petty and banal society, and irresponsibly withdraws from it, brooding on his wife's behavior and on the deplorable condition of the world —the two are somehow connected for him. Her insubordination gradually turns into sexual betrayal in his mind, and this leads to his insanity and his complete misanthropy.

The sexual obsession of Trevelyan helps explain more fully the whole strange Victorian obsession with sex. His illogical switch from blaming Emily's stubbornness to blaming her for adultery is a brilliant piece of psychological intuition on Trollope's part—not only about one man but about the whole age. Behind all the male resentment of female emancipation in the last century lies conscious or unconscious panic at the idea of equal sexual freedom for women. If the role of woman is changing, and if a wife may disobey her husband and demand her rights, what will prevent her from going off the double standard and behaving with the promiscuity of a man? Nothing, according to Trevelyan, and he takes his paranoid suspicion for fact. The continuing traumatic shock to the male psyche which the loss of power over women has caused is one of the major sociological facts of modern times. Trollope saw it bringing about everything from Trevelyan's psychosis to Plantagenet Palliser's sublimating devotion to political work.

---

[17] *He Knew He Was Right* (London, 1948), chap. I, p. 1.

Wifely chastity was to a Victorian husband both a possession and an ideal. The case of Bloom in Joyce's *Ulysses* makes us see why Trollope would imagine a Trevelyan or a Kennedy going out of his mind on the subject of adultery. Joyce uses Molly Bloom's infidelity to point up the ironic contrast between the idealism of the past (Penelope) and the earthiness of the present and to emphasize, like Bloom's alien birth and religion, modern man's essential isolation in the world. Bloom is more or less reconciled to his fate, but in Trevelyan's time the supposed mystical union of marriage still gave man an idealistic support against loneliness. The possibility that a wife might choose to be unfaithful was like the possibility that God did not exist: each knocked down a prop on which Victorian man built his life and made it more clear that he lived only in a physical, material world where ideals were delusions.

Change the status of women and you threaten the sexual code. A society orders itself by its sexual code as well as by its religious or political code; when you threaten it you threaten the whole society. Yet Trollope shows here how the obsessed man longs for what he fears because he needs to vindicate his obsession and relieve his guilt. He needs the apocalyptic fact in order to justify neglecting the "ordinary" matters of life—and Trollope is always stressing that this sort of neglect for everyday living withers a culture. At one point Trevelyan makes his wife swear falsely that she has cuckolded him, revealing the tendency of paranoia to bring into being the very object of the paranoid terror. Trollope is very good at getting down Trevelyan's schizophrenic thinking: at the same time that he condemns his wife, he condemns the artificial puritanical code of feminine behavior which *makes* him condemn her.

It is impossible not to feel sympathy for Trevelyan's hatred of his aimless, trivial society. It is full of worldly, uncharitable, pushing people accomplishing little of value, and Trollope understands perfectly why a sensitive man might want to detach himself from it. Henry James greatly admired the

climactic scenes of the novel with the picture of Louis, "separated from his wife, alone, haggard, suspicious, unshaven,
undressed, living in a desolate villa on a hilltop near Siena
and returning doggedly to his fancied wrong, which he has
nursed until it becomes an hallucination." "Here," says
James, "Trollope has dared to be thoroughly logical; he has
not sacrificed to conventional optimism; he has not been
afraid of a misery which should be too much like life."[18]

In one of the most remarkable chapters he ever wrote,
"Trevelyan Discourses on Life," Trollope gives Louis the
quality of a mad, possessed seer and lets loose some of his
own fierce resentment against Victorian society and the
petty tyranny of social convention. An up-and-coming young
reporter for *The Daily Record*—a popular newspaper which,
in fact, records quotidian junk—comes out to visit Louis and
persuade him to return to his wife and home. Trevelyan,
dressed in motley fashion and playing the wise fool, greets
him:

> "Sit down and let us two moralize. . . . I spend my life
> here doing nothing,—nothing,—nothing; while you cudgel
> your brain from day to day to mislead the British public.
> . . . Which of us two is taking the nearest road to the devil?"
> . . . "They used to tell us," said Stanbury, "that idleness is
> the root of all evil."
> "They have been telling us since the world began so many
> lies, that I for one have determined never to believe any-
> thing again. Labor leads to greed, and greed to selfishness,
> and selfishness to treachery, and treachery straight to the
> devil,—straight to the devil. Ha, my friend, all your leading
> articles won't lead you out of that. What's the news? Who's
> alive? Who dead? Who in? Who out?"

Trevelyan of course echoes Lear here, and Trollope consciously uses him, as Shakespeare uses Lear in *his* madness,
to point out the insanities and contradictions of the sup-

---

[18] Henry James, "Anthony Trollope," in *The Future of the
Novel*, ed. Leon Edel (New York, 1956), p. 257.

posedly sane world: " 'Look at me here. I have got rid of the
trammels pretty well,—haven't I?—have unshackled myself,
and thrown off the padding, and wrappings, and the swad-
dling clothes. I have got rid of the conventionalities, and can
look Nature straight in the face. I don't even want *The Daily
Record*, Stanbury:—think of that.' " A short while later, in a
perfectly phrased piece of invective, he exclaims: " 'England
is the most damnable, puritanical God-forgotten and stupid
country on the face of the globe.' "[19]

Like Milton when he wrote Satan's lines, Trollope had a
good deal more anarchic rebellion in him than he knew. The
forces of alienation were building, and there was attraction
in the sort of strong character that could stay aloof from a
grubby world and defy the tyranny of public opinion. But
Trollope means to show, through Trevelyan's miserable
death, that withdrawal and righteous misanthropy are self-
defeating. They lock one in a jail of self where one no longer
has the power to see reality.

V

Nevertheless, he strongly felt a Trevelyan-like urge to denounce the meanness and contradictions of English life. In
The Vicar of Bullhampton (1868), the sanest man in town
looks around at his neighbors and muses, "How was it possible for a man to live among such people in good humor
and Christian charity?" Bullhampton, as the name shows,
supposedly represents England, and it is a claustrophobic
little community ruled by closed-minded public prejudice.
As in Trollope's short continental novel, *Linda Tressel*
(1867), the characters, especially the women, are fanatical
about their religious sects. These ingrown sects have little to
do with real Christianity. Breeding suspicion and conformity
among people, they actually prevent communal goodwill
and progress. Organized religion has become more negative
than positive.

---

[19] *He Knew He Was Right*, chap. xcii, pp. 862–871.

This society is also obsessed with sexual purity and equates it with sanctity. One of the main characters is a prostitute whom the vicar tries to rehabilitate; but the rest of the towns-people, in the name of morality, virtually run to see who can throw the first stone at her. They react to the mire of reality with the irrational rage and the herd instinct. Even the vicar's wife exclaims, " 'It is permitted . . . not to forgive that sin.' "[20]

Trollope seems to have felt that conventional semireligious assumptions of female virtue were strangling part of his culture in dogmatic ignorance so that it could not face its problems—such as prostitution—realistically. Both *An Eye for an Eye* (1870) and *Sir Harry Hotspur of Humblethwaite* (1868–1869) in this period show how prevalent seduction and the keeping of mistresses were among the better-class Victorians. Bullhampton and England lack flexible intelli-gence and charity partly because of what he devastatingly calls "the tawdry sentimentality of an age in which the mawk-ish insipidity of women was the reaction from the vice of the age preceding it."[21] This tyranny of sentimentality and insipidity is precisely what Glencora and Madame Goesler have to fight.

The drive for identity amidst conformity led to an obses-sion with family tradition, as Glencora shows when she battles for her son's future claim to a title. Dickens's Peck-sniff speaks an article of Victorian faith when he says, " 'In our children we live again.' " With belief in the immortal soul weakening, people looked to the family for perpetual identity and a role in the future. George Orwell, writing about Dickens, makes fun of the Victorian vision of happi-ness: "A huge loving family of three or four generations, all crammed together in the same house and constantly multi-plying, like a bed of oysters." But reverence for oyster fami-lies, like the reverence for most modern visions of a happy future—cybernetic heaven, socialist paradise, joyous people's communes—comes from man's need to believe in something

---

[20] *The Vicar of Bullhampton* (London, 1924), chap. xxxix, p. 276.
[21] Chap. XXXVII, p. 260.

more enduring than himself and which he helps to create.

In *Sir Harry Hotspur of Humblethwaite*, Trollope's Hotspur has an almost religious compulsion to continue his family heritage in his only surviving child, a daughter. In the psychology of nineteenth-century fiction, Electra loomed as large as Oedipus. The middle-class concern with family identity and loyalty intensified relationships between fathers and daughters, and Trollope shows in the tangled affair of Harry and his girl how the Electra syndrome could foster clannishness, social rigidity, feminine independence, and guilt. (One need only cite a few names, for example, the real-life Barretts, Brontës, Dickenses, and Evanses, and the fictional Dombeys, Dorrits, Garths, and Henchards, to point out the imaginative impact that intense father-daughter relations had on Victorian minds.)

We find in *Harry Hotspur, Ralph the Heir* (1869), and indeed, scores of novels by Trollope and the rest of the Victorians, all kinds of business about wills and inheritances. Much of this reflects the privileged-class impulse to form the future from beyond the grave, and perpetuate personal will on posterity. In *The Golden Lion of Grandpère* (1867), *An Eye for an Eye*, *Ralph the Heir*, *Lady Anna* (1871), and other novels of this period, he imagines old people, obsessed with family rank, shutting out compassion and communal responsibility and acting ruthlessly to enforce their wishes on the young.

Family loyalty shades into class loyalty in these books, and the English obsession with class standing becomes one of Trollope's large, explicit themes. Trollope's class feelings have all the confused ambivalence of the middle class itself. Intellectually he dislikes the idea of class and favors eventual equality; emotionally he is scared to death of the lower classes and has visions of crowds smashing decent order and property. In *Ralph the Heir*, for instance, at one moment he patronizes and sneers unconscionably at lower-class pretensions, and then a few pages later he argues the justice of lower-class grievances. On a personal level, Trollope knew the strength of class feelings; the lower-class determination to rise no matter what and the upper-class will to stay up and keep others down by all means. In *Lady Anna*, written just after *Phineas Redux*, a countess actually tries to shoot the tailor's son who wants to marry her daughter, and in *An Eye for an Eye* the mother of a poor Irish girl does kill the heir to an English title when he refuses to marry the girl.

Ralph the Heir is full of equivocal middle-class ditherings about the undeclared class war. Sometimes Trollope seems to condemn the whole class structure, at other times he comes close to identifying himself with one of his sympathetic conservatives' twaddle about "children whose mother would not be a lady, and whose blood would be polluted by an admixture so base."[22] He creates a character named Neefit, a tailor, who is marrying his daughter to a gentleman. For a while Trollope pokes bitter fun at him as a modern-day Giles Overreach, but suddenly he turns him into an English Père Goriot, pathetically assuring a prospective son-in-law, "'You needn't be seen about with me, you know.'"[23]

Trollope could sympathize with the aims of the lower classes, but he could not identify with the people themselves and imagine what it was like to be a worker. On the other hand, he knew and communicated exactly what it was like to be a member of the privileged middle class and to suffer from its phobias, its guilt, and its touchy defensiveness which, in an ironic counterrevolution, were to engulf the whole population of the Western world. Trollope's great character from *Ralph the Heir*, Sir Thomas Underwood, is one of the best studies in nineteenth-century fiction of paradoxical middle-class psychology. Underwood, a "successful" lawyer, has the typically middle-class Protestant longing to distinguish himself through work—to be special, to be "chosen"—but he also has the middle-class obsession with failure. Through this man's obsessive guilt and dissatisfaction with

---

[22] *Ralph the Heir* (London, 1951), "double volume" (see Author's Note, p. viii), chap. x, p. 119 (I).
[23] Chap. XXIV, p. 283 (I).

self, Trollope connects the prevalent feelings of inadequacy and loneliness to the overpowering appeal which social convention, conformity, and the tyranny of public opinion have for the middle classes. The driving ambition of Underwood's life has been to "write a book that should live," a biography of Sir Francis Bacon which will epitomize all human nature. He spends the best part of a lifetime preparing, but he never writes a single line. "He had been divorced from the world, and Bacon had done it. By Bacon he had justified to himself —or rather had failed to justify himself—a seclusion from his family and from the world which had been intended for strenuous work, but had been devoted to dilettante idleness. . . . He was for ever doubting, for ever intending, and for ever despising himself for doubts and unaccomplished intentions."[24] Compared to Underwood and his pitiful, pedantic obsession, George Eliot's characterization of Casaubon, good as it is, seems almost crude.

Trollope put a lot of his father into Sir Thomas who, like the elder Trollope, "thought himself capable of something that would justify him leaving the common circle," but then finds that it had "all been vanity." He has lived without a personal God, without the ability to communicate well with others, and—worst of all—without the grand achievement which would have justified his life—without, in other words, any real outside support. Obsessed finally with his own weakness and guilt, he comes to loath his individuality and his former freedom:

Why had he dared to leave that Sunday-keeping, church-going, domestic, decent life, which would have become one of so ordinary a calibre as himself? . . . To walk as he saw other men walking around him,—because he was one of the many; to believe, that to be good which the teachers appointed for him declared to be good; to do prescribed duties without much personal inquiry into the causes which had made them duties; to listen patiently, and to be content

---

[24] Chap. XL, pp. 138–139 (II).

without excitement; that was the mode of living for which
he should have known himself to be fit. But he had not
known it, and had ventured to think that he could think,—
and had been ambitious. And now he found himself stranded
in the mud of personal condemnation. . . .[25]

That is a terrifying passage in what it says about human
capability. It tells us why people—and not just Victorian
people—choose to live under a tyranny of public opinion.
Most men are mediocre—literally middle class. They cannot
stand self-reliance and nonconformity and the responsibility
of free choice; and so they create societies of convention and
"normality."

<h2 style="text-align:center">VI</h2>

And yet Trollope knew that if man fails to choose his
values, then life becomes meaningless. In *The Eustace Diamonds* (1869–1870) he becomes bitterly satirical about the
urge to renounce personal responsibility and merely do as
the world expects. The compassion in *Ralph the Heir* for
Underwood turns into a scathing attack on the compulsion
to live only for the eye of the public. Like Hannah Arendt,
Trollope believed in the banality of evil. Evil is shallow
weakness, not misguided force. It is a series of negatives—
an absence of conscience, self-knowledge, conviction, and
kindness, an inability to tell the difference between appearance and reality. The society of *The Eustace Diamonds* turns
rotten with public-relations mentality. Posing falsely and
ridiculously for the world, madly worrying about status, Lizzie Eustace and her circle live the demoralizingly empty lives
of Lilliputians. The satire of the book is fresh and sometimes
wildly funny, but its subject is nothing less than the loss of
the self.

Trollope calls Lizzie his "opulent and aristocratic Becky
Sharp," and as a character she has the same kind of literary
stature that Becky has. We see, in Lady Eustace as in

---

[25] Chap. LI, p. 286 (II).

Becky, an important configuration in modern life. But she has none of Becky's self-knowledge, her sense of fun, her ability to control people and events. "To be always acting a part rather than living her own life was to her everything," Trollope says of her, and he makes clear that she *has* no life of her own: "There was no reality about her."[26] Trollope's moral criticism is more subtle than Thackeray's and just as shrewd. Becky is a selfish and wicked schemer, but she has a defiant courage and an existential egotism that makes her appealing. Lizzie has no personality at all. Whatever she does, she does for the sake of a real or imagined audience. Keeping the diamonds of her husband's estate, lying about them, reading poetry and the Bible, accepting the hand of a smooth-tongued preacher in the end—she does it all to look well in the eye of some omnipotent public. Existence to her means only how she appears to others, what others say about her, and what she ought to say and do to impress others. Trollope's image of a brainwashed nullity blown about like a tumbleweed on the winds of public opinion still makes *The Eustace Diamonds* one of the most powerful and relevant satires in the language.

Time and again in Lizzie's preference for gesture over sincerity, sham over intelligence, and the stale clichés of pseudoromanticism over genuine individuality, one sees the conventional vacuity which debases human life. Here she is in a typical moment, alone but still playing for an imaginary public:

She began her reading, resolved that she would enjoy her poetry in spite of the narrow seat. She had often talked of "Queen Mab," and perhaps she thought she had read it. This, however, was in truth her first attempt at that work. "How wonderful is Death, Death and his brother Sleep." Then she half-closed the volume, and thought that she enjoyed the idea. Death—and his brother Sleep! She did not know why they should be more wonderful than Action, or Life, or Thought; but the words were of a nature which

---

[26] *The Eustace Diamonds* (London, 1952), chap. xix, p. 175.

would enable her to remember them, and they would be good for quoting. "Sudden arose Ianthe's soul; it stood All beautiful in naked purity." The name Ianthe suited her exactly. And the antithesis conveyed to her mind by naked purity struck her strongly, and she determined to learn the passage by heart. Eight or nine lines were printed separately, like a stanza, and the labour would not be great, and the task, when done, would be complete. "Instinct with inexpressible beauty and grace, Each stain of earthliness Had passed away, it reassumed Its native dignity, and stood Immortal amid ruin." Which was instinct with beauty, the stain or the soul, she did not stop to inquire, and may be excused for not understanding. "Ah," she exclaimed to herself, "how true it is; how one feels it; how it comes home to one!—'Sudden arose Ianthe's soul.'" And then she walked about the garden, repeating the words to herself, and almost forgetting the heat. " 'Each stain of earthliness had passed away.' Ha; yes. They will pass away and become instinct with beauty and grace." A dim idea came upon her that when this happy time should arrive, no one would claim her necklace from her, and that the man at the stables would not be so disagreeably punctual in sending in his bill. " 'All beautiful in naked purity!'" What a tawdry world was this in which clothes and food and houses are necessary! How perfectly that boy poet had understood it all. " 'Immortal amid ruin'!" She liked the idea of the ruin almost as well as that of the immortality, and the stains quite as well as the purity. As immortality must come, and as stains were instinct with grace, why be afraid of ruin? But then, if people go wrong—at least women—they are not asked out anywhere! " 'Sudden arose Ianthe's soul; it stood all beautiful—'" And so the piece was learned, and Lizzie felt that she had devoted her hour to poetry in a quite rapturous manner. At any rate she had a bit to quote; and though in truth she did not understand the exact bearing of the image, she had so studied her gestures and so modulated her voice, that she knew that she could be effective. She did not then care to carry her reading further, but returned with the volume into the house. Though the passage about Ianthe's soul comes very early in the work, she was not quite familiar with the poem, and when in after days she spoke of it as a thing of beauty that she had made her own by long study, she actually did not know that she was lying.[27]

Doing things for effect is common enough, but it is seldom harmless, despite the comedy of this passage. It leads to disastrous confusion about what is real and what is false. Liking lies, "thinking them more beautiful than truth," Lizzie is led, among other things, to marry a criminal confidence man. And as Trollope shows in *Phineas Redux*, such personal error spreads, causing infinite mischief not just to herself but to a whole society. In a world of change and doubt, he sees the greatest dangers for mankind not in the force of evil will, but in the moral vacuum left by people who do not even realize that they have become slaves to public opinion. Public opinion can annihilate human identity as surely as nuclear weapons.

Trollope makes his satirical point brilliantly at the close. From time to time he uses the Palliser set from *Phineas Finn* as a kind of chorus of public opinion to comment on Lady Eustace and the diamonds. At last, in the final chapter, Lizzie does not even appear. Instead, after all her ups and downs, she exists only as a thing that the senile, dying Duke of Omnium, Glencora, and her friends and relations spend a few idle moments talking about, then put out of mind:

"I never was so sick of anything in my life as I am of Lady Eustace. People have talked about her now for the last six months."

"Only three months, Lord Chiltern," said Lady Glencora in a tone of rebuke.

"And all that I can hear of her is that she has told a lot of lies and lost a necklace."

"When Lady Chiltern loses a necklace worth ten thousand pounds, there will be talk of her," said Lady Glencora.

At that moment Madame Max Goesler entered the room and whispered a word to the hostess. She had just come from

---

[27] Chap. XXI, pp. 194–196.

the duke, who could not bear the racket of the billiard-room. "Wants to go to bed, does he? Very well. I'll go to him."

"He seems to be quite fatigued with his fascination about Lady Eustace."

"I call that woman a perfect god-send. What should we have done without her?"[28]

And that is the end—the reward for all her efforts. Her life adds up to nothing more than a piece of gossip!

Trollope imagines Lizzie Eustace, however, as a kind of Dunciad queen for much of the novel's society. She epitomizes a world obsessed with public opinion, and that epidemic obsession turns people into objects as incapable of thought as the Eustace diamonds themselves. Lord Fawn, for example, the stupid member of the Liberal Establishment, dreads "the breath of public opinion." "His prevailing motive," Trollope says, "in all that he did or intended to do . . . was above all things . . . that he should 'put himself right in the eye of the British public.' "[29] Supposedly an up-and-coming leader, he is more shuttlecock than man. And in the blackest part of the novel Lucinda Roanoke, hawked about like a chattel on the marriage market and forced by the tyranny of the world to accept a man she hates, literally loses her mind and ends up a witless lump of flesh.

Sometimes with Swiftian bitterness, sometimes playfully, Trollope satirizes in *The Eustace Diamonds* personal cowardice and foolish irresponsibility in the face of change. Most of the characters realize that they live in changing times, but they frantically run around looking for external guides to behavior in bogus or nonexistent public standards. Still, Trollope longs to keep his faith in human will and independence. Lucy Morris, the foil for Lady Eustace, has a positive self, drab though she may seem: "A most unselfish little creature she was, *but one who had a well-formed idea of her own identity*. She was quite resolved to be somebody among her

---

[28] Chap. LXXX, p. 726.
[29] Chap. LXVII, p. 601.

fellow-creatures . . . somebody as having a purpose and a use in life. She was the humblest little thing in the world in regard to any possible putting of herself forward or needful putting of herself back; and yet, *to herself nobody was her superior.*"[30] One sees in Lucy's Biedermeier existentialism how explicit Trollope's concern is with identity—something that the Victorians obviously could not take for granted. Frank Greystock also has an independent will that lets him defy the world's injunction to marry money. Deciding for themselves what is right and wrong rather than letting other "people" decide, they end up happily.

Trollope, however, remains very skeptical about this world. He never succeeds in making Lucy much more than a bloodless figure of affirmation. Frank tends to be more convincing when he almost succumbs to Lizzie than when he stays true to Lucy. An offhand remark full of wonder about the oddity of one of his characters—"She went to church, not merely that people might see her there, . . . but because she thought it right"[31]—sums up the sardonic quality that prevails in the novel. Trollope even mocks Plantagenet Palliser, who resists the triviality of "the world" only to get himself bogged down in the most trivial of political projects imaginable, the creation of a five-farthing penny. Politics has been reduced to a little comic obsession. Trollope's feelings about his society at this time seem to resemble Lady Fawn's melancholy thoughts on the direction of her world: "When she was told that under the new order of things promises from gentlemen were not to be looked upon as binding, that love was to go for nothing, that girls were to be made contented by being told that when one lover was lost another could be found, she was very unhappy. She could not disbelieve it all, and throw herself back upon her faith in virtue, constancy, and honesty. She rather thought that things had changed for the worse since she was young . . ."[32]

---

[30] Chap. III, p. 25, italics mine.
[31] Chap. I, p. 40.
[32] Chap. LX, pp. 538–539.

VII

Skepticism colors the mood of *Phineas Redux*. In *Phineas Finn* Mr. Monk confidently speaks out for reform: " 'It seems to me that they who are adverse to change . . . ignore the majestic growth of the English people, and forget the present in their worship of the past. . . . With population vice has increased, and these politicians, with ears but no eyes, hear of drunkenness and sin and ignorance. And then they declare to themselves that this wicked, half-barbarous, idle people should be controlled and not repre-sented. A wicked, half-barbarous, idle people may be controlled;—but not a people thoughtful, educated and in-dustrious.' "[33] In *Phineas Redux* (1870–1871), there is no such political optimism. When Trollope came to finish the Phineas novel, he was changed. He had imagined and felt deeply the mad alienation of Trevelyan and the wretched isolation of Underwood, and afterwards he never could feel the same confidence in a healthy relationship between a man and his community. He had also seen at firsthand the vicious, scum-my side of political life in his own bitterly disappointing race for Parliament. And in *The Eustace Diamonds* he had cre-ated a satirical vision of a corrupt society. Finn's life turns much blacker, and Trollope closely identifies with Phineas's disillusionment. *Phineas Redux* shows the inevitable ravages of time on people and the dangerous soul-killing tendencies of his world, but Trollope tries also to locate the qualities in his world on which a good life might be built. The world is diseased but not yet beyond redemption.

Anthony Cockshut, in his excellent critical study, calls Trollope's career a "progress to pessimism." This needs quali-fying, as the *The Duke's Children* and other late novels show, but Trollope did feel that as most men grow older they become more pessimistic. They see that the world can-not keep them happy, that it is impersonal and overwhelm-

---

[33] *Phineas Finn*, chap. xxxv, p. 410 (I).

ing. Certainly as he himself aged, he more and more felt what he had known as a child—his own impotent loneliness and the hostility of the world. Finn also progresses to pessimism. As the moral sense that began developing at the end of *Phineas Finn* grows sharper in *Phineas Redux*, he finds himself appalled at what he sees: the brutality and insensitivity of political life, the weakness of self, the strength of obsession, and the flimsiness of reputation. In *Phineas Finn*, Trollope caught the glory of being young. But the exuberant images of Finn thrilled with the glamor of Lady Laura's upper-class world, wildly in love with several women at once, petrified over his maiden speech in Parliament, frantic about keeping up appearances, happy with pride at pulling off a political ruse, feeling himself the center of the universe—all these give way in *Phineas Redux* to the quiet desperation of maturity. Laura changes into a guilt-ridden hag, Mr. Kennedy becomes a gun-toting madman, grand politicians turn sleazy, and Phineas himself is put in jail.

At first, Phineas's change from bright young politician to a despondent prisoner, accused of murder and on trial for his life, may seem like cheap Victorian sensationalism (all the business about coats and keys and clues at Finn's trial reads like second-rate Wilkie Collins). But in a metaphoric sense the murder charge against Phineas and the trial work powerfully and well, like Kafka's trial, to show the absurd arbitrariness of life and the fickle might of public opinion. Trollope says that the world is necessarily cold. The case of the man in court whose life depends on the opinions of a jury is merely an extreme example of the fate of any man: each person is at the mercy of other people, who can never know him and never feel for him or care about him as he would hope and expect. Life is inevitably unjust, and the realization of this awful truth is part of maturing.

In criticizing his society Trollope carefully shows the reasons why Finn is in the dock. Competition between men has turned murderously violent, and a portion of the upper classes (Lord Fawn, Lizzie Eustace—even Gresham, the

Prime Minister) stupidly fail to discriminate between honesty (Finn) and sham (Emilius and Bonteen). We find the same sort of breakdown in responsibility that we saw in *The Eustace Diamonds*, but now with even more ominous overtones. Basically callous, those in power or near power lack moral and political conviction. The politicians generally behave insincerely—toward Finn, for example, or toward Church disestablishment. In much the same amoral way as Lizzie Eustace, they regard only what gesture will please a public.

Phineas, the one-time ambitious lover of political life, says near the end, " 'What does it matter who sits in Parliament? The fight goes on just the same. The same falsehoods are acted. The same mock truths are spoken. The same wrong reasons are given. The same personal motives are at work.' "[34] This is cynicism born of trauma, but it comes close to Trollope's own view in the book. Unable to conceive of such a thing as an honest election anywhere in his work, he naturally presents the dishonesty of Finn's election as a routine matter. But that is only the beginning. *Phineas Redux* has more politics than *Phineas Finn*, and it is also more parochial and remote from communal problems. The question that concerns Parliament throughout the book is Church disestablishment (how symbolically fitting, by the way). In a perfect satirical stroke, Trollope makes Daubeny, the Disraeli-like Conservative Prime Minister and master manipulator of public opinion, propose and back the assault on the Church, against all the principles of his party, simply to keep himself in power. But the Liberals, who believe in disestablishment, foil him by voting down his bill. The leaders and the majority of each party vote precisely against what they supposedly believe in and stand for. Parliament plays its own little power game and ignores its public duties, while trying to build a good public image. Paid political propagandists like Editor Slide flourish, and the light of statesmanship dies before

---

[34] *Phineas Redux*, (London, 1957), "double volume" (see Author's Note, p. viii), chap. LXVIII, p. 306 (II).

their uncreating words. Trollope sees his political leaders, in their concern with technicalities and personal power, losing touch with people—losing the greatest of all political gifts, the power of sympathy. Finn's disillusion, in fact, comes about because he understands that politicians really cannot allow themselves to be influenced by the affairs of individual people such as himself. They must sacrifice the interest of the single man to the broad interest of staying in power. They coolly react as public figures, not as private men.

Phineas's disgust with politics falls into one of the major patterns of Trollope's later novels, the alienation of man from his profession. Carlyle preached salvation through work to an audience of believers, and Trollope, as we have seen, did more than any other novelist to make modern man's work a subject of imaginative literature. Yet, starting with Crawley, his greatest characters cannot satisfy themselves in their work, though they are somehow obsessed with it.

In this book, however, Trollope still holds some hope, despite Finn, that obsession with work *can* be a positive good. Different as they are, Lord Chiltern and Palliser both show this. Chiltern, hating the modern world, becomes a master of hounds, in the eyes of his world a trivial occupation for a nobleman. But he does not care what others think, and in riding and working outdoors, carrying out hunt traditions, he finds a ritualistic discipline and a way of life that let him get rid of his aggressive violence harmlessly. Such a character grows out of the important romantic reaction to the industrialized civilization that we see, for instance, in the heroes of Byron, Lawrence, and Hemingway. Trollope describes his ideal master of hounds, Chiltern:

He should be a man with whom other men will not care to argue; an irrational, cut and thrust, unscrupulous, but yet distinctly honest man; one who can be tyrannical, but will tyrannize only over the evil spirits; a man capable of intense cruelty to those along side of him. . . . He should be savage and yet good-humoured; severe and yet forebearing; truculent and pleasant in the same moment. He should exercise unflinching authority. . . . He must so train his heart to feel for the fox a mingled tenderness and cruelty which is inexplicable to ordinary men and women. His desire to preserve the brute and then kill him should be equally intense and passionate. And he should do it all in accordance with a code of unwritten laws, which cannot be learnt without profound study.[35]

Substitute "bull" for "fox" and this could be straight out of *Death in the Afternoon.* That Trollope, the social novelist par excellence, understands so well the antisocial sentiment which has created everything from *The Giaour* to the fiction of private detectives, lone rangers, and international spies (not to mention actual world wars), proves how strong that feeling is in most men who have lived during or after the Industrial Revolution. The problem is to find or preserve ways of safely getting rid of men's deep uncivilized urges, and Chiltern finds it possible to purge himself in his work.

Palliser, of course, loves public affairs as much as Chiltern detests them. At the death of his uncle, he regretfully becomes Duke of Omnium, which means he has to give up high office. Still, he chooses to take a menial spot in the government and to work, despite what people say about its lowering his dignity. When Glencora sarcastically tells him, " 'You would clean Mr. Gresham's shoes for him, if—the service of your country required it,' " he replies, " 'I would even allow you to clean them,—if the service of the country required it.' "[36] Subtly Trollope shows how guilt over the irresponsible life of his uncle drives him to work for the public good. And as silly as his compulsive manner sometimes is, Trollope makes him the model politician—the political hope in the novel's world—interested in making the process of government work and willing to forgo personal prestige.

But even he, in his obsession with *system,* has fatal detachment from the reality of emotions. Glencora and Madame

---

[35] Chap. VII, pp. 73–74 (I).
[36] Chap. LVIII, pp. 193–194 (II).

Goesler carry more real hope in *Phineas Redux* than the Duke. When Finn is accused, Glencora intuitively believes him innocent and hounds her husband until he tells her to keep quiet. She answers him: " 'Out of the full heart the mouth speaks, and my heart is very full. What harm do I do?' 'You set people talking of you.' 'They have been doing that ever since we were married;—but I do not know that they have made out much against me. We must go after our nature, Plantagenet. Your nature is decimals. I run after units.' "[37] "Heart," as Frank O'Connor says, is the magic word in Trollope, signifying the capacity for sympathy and affection. Glencora and Marie Goesler have "heart," and they have the playful humor which can put things in perspective and release aggression. Like Glencora, Trollope believes in units rather than percentages. Political solutions are still possible in this world, as the settling of the Trumpeton Wood feud between Chiltern and the Pallisers shows, but politics, to work, must be based on affection for people and the sympathetic imagination to sense what it would feel like to be in someone else's shoes.

Trollope's rendering of Marie Goesler's sympathetic imagination, in particular, restores balance to the world, however precarious. Even in the midst of her social success, she retains a genuine inner life: "There was ever present a gnawing desire to do something more and something better than she had as yet achieved."[38] She can appreciate the feeling of Glencora and refuse the old Duke's money, and she can relieve the troubles of young lovers by giving them money. And in Finn's crisis, risking her reputation, she can feel with him, build his defense, and then bring him out of the depths with love. One of her best saving qualities is that ego-checking humor which she often uses against herself. Near the end Glencora breaks in on her just after Phineas proposes

[37] *Ibid.*, p. 195 (II).
[38] Chap. XIV, p. 150 (I).

to her and asks if she is interrupting anything: "Marie replied, 'It is only a trifle. Mr. Finn has asked me to be his wife.' 'Well?' 'I couldn't refuse Mr. Finn a little thing like that.' "[39]

Phineas earlier remarked how grim his imprisonment was, but, he says, " 'The grimness and the jokes are always running through my mind together.' "[40] His comic sense keeps him sane in prison in the same way that Trollope's comic sense can still bring balance and gaiety to his darkening world. Much is grim in *Phineas Redux*, but one keeps coming on remarks like this one describing a fat marchioness at the deathbed of her old flame, the Duke of Omnium: "She did not look like a romantic woman; but, in spite of appearances, romance and a duck-like waddle may go together."

One scene in particular shows the kind of equilibrium which is possible—just barely—in Trollope's world. Glencora has brought Finn and Marie together in her home after his release, for which Marie worked so hard. Phineas has never yet acknowledged that she is anything to him but a pleasant friend—like Glencora or Lady Laura:

"Yes, there she is," said the Duchess, laughing. She had already told him that he was welcome to Matching, and had spoken some short word of congratulation at his safe deliverance from his troubles. "If ever one friend was grateful to another, you should be grateful to her, Mr. Finn." He did not speak, but walking across the room to the window by which Marie Goesler stood, took her right hand in his, and passing his left arm round her waist, kissed her first on one cheek and then on the other. The blood flew to her face and suffused her forehead, but she did not speak, or resist him or make any effort to escape from his embrace. As for him, he had no thought of it at all. He had made no

---

[39] Chap. LXXIX, p. 429 (II). See Arthur Mizener, "Anthony Trollope: The Palliser Novels," in *From Jane Austen to Joseph Conrad* (Minneapolis, 1958), p. 172, for discussion of this passage.
[40] *Phineas Redux*, chap. LXXIII, p. 359 (II).

plan. No idea of kissing her when they should meet had occurred to him till the moment came. "Excellently well done" said the Duchess, still laughing with silent pleasant laughter.[41]

In the midst of Parliament debates, Cabinet meetings, murders, trials, political infighting, private obsession, and public tyranny, such a passage might seem almost nothing; and yet it is everything. In it Trollope sees the grace, the emotional intensity, the individual poise, and the will to communion and love on which civilization depends.

---

[41] Chap. LXXIV, pp. 362–363 (II).

8
The Dark
New World

After *Phineas Redux*, Trollope gave up on his society. The image of humanity groping for moral balance, sanity, and freedom in a confusing new age gives way to a much darker image of people living in a commercial Victorian wasteland filled with dishonesty and impotence. The world of *The Way We Live Now* and *The Prime Minister*, and of the lesser novels *Is He Popenjoy?* and *The American Senator*, runs out of control, like the dynamo world of Henry Adams. It is much the same world that Marx and Engels describe in the Communist Manifesto—a world where "there is no other bond between man and man but crude self-interest and callous cash-payment," a place which "has degraded personal dignity to the level of exchange value" and created "exploitation that is open, unashamed, direct and brutal."

But Marx was an optimist and Trollope now had become a profound pessimist. His writing in the years just preceding his *Autobiography* and *The Duke's Children* makes Lytton Strachey seem like a panegyrist of the Victorian age. He saw no hope for his world—nothing on which to build or preserve moral and communal values. His characters can no longer adapt to change or live good lives. Ambitious parvenus and speculators create vicious excesses of capitalism and competitive individualism, but the ultimate responsibility for the bad new world lies with the "established" people, whose incompetence and selfishness disgust Trollope.

The seventies were comparatively bleak and disillusioning

years for Victorian intellectuals. Confidence in the future
faded, Victoria's reign was at its nadir, she was in seclusion,
"progress" seemed more and more a naïve outworn creed.
The old order, with its flaws now obvious, was passing, but
the economic Darwinism that was replacing it seemed harsh
and uncivilized. Books of the period as different as Mallock's
The New Republic and Butler's *The Way of All Flesh* convey
the prevailing mood of pessimism.

Trollope also had strong personal reasons in 1873 for seeing black. Now almost sixty, he was moving into old age and
edging toward death. His popularity was on the wane. On
a trip around the world, from which he had just returned, in
Australia he had seen his disappointing son Frederick squan-
dering the money he had given him.[1] He also saw the tremendous global expansion of capitalism being carried out
by ruthless adventurers. At home a seemingly imperceptive,
degenerate English society was being corrupted by mammonism. People were becoming more vulgarly covetous, more
obstinate, more stupid, more uncooperative, and more insecure than before.

I

Out of this angry old man's revulsion came *The Way We
Live Now* (1873), the most vitriolic satire of the Victorian
era and one of the most powerful satires on capitalism ever
written. Although Trollope more or less confined himself to
the "genteel" classes, no novelist has ever made the economic
savagery of life more clear. His world has become a jungle
full of sham and cruelty which no amount of pomade could
gloss over. He believed that a good society must be based
on strong, trusting personal relationships. But in *The Way
We Live Now*, the profit motive poisons even the most intimate human relationships, and the power of sympathy is
completely lost.

Trollope tosses off a good one-sentence summary of the

---

[1] See Anthony Trollope, *An Autobiography* (London, 1953),
chap. XIX, pp. 298–300.

book: "It seemed that there was but one virtue in the world, commercial enterprise—and that Melmotte was its prophet." The Midas of capitalism has touched this world, turning men into economic objects, and love, friendship, religion, marriage, generosity, diplomacy, and literature into commodities of exchange. Credit and trust make the world go around, but they have only an economic meaning now. The swindling capitalist Melmotte has pushed aside priest, politician, and aristocrat to become the central figure in Trollope's new vision. Melmotte has the power now; people think of him as a modern earth-shaker. "It was said that he had made a railway across Russia, that he provisioned the Southern army in the American civil war, that he had supplied Austria with arms, and had at one time bought up all the iron in England. He could make or mar any company by buying or selling stock, and could make money dear or cheap as he pleased."[2] The Victorian age has changed into an international Gilded Age, and Melmotte sets its tone. Humanity goes on the gold standard. Trollope sees the world consciously accepting the view that economic activity and worth are the most important things in life, and he sees also that this idea can destroy people.

He brings, as Edgar Rosenberg says, "a vast amount of inside information"[3] from the times to his portrait of Melmotte. We know infinitely more about what Melmotte does, how he does it, and how he spreads the capitalistic fever than we do about earlier tycoons like Dickens's Merdle in *Little Dorrit*. Melmotte doing favors for royalty and politicians, floating a railroad company on a fake American project to build a railway from Salt Lake City to Mexico, running board meetings, handpicking his dummy directors, stretching out his credit, keeping up a front through conspicuous consumption,

---

[2] *The Way We Live Now* (London, 1951) "double volume" (see Author's Note, p. viii), chap. IV, p. 31 (I).

[3] Edgar Rosenberg, *From Shylock to Svengali* (Stanford, 1960), p. 150.

has the authentic stamp of the robber baron on him. Trollope understands Melmotte's appeal for the age, though he detests it. One of the most sympathetic characters, the American Mrs. Hurtle, defends him in almost Nietzschean terms:

". . . he is bold in breaking those precepts of yours about coveting worldly wealth. All men and women break that commandment, but they do so in a stealthy fashion, half drawing back the grasping hand, praying to be delivered from temptation while they filch only a little, pretending to despise the only thing that is dear to them in the world. Here is a man who boldly says that he recognizes no such law; that wealth is power, and that power is good, and that the more a man has of wealth the greater and the stronger and the nobler he can be."[4]

This description of the worship of power may read like a passage out of Ayn Rand, but it expresses neatly both late nineteenth-century exasperation with religious and economic hypocrisy and the romantic longing for heroes in an industrial age. The trouble is that when people think that way, you get a grubby world of lonely, deceitful, joyless men and women, as in *The Way We Live Now*.

Actually Melmotte is not great or noble, but hollow, and he depends entirely on the opinion of others, on "credit." When he loses that, he has nothing left. The need for wealth and power as ends in themselves shows a spiritual emptiness that Trollope thought characteristic of the times.

It is difficult to suggest in a few excerpts or paraphrase the cumulative effect of his satire. With black humor, constant irony, pointed understatement, caricature, invective—in a thousand different ways—he brings home the degraded condition of a society which bows down in honor before the moneymaking power. In one typical scene, the most idealistic character in the novel, a Roman Catholic priest, visits Mel-

---

[4] *The Way We Live Now*, chap. XXVI, p. 246 (I).

motte. Melmotte, running for Parliament in a heavily Catholic district, has donated an altar to "St. Fabricius," and the priest, hearing of this, calls on him to find out if he is a Roman Catholic, convinced that he will be God's agent for spreading the faith. He barges in by accident on Melmotte and two of his paid flunkeys—Lord Alfred and his son Miles Grendall who, in Trollope's sardonic vision, naturally belong to one of Britain's oldest and noblest families:

"Who the devil are you?" . . .
"I am the Rev. Mr. Barham," said the visitor. "I am the priest of Beccles in Suffolk. I believe I am speaking to Mr. Melmotte."
"That's my name sir. And what may you want? I don't know whether you are aware that you have found your way into my private dining-room without any introduction. Where the mischief are the fellows, Alfred, who ought to have seen about this? I wish you'd look to it, Miles. Can anybody who pleases walk into my hall?"
"I came on a mission which I hope may be pleaded as my excuse," said the priest. . . .
"Is it business?" asked Lord Alfred.
"Certainly it is business," said Father Barham with a smile.
"Then you had better call at the office in Abchurch Lane,—in the City," said his lordship.
"My business is not of that nature. I am a poor servant of the Cross, who is anxious to know from the lips of Mr. Melmotte himself that his heart is inclined to the true Faith."
"Some lunatic," said Mr. Melmotte. "See that there ain't any knives about, Alfred."
"No otherwise mad, sir, than they have ever been accounted mad who are enthusiastic in their desire for the souls of others."
"Just get a policeman, Alfred. Or send somebody; you'd better not go away."
"You will hardly need a policeman, Mr. Melmotte," continued the priest. "If I might speak to you alone for a few minutes—"
"Certainly not;—certainly not. I am very busy, and if you

will not go away you'll have to be taken away. I wonder whether anybody knows him."

"Mr. Carbury, of Carbury Hall, is my friend."

"Carbury! Damn the Carburys! Did any of the Carburys send you here? A set of beggars! Why don't you do something, Alfred, to get rid of him?"

"You'd better go," said Lord Alfred. "Don't make a rumpus, there's a good fellow;—but just go."

"There shall be no rumpus," said the priest, waxing wrathful. ". . . Have I been uncivil that you should treat me in this fashion?"

"You're in the way," said Lord Alfred.

"It's a piece of gross impertinence," said Melmotte. "Go away!"

"Will you not tell me before I go whether I shall pray for you as one whose steps in the right path should be made sure and firm; or as one still in error and darkness?"

"What the mischief does he mean?" asked Melmotte.

"He wants to know whether you're a papist," said Lord Alfred.

"What the deuce is it to him?" almost screamed Melmotte; —whereupon Father Barham bowed and took his leave.

"That's a remarkable thing," said Melmotte,—"very remarkable." Even this poor priest's mad visit added to his inflation. "I suppose he was in earnest."

"Mad as a hatter," said Lord Alfred.

"But why did he come to me in his madness—to me especially? That's what I want to know. I'll tell you what it is. There isn't a man in all England at this moment thought so much of as—your humble servant." . . .

Father Barham went away certainly disgusted; and yet not altogether disheartened. The man had not declared that he was not a Roman Catholic. He had shown himself to be a brute. He had blasphemed and cursed. He had been outrageously uncivil to a man whom he must have known to be a minister of God. . . . But, not the less might he be a good Catholic,—or good enough at any rate to be influential on the right side. . . .

"Think what such a man might do, if he be really the wealthiest man in the world! And if he had been against us would he not have said so?" Father Barham with a simplicity that was singularly mingled with religious cunning, made himself believe before he returned to Beccles that Mr. Melmotte was certainly a Roman Catholic.[5]

Behind the comic tone of this passage lie serious moral and historical observations. The business of this world is now business, and there is nothing left in the old religious tradition of Barham or the aristocratic tradition of the Grendalls to counteract Melmotte's idea that peopl, exist to be commercially exploited. Consciously or not they accept his values. Father Barham really wants a testimonial from Melmotte to boost the credit rating of his Church; and we read that "Lord Alfred when he was called by his Christian name felt no aristocratic twinges. He was only too anxious to make himself more and more necessary to the great man."[6] Everybody tries to *use* everybody else. One of the ironies that Trollope saw in the marriage of utilitarianism and capitalism was that it helped people to regard each other as useful *things*.

All around him in the seventies he heard proper Victorians complaining about pushing, greedy Jews, who were somehow climbing high in the British world and taking financial control. Anti-Semitic visions of Disraeli deceit and Rothschild rascality ran through prejudiced English minds, and even Trollope himself, having spent much of his youth in debt to moneylenders, had his share of bigotry (though, to be fair to him, there is no more attractive or finely drawn character in all his work than Madame Goesler). He made Melmotte a Jew, imagined other crude, materialistic Jews moving in on "polite" society, and threw in some supposedly vulgar Americans as well. And the outsiders are just as bad as middle-class insular snobbery would have it. But Trollope was saving his real venom for the staunch old guard—the Carburys, the Longstaffes, the Monograms, the Grendalls, the

---

[5] Chap. LVI, pp. 55–59 (II).
[6] Chap. XXXV, p. 330 (I).

hierarchy of the Conservative Party who put Melmotte up
for office, and the rest of the Establishment.

He makes it painfully clear how much worse they are than
the Jews and the parvenus. They pile moral outrage on outrage as they join in a vicious race to exploit people. Lady
Carbury tries to corrupt the reviewers to get good notices
for her trashy books; then for money she tries to palm off her
degenerate son as a husband for Melmotte's daughter. Dolly
Longstaffe starts to sue his own father. Lady Monogram pays
for invitations to parties which she regards as business prop-
ositions. Marriage for the Carburys, Longstaffes, Lord Nidderdale, and the others becomes a kind of auction where
they sell themselves to the highest bidders. Miles Grendall
cheats his friends at cards because he needs cash. Felix Carbury treats the lower-class girl Ruby as a sexual object and
not as a person; she falls in love with him, and he uses her
with listless obscenity: " 'I can give you a couple of sover-
eigns. . . . I don't ever mean to marry. It's the greatest bore
out. I know a trick worth two of that.' "[7] Trollope here is
talking about the sexual exploitation that was so common to
the Victorian scene, as Steven Marcus brilliantly shows in
The Other Victorians.

The Beargarden, a club for overprivileged young men like
Dolly Longstaffe and Sir Felix Carbury, contains the most
odious spawn of nineteenth-century parasites existing outside of Miss Havisham's wedding cake in *Great Expectations.*
Trollope keeps drawing the parallel between the gambling,
cheating, and bad faith among the club members and the
shady capitalistic deals of Melmotte. Fittingly, he chooses
most of his company's directors from the ranks of the Beargarden, and by coincidence the club folds just at the time of
Melmotte's collapse.

For Trollope, the cream of the aristocracy had curdled. In
the naïve cynicism, ennui, selfishness, and ignorance that
makes up the talk and behavior of the Beargardeners, he

---

[7] Chap. XLIII, p. 405 (I).

satirizes the degeneracy of a ruling class. Obviously they are morally and intellectually incapable of dealing with the problems of a changing world. Near the end someone mentions to Dolly Longstaffe that Melmotte's death was rather awful, and he answers, " 'Not half so awful as having nothing to amuse one.' " That is the level of compassion and seriousness of the young generation. And yet they all can wax sentimental about the end of the Beargarden, where they did nothing but loaf, gamble, squabble, and bilk creditors: " 'Dear old place! I always felt it was too good to last,' " says Lord Nidderdale; and Dolly commiserates, " 'I never felt so much like crying in all my life. . . . Good-night old fellows; good-bye . . . I shouldn't wonder if I didn't drown myself.' " In the next sentence Trollope reports what he actually does do to the foreclosing creditor of the club: "Dolly . . . utterly confounded . . . and brought that ingenious but unfortunate man, with his wife and small family, to absolute ruin. . . ."[8]

The whole Longstaffe family is particularly interesting because they belong to the old squirearchy for which Trollope had always had a sentimental affection. Now he blasts them with a measured rage. Brehgert, an honest Jew, helps old Longstaffe out of money difficulties, and the snobbish squire deigns to have a private dinner with him. Georgiana, one of the Longstaffe daughters, has negotiated shamelessly about marrying Brehgert and when the match does not come off, Brehgert feels he must now tell the father that he has acted toward the girl like a gentleman. Longstaffe agonizes over the bare mention of the possibility that his daughter would marry a Jew, and when Brehgert leaves, he reacts like the stupid, hypocritical bigot he is:

Mr. Longstaffe opened the door and walked about the room and blew out long puffs of breath, as though to cleanse himself from the impurities of his late contact. He told himself that he could not touch pitch and not be defiled! How vulgar had the man been, how indelicate, how regardless

---

[8] Chap. XCVI, p. 438 (II).

of all feeling, how little grateful for the honour which Mr.
Longstaffe had conferred upon him by asking him to dinner!
Yes;—yes! A horrid Jew! Were not all Jews necessarily an
abomination? Yet Mr. Longstaffe was aware that in the
present crisis of his fortunes he could not afford to quarrel
with Mr. Brehgert.[9]

That is how Trollope now sees the gentry which for him had
once been the backbone of English greatness.

Georgiana reveals everything about this world when her
mother tells her that she never could have loved Brehgert:
" 'Loved him! Who thinks about love nowadays? I don't know
any one who loves any one else.' "[10] This society is totally
disoriented by change, as is shown by the recurring confusion over what people ought to do "nowadays" and the implicitly damning title *The Way We Live Now*. The one
really admirable man of principle in the book is Roger Carbury, the bachelor head of the Carbury family and a careful
defender of old values. His relation Lady Carbury, whose
amorality sets the norm for the book, sums him up this way:
" 'Dear Roger was old-fashioned and knew nothing of
people as they are now. He lived in a world which, though
slow, had been good in its way; but which, whether bad or
good, had now passed away.' "[11] Trollope sadly agrees with
Lady Carbury's thinking here, though in context he is also
ironically criticizing her. When someone mentions to Roger
that the country is changing, he snaps, " 'It's going to the
dogs, I think;—about as fast as it can go.' "[12] He is right, but
ineffectual—a fine and good man in a new world which has
little use for him and turns him into a crotchety misanthrope.
He *is* one who thinks about love and loves deeply; but his
cousin Hetta turns him down, and he ends up single and disappointed, presumably one of a dying breed.

Trollope finds no redeeming love in *The Way We Live*

---

[9] Chap. LXXXVIII, p. 363 (II). See also Edgar Rosenberg,
From Shylock to Svengali, p. 143, for discussion of this passage.
[10] *The Way We Live Now*, chap. xcv, p. 425 (II).
[11] Chap. XXX, p. 283 (I).
[12] Chap. LV, p. 45 (II).

Now. His passive, equivocal romantic leads, Hetta Carbury
and Paul Montague, are peculiarly pale and boring figures.
The "happy ending" for them reads as if he turned it out as
an afterthought for the simpering Mudie's crowd. But Hetta's rival for Paul, the "liberated" American woman Mrs.
Hurtle, is a fascinating character—at least whenever Trollope lets his sympathy for her break through his caricature
of her as a wild American. Like Roger, the other ardent lover
in the book, she fails. She has sex appeal, courage, and intelligence, but men still prefer to marry gentility.

The commercialization of women and their *awareness* that
they are being commercialized were favorite topics of Trollope in these years. Women had always been used as economic pawns, but now the Victorian circle of ignorance sur-
rounding them was disappearing. The crinoline façade of
innocence could not be kept up in places like the American
Far West, where Mrs. Hurtle comes from, nor could better-
educated, intelligent girls help seeing the contradictions between Victorian sentimentalization of "wives and daughters"
and the often harsh pragmatism which disposed of their
lives. A short but typical discussion of marriage in *The Way
We Live Now* goes like this: "Rank squanders money; trade
makes it;— and then trade purchases rank by re-gilding its
splendour."[13] That is the formula for the central marriage
episode in *Is He Popenjoy?* No wonder Melmotte's daughter Marie bursts out, " 'I'll marry Lord Nidderdale, or that
horrid Mr. Grendall . . . , or his old fool of a father,—or the
sweeper at the crossing,—or the black man that waits at
table, or anybody else that he [Melmotte] chooses to pick
up. . . . But I'll lead him such a life afterwards!' "[14]

As women became more independent in their thinking,
Trollope saw them getting more and more confused about
their roles. A Marie Melmotte, a Georgiana Longstaffe, or an
Arabella Trefoil in *The American Senator* sees the economic

---

[13] Chap. LVII, p. 59 (II).
[14] Chap. LXVIII, p. 169–170 (II).

and class motives behind marriage and grows cynical, but
cynicism is always a desperate defense against pain. Women
sensitive enough to realize that society buys, sells, and uses
them like pedigreed cattle naturally turn hard, but then they
feel guilty. When Montague jilts Mrs. Hurtle, she first writes
him a very "feminine" letter meekly forgiving him, then another telling him that she will horsewhip him on sight. Finally she sends neither. All of Trollope's clever women in these
books are wavering and unhappy creatures, rejecting the
part of the docile female, yet conscience-stricken at their
own aggressiveness. Each carries the bitterness of self-
conscious failure.

II

The image of failure is everywhere in *The Way We Live
Now*—failure in love, in feeling, in morality, in business—the
colossal, cosmopolitan failure of a world where men and
women, in exploiting each other, inevitably brutalize life.
Even so, this masterpiece of satire does not have the overwhelming pessimistic power of *The Prime Minister* (1874).
As Trollope remarked, "*The Way We Live Now* has the fault
which is to be attributed to almost all satires, whether in
prose or verse. The accusations are exaggerated."[15] In it he
said nearly everything that can be said against his society,
but in *The Prime Minister* he says nearly everything that can
be said *for* his society, and still it is hopeless.

He is dealing here not just with the kinds of people that
he despises, but with those that he loves and understands—
the Pallisers, the upright Wharton clan, the strong-willed,
moral girl Emily, and others. He sees, however, that they
cannot accommodate themselves to change. They lose the
ideals of communal sympathy and political harmony in the
fragmentation of their lives. The forces that pull people apart
are stronger than the cohesive forces in the world. The sturdy
old bourgeois Abel Wharton catches the spirit of the novel

---

[15] *An Autobiography*, chap. xx, p. 267.

when he says, " 'Everything has to be broken up sooner or later. One feels that as one grows older.' " That "everything" for Trollope includes hearts and marriages as well as plans and political alliances. The vision of life in *The Prime Minister* as a series of coalitions—personal, social, and political—doomed to failure turns out to be one of the toughest and most impressive in our literature.

John Donne had a habit of using profane terms to describe sacred love and sacred terms to describe profane love in order to stress the unity of human experience. Trollope, in much the same way, particularly in this novel, treats personal life in political terms and political life in personal terms. He organized the book around the word and the concept of *coalition*: Palliser presides over a coalition government; he and Glencora live together as usual in uneasy coalition; and the marriage of Emily Wharton, from a solid, middle-class, old-family background, to the Portuguese Jew Ferdinand Lopez, an ambitious outsider, forms a coalition of the greatest significance. Since for Trollope man is a social animal, and society is an organic whole, a good life always depends on the possibilities of coalition of some kind, as we see in the Barset and the Finn books. All the parts of *The Prime Minister* reinforce and comment on each other in showing the misunderstanding and aggression that break up coalition. Different points of view cannot be reconciled, and selfish party spirit prevails.

The old inflexible codes of the Whartons and Plantagenet Palliser do not work in the dark new world. Instead, a money craze and a power craze take hold of everybody. For Lopez, the new man and the would-be capitalist, money means acceptance, respectability, even love. Trollope attempts much more with Lopez than he did with Melmotte; he humanizes him, shows what motivates him, gives him good qualities, and tries to hold reader sympathy for him, even while he makes it clear that Lopez lives like a scoundrel by a ruthless, self-defeating ethic. " 'Them men [says his partner's wife]

when they get on at money-making . . . are like tigers clawing
one another. They don't care how many they kills, so that
they has the least bit for themselves. There ain't no fear of
God in it, nor yet no mercy, nor ere a morsel of heart.' "[16]
Lopez, like Fitzgerald's Gatsby, thinks that if you make
money you can buy gentility; for the low-born, money and
only money, will open the right doors, cut across class and
racial lines, make you that marvelous person in Victorian
eyes, a "gentleman." " 'Equality is a dream [says Palliser],
but sometimes one likes to dream.' " For Lopez and much of
the world, money is what makes the dream come true. But
not for Trollope. In what we might call his own excremental
vision, he imagines Lopez speculating in guano manure and
Kauri gum, hoping they will turn to gold; but his cargo of
excreta remains worthless, and Lopez himself perishes as a
pulverized waste-product of his society.

Trollope begins the novel by describing him: "He was
essentially one of those men who are always, *in the inner
workings of their minds*, defending themselves and attack-
ing others."[17] The irony is that we come to see how neatly
this fits nearly everyone in the book, including his wife,
Emily, and his father-in-law, Wharton. The established classes, instead of trying to assimilate and civilize the new man's
energy and intelligence, react to him with an enmity which is
no less savage for being unconscious. Once Lopez decides
to marry Emily and move in on the Establishment, the novel
settles into deadly conflict between his ambition and the defensive rigidity of the Wharton family and its friends.

We find in *The Prime Minister* one of the classic and most
relevant treatments of middle-class power in fiction. In artistry and depth of understanding, Trollope's picture of the
Wharton faction—perfect representatives of the nonaristo-
cratic property-owning class which has more or less run

---

[16] *The Prime Minister* (London, 1951), "double volume" (see
Author's Note, p. viii), chap. XLVII, p. 74 (II).

[17] Chap. I, p. 7 (I), italics mine.

things for the last century or so in the Western democracies—compares favorably with the views of the middle classes in Balzac, Flaubert, Thackeray, Dickens, and Howells. In fact, Trollope's middle class generally seems less dated. Dickens's Podsnappery, for example, catches certain ugly bourgeois attitudes perfectly, but it is so blatantly unattractive and crude that it does not explain the continuing power and success of the middle classes. But Trollope shows the wonderful ability of the Wharton class to justify itself and put itself in a good light. He gives it full credit for meaning to do right, for its endurance, for its sense of principle and duty, its family loyalty, its integrity (though an integrity that is, as someone in the book remarks, " 'a sort of bastard honesty,—by precept out of stupidity' "[18]). Most critiques and satires of the bourgeoisie fail because they underestimate it. Trollope, who had a lot of Wharton in him, did not. He bends over backward to be fair toward the class and to sympathize with the characters who embody it—Emily, her father, and Arthur Fletcher in particular. He presents things from their point of view and seldom criticizes them in his own voice. His indictment of them and what they stand for seems to come almost against his will, and that is why it carries such convincing force.

Ignorance for Trollope is the true repository of cruelty, and out of ignorance about the feelings of other people unlike themselves and the willful and repressed ignorance of their own aggressive motives, Emily and the Wharton faction act with an inadvertent cruelty that is absolutely frightening. Old Wharton calls Lopez " 'a greasy Jew adventurer out of the gutter,' " and refuses him the money he had set aside for a prospective son-in-law; his brother-in-law Everett cuts him even though Lopez saved his life; Arthur Fletcher accuses him of dishonesty after making love to Lopez's wife. Emily rejoices at her baby's death, "telling herself that it was per-

---

[18] Chap. LXVI, p. 293 (II).

haps better . . . with such a father as she had given him."[19]
Greater hate hath no woman, and still these people have no
idea that they are anything but fair-minded. She originally
chooses to marry Lopez instead of Fletcher because she
rebels against the genteel class: "It could exist without intellect, without heart, and with very moderate culture. It
was compatible with many littlenesses and with many vices.
As for that love of honest, courageous truth which her father
was wont to attribute it, she regarded the theory as based
upon legends . . ."[20] Ironically, her behavior agrees with her
description of her class. Real independence and adaptability
have been bred out of her, and after her marriage she re-
verts to the outlook of her father in condemning her husband. He breaks the accepted code of bourgeois morality,
and that seems unforgivable to a logical bourgeois girl.

Unconscious motivation as the determiner of life is as old
in the English novel as *Pamela*, but Trollope gives Emily's
unconscious motivation a new twist: he uses it to reflect crucial political attitudes of a whole dominant class. The point
is that Emily and the Whartons are not by mere chance in
a novel called *The Prime Minister* dealing with political life:
they are there because they control that life. Late in the
book Glencora the Duchess says of " 'such people as the
Whartons . . . that as a class, they are more impregnable,
more closely guarded by their feelings and prejudices against
strangers than any other. None . . . are less willing to see
their rules of life changed or abolished.' "[21]

In Emily's unconscious drives to make Lopez conform to
her father's orthodoxy, to punish him and cast him away for
being different, and to atone for her own nonconformity in
marrying him, we find the middle-class obsession with making the world over in its own narrow image. Almost everything that Emily does or thinks tends to preserve her righ-

---

[19] Chap. XLIX, p. 103 (II).
[20] Chap. XXXI, p. 351 (I).
[21] Chap. LXXVII, p. 429 (II).

teous sense of the Wharton and Fletcher moral superiority
and to show the incredible strength of middle-class convention. With an irony that commentators have missed, Trollope shows her convenient double-think habits of mind:

> She soon knew that her marriage had been a mistake. . . .
> Then there would come upon her unbidden, unwelcome
> reminiscences of Arthur Fletcher,—thoughts that she would
> struggle to banish. . . . She remembered his light wavy hair,
> which she had loved as one loves the beauty of a dog, . . .
> Ah,—that she should ever have been so blind, she who had
> given herself credit for seeing so much clearer than her
> elders! . . . She must bear it all in silence, and live with it,
> and still love this god of clay that she had chosen. And,
> above all, she must never allow herself even to think of that
> other man with the wavy light hair,—that man who was ris-
> ing in the world of whom all people said all good things,
> who was showing himself to be a man by the work he did,
> and whose true tenderness she could never doubt.[22]

A while later she somehow manages to break her silence and
talk to Arthur Fletcher about her miserable marriage to Lopez: " 'Thank God, Arthur, I have no baby to suffer with
me.' " Arthur then says of her husband, " 'Of course, I know,
—and you know. He is—a scoundrel!' 'I will not hear it,' said
she rising from her seat on the sofa with her hands up to her
forehead, but *still coming nearer to him as she moved.*"[23]

This is more than just harmless self-deception; it gives a
key to the strength and solidarity of her group. The Whartons and the Fletchers simply do not subject themselves to
the rigid moral scrutiny that they apply to outsiders. They
do what they want to do and rationalize it or deny to themselves that they do it. They are masters at idealizing what
benefits them. The Fletchers, for example, want Emily to
marry Arthur instead of Lopez: "Something of the truth as to
Emily Wharton's 60,000 pounds was, of course, known to the

---

[22] Chap. XXXIX, p. 452–453 (I).
[23] Chap. LIX, p. 219 (II), italics mine.

Longbarns people. Not that I would have it inferred that they
wanted their darling Arthur to sell himself for money. The
Fletchers were great people, with great spirits, too good in
every way for such baseness. But when love . . . can be joined
to money, such a combination will always be thought pleasant."[24] Lopez makes them all insecure because he threatens
their easy consciences. His crude ambition reminds them of
what they want to repress: that living is a hard and sometimes dirty struggle and that there are many people who hate
them and covet their ease and wealth—people who must be
kept down if the status quo of their own physical and mental comfort is to be preserved.

Whining self-pity and complaints about the deteriorating
morality of the times are the opiates of the middle class.
Wharton sorrowfully muses, "The world as it was now didn't
care whether its sons-in-law were Christian or Jewish;—
whether they had the fair skin and bold eyes and uncertain
words of an English gentleman, or the swarthy colour and
false grimace and glib tongue of some inferior Latin race.
But he cared for these things and it was dreadful to him to
think that his daughter should not care for them. 'I suppose
I had better die and leave them to look after themselves,' he
said."[25] But of course it is Lopez who dies instead, and Wharton has a stronger grip on his children than he knows.

His son Everett, after calling his Wharton cousins a "prejudiced set of provincial ignoramuses," marries one and takes
up their opinions. Everett begins as a middle-class liberal
whose type has become so familiar: "He had read much,
and, though he generally forgot what he read, there were
left with him from his readings certain nebulous lights. It
cannot be said of him that he did much thinking for himself
but he thought that he thought. . . . He was quite clear on
questions of finance, and saw to a 't' how progress should
be made towards communism, so that in the due course of

[24] Chap. XV, p. 163 (I).
[25] Chap. XIV, p. 159 (I).

centuries all desire for personal property should be con-
quered and annihilated by a philanthropy so general as hardly to be accounted a virtue."[26] He ends up inheriting a large
property and living in the country as a conservative landowner. Emily, after Lopez's suicide, finally gets her father's
favorite, Arthur, and returns to the fold in a kind of sociological incest. The class has a built-in resistance to change.
It closes ranks, holds on to its own, perpetuates its ideology,
and stagnates in its prejudices.

The Whartons and Fletchers remain firmly entrenched in
power, but the hope of coalition dies. They, like Lopez ironically, feel little responsibility to the community and little
love or pity for people beyond their immediate circle. They
are, however, amazingly tough, and after reading *The Prime
Minister*, one sees how much the middle classes contributed
to the idea of class warfare. Lopez, the new man, is alone,
but the members of the Wharton clan look upon themselves
as *the elect* and protect each other.

All this does not mean that Trollope sentimentalizes Lopez any more than Shakespeare sentimentalizes Shylock, to
whom Lopez compares himself (both authors are a bit ambiguous about whether their Jewish speculators are more
sinned against than sinning). Of memorable outsiders in
nineteenth-century fiction—Julien Sorel, Bazarov, Raskolni-
kov, Hyacinth Robinson, for example—Lopez is one of the
meanest and least appealing because his goal is simply to
have money. For the same reason, however, he is more typical of the capitalistic age. He sees reality in economic terms,
as does his world, and uses people as commodities. He even
agrees to sell Emily back to her father. But Lopez's businesslike attitude toward life is ultimately self-defeating. He loves
Emily and needs her love, but he destroys it by his overt
greed for her father's money. Like Melmotte, when he loses
his money he has nothing left. Near the end he wails with
black irony the complaint everyone feels from time to time

---

[26] Chap. II, p. 17 (I).

in a business culture, " 'There is no mercy, no friendship, no kindness, no forebearance anywhere!' " A company agent replies, " 'If you have any complaint to make . . . you had better write the directors.' "[27] Such is the solace of a commercial era.

III

Lopez's death in the great chapter "The Tenway Junction" illuminates the whole tragedy of the Lopez–Wharton story, but its implications extend far beyond the limits of the novel. Trollope achieves in the suicide scene an important metaphoric vision of modern existence. Lopez takes a train to the Tenway rail junction:

From this spot, some six or seven miles distant from London, lines diverge east, west, and north, northeast, and northwest, round the metropolis in every direction, and with direct communication with every other line in and out of London. It is a marvelous place, quite unintelligible to the uninitiated, and yet daily used by thousands who only know that when they get there, they are to do what someone tells them. The space occupied by the convergent rails seems to be sufficient for a large farm. And these rails always run one into another with sloping points, and cross passages, and mysterious meandering sidings, till it seems to the thoughtful stranger to be impossible that the best-trained engine should know its own line. Here and there and around there is ever a wilderness of wagons, some loaded, some empty, some smoking with close-packed oxen and others furlongs in length black with coals, which look as though they had been stranded there by chance, and were never destined to get again into the right path of traffic. Not a minute passes without a train going here or there, some rushing by without noticing Tenway in the least, crashing through like flashes of substantial lightning, and others stopping, disgorging and taking up passengers by the hundreds. Men and women,— especially the men, for the women knowing their ignorance

---

[27] Chap. LVIII, p. 212 (II).

are generally willing to trust to the pundits of the place,—
look doubtful, uneasy, and bewildered. But they all do get
properly placed and unplaced, so that the spectator at last
acknowledges that over all this apparent chaos there is pre-
siding a great genius of order. From dusky morn to dark
night, and indeed almost throughout the night, the air is
loaded with a succession of shrieks. The theory goes that
each separate shriek,—if there can be any separation where
the sound is so nearly continuous,—is a separate notice to
separate ears of the coming or going of a separate train. . . .
Now Tenway Junction is so big a place, and so scattered,
that it is impossible that all the pundits should by any combined activity maintain to the letter . . . order. . . . At that
moment there came a shriek louder than all the other shrieks,
and the morning express down from Euston to Inverness was
seen coming round the curve at a thousand miles an hour.
Lopez turned round and looked at it, and again walked
toward the edge of the platform. But now it was not exactly
the edge that he neared, but a descent to a pathway,—an inclined plane leading down to the level of the rails, and made
there for certain purposes of traffic. . . . With quick, but still
with gentle and apparently unhurried steps, he walked down
before the flying engine—and in a moment had been knocked
into bloody atoms.[28]

Like those great set-pieces of symbolism in Dickens, this
astonishingly dense image opens up a world of meaning and
the meaning of a world. It suddenly puts not only Lopez but
also the Whartons, Prime Minister Palliser, and all the rest
in proper perspective. How overwhelming and bewildering
the swirling pressure of the new mechanized urban life is,
and how helplessly unfit all these people are to meet it and
control an industrial society! Tenway is the new pandemo-
nium of big machines and little men, of commerce, of lonely
individualism, of alienation in the middle of crowds, of des-

[28] Chap. LX, pp. 231–235 (II). See Beatrice Curtis Brown, *Anthony Trollope* (London, 1950), pp. 70–73. The same passage
is quoted in full in this incisive monograph.

perate longing for order in chaos, of blind faith in pundits, of *literally* fragmented humanity. It is a deadly place.

Since the middle of the last century at least, an apocalyptic image of death by mechanism (locomotive, auto, bomb, computer) has haunted the modern psyche the way the Last Judgment haunted the medieval mind. If we compare Lopez's suicide with the two more-or-less contemporary scenes most like it, Carker's death in *Dombey and Son* and Anna Karenina's death,[29] we find Trollope less interested in the psychology of his victim and more intent on symbolizing broad historical and sociological conditions. The fact that Lopez dies at the Tenway Junction is as important as the fact that he dies at all. We see that in a sense he is a product of the same forces that have produced Tenway and has lived his life in exactly the same kind of ugly maze.

When Glencora, speaking of Lopez, says, " 'I have a sort of feeling, you know, that among us we made the train run over him,' "[30] she not only acknowledges the guilt of the "nice" people, she also points up the inability of Trollope's Establishment to manage the world competently. Trollope knew that the days of amateur political pundits like Planty Pal were numbered. Despite his virtue and idealism he cannot preserve communal harmony, and that is the reason for the aura of defeat which hangs over his ministry. Palliser's qualities—integrity, moral sensitivity, good will, and personal loyalty—are the qualities Trollope most admires, but they are hardly the qualities it takes to govern a Tenway Junction. He, like the Whartons, indicates a kind of social

---

[29] See N. N. Glisev, *Chronicle of the Life and Work of L. N. Tolstoy 1828–1890* (Moscow, 1958). Tolstoy, who notes, "Trollope kills me with his mastery" (p. 315), was writing *Anna Karenina* while *The Prime Minister* was appearing. Evidence suggests that he may have had Lopez's death in mind when he imagined Anna's suicide. He read *The Prime Minister* and called it "a beautiful book" (p. 466) just at the time when he was about to complete the story of Anna.

[30] *The Prime Minister*, chap. LXXVI, p. 425 (II).

paralysis falling over the British ruling classes. He obviously does not have the political intelligence to cope with the new world, but Trollope worries about what will come after him.

Trollope's pessimism comes through in a passage of high satire. A member of the coalition government begins complaining to Palliser that they do not do anything, and the Prime Minister answers:

" 'Things to be done offer themselves, I suppose, because they are in themselves desirable; not because it is desirable to have something to do.'"

" 'Just so;—no doubt. But still, if you will think of it, no ministry can endure without a policy. During the latter part of the last Session it was understood that we had to get ourselves in harness together, and nothing more was expected from us; but I think we should be prepared with a distinct policy for the coming year.'"

Palliser seems here to be like one of Dickens's do-nothing Boodles and Coodles, and we think how outrageously silly it is that a government should not have a policy. But then the activist member suggests one: " 'For myself, I think, I am in favour of increased armaments.' "[31] How chillingly prophetic that is! The end of power sooner or later becomes power itself. How many policies of the last century have been essentially nothing more or less than "increased armaments."

The Coalition founders on political ambitions, and Glencora, who understands the selfishness of politics better than her husband, gives a little speech on the art of ruling.

"They should have made me Prime Minister, and have let him be Chancellor of the Exchequer. I begin to see the ways of Government now. I could have done all the dirty work. I could have given away garters and ribbons, and made my bargains while giving them. I could select sleek, easy bishops who wouldn't be troublesome. I could give pensions or withhold them, and make the stupid men peers. I could have the big noblemen at my feet. . . . I could dole out secretary-

---

[31] Chap. XX, pp. 229–230 (I).

ships and lordships, and never a one without getting something in return. I could brazen out a job . . . and I think I could make myself popular with my party, and do the high-flowing patriotic talk for the benefit of the Provinces."[32]

This is the Lopez method of using people, and that Trollope should have shown one of his favorite characters thinking this way—in fact, that he should draw so many parallels between Glencora and Lopez—shows the hold of cynical utilitarianism in his world. To be successful, you must handle people like the levers of machines. One must be *objective*, which means that life becomes dehumanized as one learns to treat people as objects.

IV

Trollope himself lapses into Glencora's kind of practical cynicism in his wry, witty, social comedy *Is He Popenjoy?* (1874–1875). It has neither the compassion nor the moral outrage of his best work. Thackeray-like, he seems resigned to the badness of a world inhabited mostly by knaves and fools, and this resignation makes the book even more pessimistic than its predecessors. He takes his depersonalization theme to its limit by making the plot turn on the legitimacy of Popenjoy, a sickly child, whom everyone regards as a potential title-deed rather than a human being. The boy's death helps clear up everything happily. Property and status mean more than life.

In *The American Senator* (1875), we get the ultimate in making a business of personal relationships. Arabella Trefoil is the hardest-working gold-digger in Victorian fiction, and she goes about getting a husband the way Memotte and Lopez go about speculation. To express her thoughts about Lord Rufford making love to her, Trollope purposely falls into a commercial vocabulary: "The loan of her lips had been for use only, and not for any pleasure which she had even in pleasing him. In her very swoon she had felt the need of be-

---

[32] Chap. LVI, pp. 186–187 (II).

ing careful at all points. It was all labour, and all care."[33] In
fact, Arabella is a cash-nexus necker. Like clever traders, she
and Rufford try to compromise each other; she lets him use
her, then deceitfully interprets his lovemaking as an "offer"
of marriage. He finally offers to pay eight thousand pounds
not to marry her. She is bad merchandise.[34]

England in *Is He Popenjoy?* and *The American Senator* is
in its decadence—a dull, dimwitted, spiritless decadence.
Trollope's remark about Lord George in *Is He Popenjoy?*—
"Birth and culture had given him a look of intellect greater
than he possessed"[35] sums up his attitude toward the whole
degenerate aristocracy, and his characters in general lack
grace and charm. His conception of particular characters,
however, wavers, and the tone in both books seems a bit confused and inconsistent—more nihilistic than anything else.
He is like a man today who thinks that traditional Western
ways of life are dried up and historically doomed but who

---

[33] *The American Senator* (London, 1931), chap. XLIX, p. 337.

[34] Did Trollope, *The American Senator,* and Arabella Trefoil
help change the course of history by preventing World War III
in 1962? After the Cuban missile crisis in the autumn of 1962, reports indicate that the United States government used the tactics
of Arabella to preserve peace with the Soviet Union. See Stewart
Alsop and Charles Bartlett, "In Time of Crisis," *The Saturday
Evening Post,* Dec. 8, 1962, p. 19: "It was Bobby Kennedy who
suggested what has since been dubbed 'the Trollope ploy.' The
Victorian novelist Anthony Trollope had a standard scene: a
young man with no marital intentions makes some . . . gesture
toward a marriage-hungry maiden—he squeezes her hand, even
kisses her. The lady instantly seizes the opportunity by shyly
accepting what she chooses to interpret as a proposal of marriage.
Robert Kennedy suggested that the President simply interpret
the . . . [Soviet] letter as a proposal for an acceptable deal." Since
this is not "a standard scene" in Trollope, but one that only occurs
in *The American Senator,* and since *Time Magazine* reports that
in the summer of 1960 John Kennedy was "browsing through
Anthony Trollope's *The American Senator*" (*Time,* August 1,
1960, p. 13), perhaps Arabella Trefoil's ultimate fate was to be
one of the great peacemakers of all time.

[35] *Is He Popenjoy?* (London, 1946), "double volume" (see
Author's Note, p. viii), chap. I, p. 7 (I).

finds the prospect of a collectivized, "programmed" future dreadful. The American senator Gotobed's criticisms of England hit home, but he, riding on a very mucky New World wave of the future, has nothing better to offer than what he attacks. Trollope makes a kind of cynical compromise with his bad world (people are ignorant, greedy, and heartless, but what can you expect?) and palms off happy endings in these two books.

V

The Prime Minister is the best of these novels and—one has to say it in the face of its comparatively small reputation —a magnificent book. Of all Trollope's creations, he loved the Pallisers the most and their marriage is probably the finest expression of his art. "Hell," says Sartre, "is other people," and, for Trollope, the major part of life—both personal and political life—is, unavoidably, getting along with other people. The lives of Glencora and Plantagenet are filled with pain and difficulty because they, like most people, are naturally competitive and hopelessly wrapped up in themselves and their own ways of seeing. No one, as they show, can ever bring enough sympathy to another person. Coalition is the fated condition of man, but he is not suited for it.

No relation among people, whether it be a marriage or a government, is ever static for Trollope. Circumstances change, people change; they must work and work to get along with each other, and yet never permanently succeed. Glencora and Palliser love each other, but each finds the other impossible. He wants everything to be quiet, honest, and orderly, and she yearns ambitiously after a vague, never-to-be reached infinite *success*. He has a fine moral sense, she has a passionate "heart," racy wit, and intelligence. They both think they are devoted to the other, but they are even more thoroughly devoted to themselves. Each keeps trying to make the other over, each knows the projects will never succeed. But no summary can do justice to the emotional intricacy, the intensity, and the development of their relationship.

In a typical scene, the Duke confronts her after her attempt to use political influence for Lopez has nearly ruined his regime. He frets, and then falls into the trite language of politicians in power. " 'Kiss me, dear,' he said. Then she stooped over him and kissed him. 'Do not think that I am angry with you because the thing vexes me. I am dreaming always of some day when we may go away together with the children, and rest in some pretty spot, and live as other people live.' 'It would be very stupid,' she muttered to herself as she left the room."[36] Of course, one person does not think like another, but the marriage of these two gives us a new awareness of what that commonplace actually means in day-to-day living. Glencora understands her husband perfectly and admires him, as we see in her conversation with Marie Finn, but she can not be close to him: " 'He is a god, but I am not a goddess;—and then, though he is a god, he is a dry, silent, uncongenial and uncomfortable god. It would have suited me much better to have married a sinner.' "[37] She cannot really appreciate him, and he does not even understand her. In the final chapter, when Glencora makes some outrageous proposition, Trollope says that Palliser, after a lifetime, "Hardly yet knew his wife well enough to understand that the suggestion had been a joke."[38]

The spirit of competition rules every phase of life in the novel, and it is especially strong between the Duke and the Duchess. It is no mere coincidence that competition between husbands and wives grew with the rise of capitalism, just as it is no coincidence that Glencora and Palliser compete so intensely with each other in a novel that contains Lopez, the Tenway Junction, and a saga of cut-throat business. The Duke, like Abel Wharton, loves serenity and hates ambition

---

[36] *The Prime Minister,* chap. LI, p. 125 (II).
[37] Chap. LVI, pp. 185–186 (II).
[38] Chap. LXXX, p. 463 (II).

in others. Yet like the Whartons he becomes suspicious, defensive, and unconsciously very competitive:

> And now, gradually,—very slowly indeed at first, but still
> with a sure step,—there was creeping upon him the idea that
> his power of cohesion was sought for, and perhaps found,
> not in his political capacity, but in his rank and wealth. It
> might, in fact, be the case that it was his wife the Duchess,—
> that Lady Glencora, of whose wild impulses and general im-
> practicability he had always been in dread,—that she with
> her dinner parties and receptions, with her crowded saloons,
> her music, her picnics, and social temptations, was Prime
> Minister rather than he himself. It might be that this had
> been understood by the coalesced parties,—by everybody,
> in fact, except himself. . . . She and she only would have the
> spirit and the money and the sort of cleverness required. In
> such a state of things he of course, as her husband, must be
> the nominal Prime Minister.[39]

There is incipient paranoia here, but it is cultural paranoia as much as anything else—a symptom of the whole new world. Even the champion of coalition must look upon his own wife as a rival.

Trollope now sees life as, among other things, a power struggle that never ends. Every act in *The Prime Minister* is a political act—political in the sense that it affects the balance of power between people, and political because, no matter how insignificant it may seem, it affects the whole community. Distinctions between public and private life do not hold. There is no escape from politics in the full meaning of the word, though the Duke and the Whartons like to pretend that there is. And conversely, public policies, such as "armaments," "coalition," or "monetary reform," always take their shape from the motives and psychological bent of particular public officials, though people usually pretend otherwise. The Pallisers always show the unity of political and personal life. Trollope ends the novel with these two, putting the

---

[39] Chap. XVIII, p. 195 (I).

stress on them because they are finally the people he cares most about. With all their faults they are the best that the Victorian age has to offer. Despite their exasperating cold war with each other, their marriage is, relatively speaking, a good marriage—in such a world. Yet in the last scenes, they both talk calmly about their sense of failure and frustration, though significantly they do not talk to each other. Life, even for the lofty Pallisers, is a shifting, disappointing, patchwork affair. People never get the sympathy they need, never do all the things they want to do or wield all the power they want to wield, never can keep all the good things they get. Glencora, mourning her husband's ministry, says, "It is done and gone and can never come back again.' "[40] But the cumulative effect of the Palliser section, ending as it does undramatically with both of them alive and kicking, is to throw us back on the idea of life as a continuing process. It is not a series of goals which one either does or does not attain, nor a package labeled "happy" or "unhappy." It is process, like history or politics. And the process of living, despite human comedy, passion, and virtue, is, as Trollope now understands his world, inevitably lonely and unsatisfying.

---

[40] Chap. LXXX, p. 467 (II).

9

An Old Man's Love:
The Plea For Tolerance

In both life and literature, cursing the darkness may be satisfying and even constructive, but it has its law of diminishing returns, especially for an old man nearing death. In his last novels Trollope puts aside moral revulsion and pleads for acceptance and readjustment to a changing world. Seeing the practical failure of all kinds of rigidity, even his own rigid assertion that his world needed moral reformation if men were to live with genuine hope, he begins to accept moral relativism. The rage and bitterness of his dark books fade, and he returns to a quiet crusade for tolerance in personal relationships.

Cultural influence as well as private motives caused him to mellow. His writing reflects what might be called, in the language of Erik Erikson, the polarities of Victorian identity. The cultural ideal of Victorian civilization was individual liberty in a moral society. This ideal contains an inherent contradiction, and it explains many of the other contradictions in the age and in Trollope's work. Sometimes individualism and freedom had to be stressed; at other times people had to be sold on conformity to idealistic standards and their responsibility to others. To pursue freedom effectively men needed to know their bondage to historical and psychological forces. They had to have hope and confidence, yet self-satisfaction would have been fatal in a time of economic scarcity. Money could be the means to make people free, but when it became an end in itself, it led to immorality. The Victorians had to accommodate and criticize all sorts of views. They needed inner purpose and self-abnegation, open-mindedness and a rigid sense of good and evil, flexibility and dogmatism. They had to believe in both human perfectibility and original sin.

Like his era, Trollope was always trying to balance opposites. The fatalistic pessimism of *The Macdermots* turns into the optimism of *Barchester Towers*; romantic love enriches life in *Rachel Ray* and sterilizes it in *The Small House*. Money brings joy and gladness in *Doctor Thorne*, trouble in *The Prime Minister*; the cancer of the ego in *He Knew He Was Right* changes into the disease of the disappearing self in *The Eustace Diamonds*. At the end of his career, the angry satirical novels which show contempt for his world give way to books preaching the necessity of reconciliation and resignation.

I

The last period begins with his autobiography. After finishing *The American Senator* and returning home from another visit to Australia and his son, he felt the time had come for summing up. The result is that fascinating, yet maddening testimony from the Victorian age, *An Autobiography* (1875–1876). The mixture of candor with evasiveness, and good sense with utter foolishness, is enough to drive one wild. Often the book takes the form of a commercial ledger that a character like Abel Wharton might have kept, and it finally reads like the success story of Trollope and Company. In the penultimate chapter we get a list of sums received for each novel; opening the book at random, we come on sentences like this: "From this time for a period of twelve years, my income averaged 4500 pounds a year."[1] We want

---

[1] Anthony Trollope, *An Autobiography* (London, 1953), chap. x, p. 144.

the record of his inner life, which he refuses to give us, and
the account of himself—which often seems to be literally just
that, an accounting of his financial state—tempts us to cry
"philistine." But how much it reveals, after all, about the
age that Trollope should tend to see his life as a series of
fiscal events. It shows how deeply embedded the capitalistic
spirit was in the consciousness of the middle class—even in
those who were most critical of it. A healthy financial history seems to have given proper Victorians the same kind of
stamp of inward approval that a healthy sex life supposedly
provides now, at least in middle-class mythology. It also
shows Trollope's tacit assumption that material well-being
is necessary for self-respect, free choice, and a rich intellectual life. And that hardheaded insistence on the materialistic
basis of the good life is one of the things that makes the
assessment of life in his novels so impressive.

The autobiography has long been notorious for passages
like this one:

There are those who . . . think that the man who works
with his imagination should be allowed to wait till inspiration moves him. When I have heard such a doctrine
preached, I have hardly been able to repress my scorn. To
me it would not be more absurd if the shoemaker were to
wait for inspiration, or the tallow-chandler for the divine
moment of melting. If the man whose business it is to write
has eaten too many good things, or has drunk too much, or
smoked too many cigars,—as men who write sometimes will
do,—then his condition may be unfavorable for work but so
will be the condition of a shoemaker who has similarly been
imprudent. . . . *Mens sana in corpore sano.* The author wants
that as does every other workman,—that and the habit of
industry. . . .
While I was in Egypt, I finished *Doctor Thorne*, and on
the following day began *The Bertrams*. I was moved now by
a determination to excel, if not in quality, at any rate in
quantity.[2]

---

[2] *Ibid.*, chap. VII, pp. 104–105.

"Sacrilegious!" James might have said, but Trollope had polemical reasons for going out of his way to make it clear that he, the writer, had the same worries about working and earning a living as other men. He felt that the rise of aestheticism and romantic theories about the specialness of the artist could have the harmful effect of separating writers from their audience. He thought that by taking on the status of rare, beautiful birds in society, writers would ultimately weaken their power to influence the life of their communities. There is an implicit worldly rhetoric in the autobiography which—put crudely—goes something like this: *I am a no-nonsense hardworking man just like you. I know what your problems are; I don't despise you for caring about mundane things because I do too, and so you can believe what I tell you, that you must change your ways.* Trollope feared the cult of elitism because he believed strongly in the moral relevance of fiction to a wide range of humanity.

Writing the autobiography seems to have liberated him from the black world-view of *The Prime Minister* and *The Way We Live Now*. Setting down the outward facts of his life made him recognize that by the standards of the world he had been extremely successful. In his own dried ink, he could see how far he had come from his early wretched days, and the obvious change for the better in his private world helped to reconcile him with a world that he had come to despise. Looking at himself in much the same way that a bank auditor looks over the assets, he got rid of some doubts about his own worth and the potential worth of his world. With a new equanimity, he was free to write the real spiritual autobiography of his last years in *The Duke's Children, Cousin Henry, Dr. Wortle's School,* and *Mr. Scarborough's Family*.

In a frenzy of working while there was still light, Trollope poured out ten and a half novels in this final period, many of them incredibly bad. *The Duke's Children* and *Cousin Henry* are distinguished works of fiction; *Dr. Wortle's School* and

Mr. Scarborough's Family are good, if spotty, and they present interesting moral problems. The others, however, show an incoherent, tired imagination. What matters is that the theme of relinquishment and the necessity of tolerance runs through them all. The heroine in *Ayala's Angel* (1878) finds that she has to marry a plodding, flawed *man*, not an angel. In *Marion Fay* (1878–1879) class rigidity breaks down; and the unfinished *Landleaguers* (1882) is about the horrors of political extremism in Ireland. In the dull futuristic novel *The Fixed Period* (1880–1881), an idealistic government of a little island has to give up its supposedly humane plan for euthanasia; and in *An Old Man's Love* (1882), the elderly man has to abandon his plan to marry his ward and gives her up to a younger man (clearly Trollope's own psychology was wrapped up in these last books). The moral imperatives are always: *relinquish rigid idealism* and *stop being judgmental*. But despite some strong scenes, these novels, along with *John Caldigate* and *Kept In the Dark*, are for the most part repetitive and flabby.

II

Good realistic literature, says Arnold Kettle, "gets hold of the extreme possibilities inherent in a situation and gains a more profound typicality through concentration on the truly significant tensions within that particular chunk of life."[3] *The Duke's Children* (1876) has this kind of realism. The tensions between the Duke and his children and, within the Duke's own mind, between the impact of the present and the psychological effects of the past on him bring us right to the heart of important problems of change in Victorian and modern life. The book could be subtitled *Letting Go*. Palliser, growing old, loses control over his children and his world. To live in the present, he must learn to let go of the past.

Glencora has died, and Trollope begins the story with one

---

[3] Arnold Kettle, *An Introduction to the English Novel*, 2 vols. (New York, 1960), II, 116.

of those strange passages that show his range of feeling:
"Had the heavens fallen and mixed themselves with the
earth, had the people of London risen in rebellion with
French ideas of equality, had the Queen persistently de-
clined to comply with the constitutional advice of her ministers, had a majority of the House of Commons lost its
influence in the country,—the utter prostration of the bereft
husband could not have been more complete. It was not
only that his heart was torn to pieces, but that he did not
know how to look out into the world."[4] The long first sentence, with its faintly ironical tone, serves to define the
Duke's conventionality and his political interests, and to
distance us from this fretful, sometimes silly figure. But the
second sentence brings home the awful perplexity of the man
and makes us sympathize with him. That beautiful, decep-
tively simple phrase, "he did not know how to look out into
the world," ought to make us feel how difficult it is to see
reality in a world of change and death. Life keeps forcing a
man to readjust his outlook, and according to Trollope the
readjustment seems to get harder and more painful as one
moves into old age and the need for it becomes more
pressing.

He saw that, in a time of change and progress, the clash
of generations would grow sharper. Fathers want to put some
sort of lasting mark on the mutable world; sons must be free
to move with the times. Politically, Palliser has always cham-
pioned progress and the march toward social equality. Ironically, he finds that he has helped produce the situation in
which his son and daughter insist against his will on marrying, respectively, an American girl and a poor commoner:
"Such drawing-near of the classes was the object to which
all this man's political action tended. And yet it was a dreadful thing to him that his own daughter should marry a man

---

[4] *The Duke's Children* (London, 1957), "double volume" (see
Author's Note, p. viii), chap. i, pp. 2–3 (I).

so much beneath her own rank."[5] We have here another of Trollope's reminders that political and private life cannot be separated.

Parents and children are always squabbling in his novels, especially in his last ones. He writes of Palliser's son Lord Silverbridge, "He thought that there were certain changes going on in the management of the world which his father did not quite understand. Fathers never do quite understand the changes which are manifest to their sons. Some years ago it might have been improper that an American girl should be elevated to the rank of an English Duchess; but now all that was altered."[6] In *John Caldigate* (1877), the novel that followed, a puritanical mother screams at her married daughter, " 'I will not be beaten by one who has been subject to my authority.' "[7] That expresses the Duke's feeling as well as the petulance of every parent who finds time has made the will of his child independent. But the revolutionary changes of the last two centuries have exacerbated the battle of the generations, and it is no historical accident that Trollope should have made this battle a major theme in his last novels or that, a few years later, Freud should have articulated the Oedipal hostility between father and son. The difference in world views of old and young was becoming greater than ever before.

"Never trust anyone over thirty," has, of course, always been an axiom of comedy, and if Palliser were merely the stock father-figure harassing young lovers, *The Duke's Children* would be trite. What makes the book so interesting is that the Duke is really a much better man than his sons and his prospective son-in-law. His loss of influence in this world means that the Victorian dream of a disciplined, responsible, compassionate society living by absolute moral standards is waning. Silverbridge is a generous and modest young man,

[5] *Ibid.*, chap. xxii, pp. 213–214 (I).

[6] *Ibid.*, chap. lxi, p. 204 (II).

[7] *John Caldigate* (London, 1946), chap. xxxvi, p. 346.

but he behaves frivolously and is not very bright. Not only does he squander a fortune on horses, but he is given to talking like this: " 'We've got to protect our position as well as we can against the Radicals and Communists. . . . The people will look after themselves, and we must look after ourselves. We are so few and they are so many, that we shall have quite enough to do.' "[8] The Duke, good old-fashioned utilitarian that he is, tries to teach him that "the greatest benefit of the greatest number was the object to which all political studies should tend." But Trollope makes clear the weakness of utilitarianism when he shows how easily Silverbridge turns its doctrine into the greatest good for *number one*. Silverbridge infuriates his Liberal father by turning Conservative: " 'In comparison with a great many men, I know that I am a fool. Perhaps it is because I know that, that I am a Conservative. The Radicals are always saying that a Conservative must be a fool. Then a fool ought to be a Conservative.' " There is a certain logic and charm in this, but no wonder the former Prime Minister "more than once clenched his fist in eager desire to turn upon the young man."[9] And no wonder he wants the boy to marry intelligent Lady Mabel Grex and has no faith in his decision to marry an American girl.

Like so much of Trollope's fiction, *The Duke's Children* is a book that gets better the more one reads it and thinks about it. It lacks the sweep of the other Palliser novels, but it deepens the characterization of the Duke. John Hagan, in an excellent study, has called the novel Trollope's psychological masterpiece.[10] He shows in detail how Palliser's feelings about his dead wife—his wish to justify their marriage, his own guilt over his exasperation with her, his unconscious resentment of her for withholding information from him about Mary's love for Tregear, his painful memories of her

---

[8] *The Duke's Children*, chap. vii, p. 69 (I).

[9] *Ibid.*, p. 70 (I).

[10] John Hagan, "Trollope's Psychological Masterpiece," *Nineteenth-Century Fiction* (June 1958), pp. 1–22.

own love for Burgo Fitzgerald, his jealousy and rivalry with her that continue even after her death, and above all his love and his new-found admiration for her—affect his relations with his children. Palliser, for example, takes Mary to Europe, hoping she will fall out of love with Tregear, just the way he took Glencora away to make her forget Fitzgerald in *Can You Forgive Her?* He thinks about his daughter's misery, but "his mind was intent on his Glencora and on Burgo Fitzgerald," and his thoughts become neurotic: "Should she be allowed to break her heart and die, or should he save her from that fate by sanctioning her marriage with Tregear? If the choice could be put to him plainly by some supernal power, what then would he choose? If duty required him to prevent this marriage, his duty could not be altered by the fact that this girl would avenge herself upon him by dying! If such a marriage were in itself wrong, that wrong could not be made right by the fear of such a catastrophe. Was it not often the case that duty required that someone should die?"[11]

For a time he is paralyzed by a combination of his own past and a slightly antiquated Victorian idealism. When he learns that the Duchess has approved of Mary's lover, he thinks: "His dear wife had been the most imprudent of women. And he recognized in her encouragement of this most pernicious courtship . . . a repetition of that romantic folly by which she had so nearly brought herself to shipwreck in her own early life."[12] He keeps telling himself that he opposes Tregear out of love for Mary and moral obligation, but ironically Trollope introduces thoughts like these: "His Cora and all her money had been saved from a worthless spendthrift. He had found a wife who *he now thought* had made him happy."[13] Palliser's motives are sometimes psychologically complex, but they are clear. He is disappointed in the children whom Glencora has borne him, and he has to go on

[11] *The Duke's Children*, chap. XLI, pp. 16–17 (II).
[12] Chap. V, p. 50 (I).
[13] Chap. XXIV, pp. 229–230 (I), italics mine.

fighting Glencora's will, which has cost him so dearly. At the same time he misses her so much that he even tries to keep her faults alive by projecting them on the daughter, a girl who is no more like Glencora than a nun. Trollope, like Proust and Freud, believed that the ghosts of the past always live with one. One is apt to be dealing with them instead of the living flesh and blood of the present moment.

III

Trollope has more charity for Palliser in this novel than ever before, partly, of course, because he identified with him and distrusted the self-indulgence of the new generation. The Duke, with his terrible reserve and all his other faults, has an idealistic feeling for others and a sense of moral obligation to the community which his sons, for all their cheerful good-humor, lack. One of Silverbridge's young friends tells the Duke about the difference in generations: "'There is a great deal of good feeling no doubt, but there's no earnestness about anything. I think you are more earnest than we; but then you are such horrid bores. And each earnest man is in earnest about something that nobody else cares for.'"[14] Palliser and the importance of being earnest bore the new young aristocrats, much as Trollope bored the bright young men of the late Victorian era; yet each is greater than his progeny because each has greater moral power and greater sympathy for humanity.

At the same time, Trollope also likes the young people better here than in a book like *The Way We Live Now*. Both Silverbridge and his younger brother, Gerald, belong to the Beargarden Club, and some of the former members, such as Dolly Longstaffe and Nidderdale, reappear. Now these young men seem good-hearted, and ignorant and irresponsible rather than vicious and mean. In one of the finest scenes of the book, Palliser and his sons breakfast together, and their conversation epitomizes their faults and virtues, the

---

[14] Chap. XXXV, pp. 329–330 (I).

difficulties of communication between generations, the changing spirit of the Victorian age, as well as the artistry and tone of the novel. The night before, the boys decided to "give the governor a turn," and knowing that he breakfasts sparingly, Silverbridge puts in an order for a big meal:

"You never seem to eat anything, sir."

"Eating is an occupation from which I think a man takes the more pleasure the less he considers it. A rural labourer who sits on the ditch-side with his bread and cheese and an onion has more enjoyment out of it than any Lucullus. . . ."

". . . You are twenty minutes late, Gerald. My father says that bread and cheese and onions would be better for you than salmon and stewed kidneys. . . ."

"I should not mind trying them at all," said Gerald. "Only one never does have such things for breakfast. Last winter a lot of us skated to Ely, and we ate two or three loaves of bread and a whole cheese at a pothouse! And as for beer, we drank the public dry. . . . I don't think things are a bit the nicer because they cost a lot of money. I suppose that is what you mean, sir."

"Something of that kind, Gerald. Not to have money for your wants;—that must be troublesome. . . ."

"I don't complain," said Gerald. "No fellow ever had less right to complain. But I never felt that I had quite enough. Of course it was my own fault."

"I should say so, my boy. . . . To be in any difficulty with regard to money . . . creates a feeling of meanness."

"That is what I have always felt," said Silverbridge. "I cannot bear to think that I should like to have a thing and that I cannot afford it."

"You do not quite understand me, I fear. The only case in which you can be justified in desiring a thing which you cannot afford is when the thing is necessary;—as bread may be, or cheese."

"As when a fellow wants a lot of new breeches before he has paid his tailor's bill."

"As when a poor man," said the Duke impressively, "may long to give his wife a new gown, or his children boots to keep their feet from the mud and snow." Then he paused a moment, but the serious tone of his voice and the energy of his words had sent Gerald headlong among his kidneys. . . . "As far as I have been able to look out into the world—"

"I suppose you know it as well as anybody," said Silverbridge, who was simply desirous of making himself pleasant to the "dear old governor."

"As far as my experience goes, the happiest man is he who, being above the troubles which money brings, has his hands the fullest of work. . . .

"Isn't it a great grind, sir?" asked Silverbridge. . . .

"But it is the grind that makes the happiness. To feel that your hours are filled to overflowing, that you can barely steal minutes enough for sleep, that the welfare of many is entrusted to you, that the world looks on and approves, that some good is always being done to others,—above all things some good to your country; that is happiness. For myself, I can conceive of none other."

"Books," suggested Gerald, as he put the last morsel of the last kidney in his mouth. . . .

"As for money," continued the father, not caring to notice this interruption, "if it be regarded in any other light than as a shield against want, as a rampart under the protection of which you may carry on your battle, it will fail you. I was born a rich man."

"Few people have cared so little about it as you," said the elder son.

"And you, both of you, have been born rich." This assertion did not take the elder brother by surprise. It was a matter of course. But Lord Gerald, who had never as yet heard anything as to his future destiny from his father, was interested by the statement. "When I think of all this,—of what constitutes happiness,—I am almost tempted to grieve that it should be so."

"If a large fortune were really a bad thing," said Gerald, "a man could I suppose get rid of it."

"No;—it is a thing of which a man cannot get rid,—unless by shameful means. It is a burden which he must carry to the end. . . ."

The two brothers then took themselves to some remote part of the house where arrangements had been made for smoking, and there they finished the conversation.

"I was very glad to hear what he said about you, old boy."
This of course came from Silverbridge. . . . "He meant you to
understand that you wouldn't be like other younger brothers."

"Then what I have will be taken from you."

"There is lots for three or four of us. . . . He's going to have
two eldest sons."

"What an unnatural piece of cruelty to me;—and so unnecessary!"

"Why?"

"He says that a property is no better than a burden. But
I'll try and bear it."[15]

What Trollope manages to accomplish in this passage is
amazing; and its comprehensiveness is typical of him in his
best moments. The father patronizes the sons, the sons
patronize the father. The Duke talks like a pompous, old-
fashioned prig, the boys seem naïvely self-centered and im-
mature. All three behave a little ridiculously, and the whole
scene is comic. But more than that, it is also in an original
way moving and serious. What Palliser says is true enough.
That he speaks a stale, ineffectual language in trying, for his
sons' own good, to inspire them with the Victorian sense of
mission and make them see the ideal of a moral society does
not make his attempt less important. The unbridgeable gulf
between saying and doing shows through here, and so does
the burden of time which makes the old man intent on com-
municating both his knowledge and his affection to them.
Trollope shows us the generosity of all three and their restrained love for each other. Silliness, sincerity, goodness,
and weakness are all mixed up together; he sees the foolishness of these characters, but he likes and respects them. He
is not sentimental about people in his last novels, but he is
extremely tolerant.

His tolerance now extends to Americans, on whom he had
been rather hard in *The Way We Live Now* and *The Ameri-*

---

[15] Chap. XXV, pp. 232–244 (I).

can Senator. Pleasant though it is, the Victorian aristocracy obviously suffers from tired blood, and Silverbridge's match with the American Isabel Boncassen seems a good tonic. Henry James, discussing Trollope, remarks "The American girl was destined sooner or later to make her entrance into British fiction," and refers to "Miss Boncassen, in *The Duke's Children*."[16] (A short while after he read Trollope's novel, James portrayed another American lady named Isabel who visits England and wins a proposal from a lord.) Trollope's Isabel punctures some of the stuffiness of the upper-class atmosphere and mocks the Victorian cultural myopia. Her energy, loyalty, and practicality are just what Silverbridge needs to open the world up to him.[17]

Trollope's late novels show the Victorians profiting from the people and wealth of the rest of the world. John Caldigate, in the next novel, makes a man of himself and a fortune to boot in the gold mines of Australia. In *An Old Man's Love* the course of true love runs smooth because a poor young man can mine diamonds in South Africa. Like Disraeli, of whom he disapproved, Trollope hoped his people could reinvigorate themselves by turning outward. There is no jingoism in him, but in his tendency to see internationalism as a crutch for his culture—an American to reinvigorate the nobility, Australian gold to achieve status—we can see how jingoism developed.

For Trollope, one of the marks of narrowness and provincialism in Victorian society was the sad plight of intelligent, ambitious women. He dramatized the marriage-market theme *ad nauseam*, but he repeats it once more in Lady Mabel Grex, the brightest of the young people in the novel.

---

[16] Henry James "Anthony Trollope," *The Future of the Novel*, ed. Leon Edel (New York, 1956), p. 251.

[17] In imagining Silverbridge's marriage to an American, Trollope may well have had in mind an actual marriage which took place in 1874 between a member of one of England's first families and a New York girl named Jenny Jerome—a match which produced Winston Churchill.

She is like Julia Brabazon, Laura Kennedy, and Arabella
Trefoil, with something of a Glencora in her. Almost compulsively, Trollope kept creating these smart, aggressive, un-
fulfilled women whose only outlet for ambition is to try to
marry money and titles. Down deep he was an unrecon-
structed utilitarian, and it pained him that women with the
most ability often seemed unable to use their talent and
ambitions positively. It was the nature of his world to see
the intelligent woman as a threat and to try to keep her in a
doll's house. Lady Mabel has nothing worthwhile to do,
and the waste of her potential in a society that badly needs
her perceptive mind is tragic. Trollope has more sympathy
for her than he had for Arabella Trefoil; Mabel is more victim than victimizer. As his antiheroine, he gives her some of
the best lines in the book and uses her to make his truce with
a world whose faults he knows very well, but which he for-
gives. She says to Frank Tregear: "'After all I think that
pious godly people have the best of it in this world. Let them
be ever so covetous, ever so false, ever so hard-hearted, the
mere fact that they must keep up appearances, makes them
comfortable to those around them. . . . A little hypocrisy, a
little sacrifice to the feelings of the world may be such a
blessing.'"[18] In Wilde and Shaw this kind of ironical insight
can become mannered and insincere, but in Trollope it can
give new perspectives on an age. For a moment, in this passage, he softens his attitude toward that evangelical side of
Victorian life. We find him much less willing in this book to
condemn people and life-styles than before.

   The Duke's Children makes a curious but appropriate ending to the Palliser series. It has less action and flashiness than
its predecessors and little of their satirical bite or their overt
political significance. It does, however, round out a man and
an era, and it is Trollope's gentlest book since *The Warden*.
"Gentle" is not an adjective which especially recommends a
novel—unless, that is, we accept his view that gentleness is

---

[18] *The Duke's Children*, chap. LXXVII, p. 350 (II).

the most valuable and indispensable of human qualities. From the time when Palliser first appeared in *The Small House at Allington*, he has never been able to convey in words his love for others or the passionate turmoil of his inner life. But in this book Trollope imagines him at a time when his reserve breaks down and he communicates to his son through a gentle action. He and Silverbridge are dining alone at the Beargarden Club. "Then the father looked round the room furtively, and seeing that the door was shut, and that they were assuredly alone, he put out his hand and gently stroked the young man's hair. It was almost a caress, —as though he would have said to himself, 'Were he my daughter, I would kiss him.' "[19] This novel does not have the power of *The Prime Minister*, but it has surprising moments like this one in which Trollope's grasp of the intensity of human emotion makes better-known novels and writers seem thin by comparison. All his life Palliser has been disappointed in his family. Glencora and his children repeatedly fail to live up to his ideal of what is fitting, and though he tries, he can never make them do as he wishes. Strenuous efforts to change other people not only do not work, they drain and isolate one: "Now in the solitude of his life, as years were coming on him, he felt how necessary it was that he should have someone who would love him."[20] Only his kindness and gentleness keep the love of his children, which he needs. They allow him to make what Trollope calls now the crucial "act of reconciliation."[21]

The last line of the book—of the whole Palliser series—is all important. The Duke says of Frank Tregear, " 'But now I will accept as courage what I before regarded as arrogance.' "[22] The wall of class, which Palliser in his public life has battered, is broken, and Palliser can now see things from

---

[19] Chap. XXVI, p. 253 (I).
[20] Chap. LXVI, p. 252 (II).
[21] Chap. LXXIV, p. 328 (II).
[22] Chap. LXXX, p. 379 (II).

Tregear's point of view, which means he can sympathize with him. The key word naturally is "accept." All one can finally do about posterity and the future is to accept it. The Duke must reconcile himself to the fact that his past is not the present, that Tregear is not Burgo Fitzgerald, that his world is different from his children's, that they will be independent of him no matter what happens. Reconcilation and acceptance, the last great themes of Trollope, are the last lessons which Palliser learns.

IV

In his odd little novel *Cousin Henry* (1878) he shows that the price which a "moral" society exacts in trying to make people live up to its ideals is too high; its righteousness feeds on victims. Surprisingly, Trollope, now over sixty, with more than forty books out, took a new tack. He went far back into his childhood to imagine the feeling of being a total outcast, and stylistically he went forward to experiment—sometimes falteringly and not always successfully, to be sure—along fascinating new lines. *Cousin Henry*, long out of print and virtually ignored, is one of the strangest and most original works in Victorian fiction. In his attack on moral rigidity, Trollope abandons the logic of cause and effect which is the mainstay of the realistic novel; the basis of the story, which is the intense revulsion that Cousin Henry produces in all the other characters, is neither logically nor realistically motivated. Here Trollope presents a subjective and unflattering picture of organized society from the perspective of a social misfit; he develops a full-blown antihero; he makes the reader sympathize with the weak and disreputable side of human nature and distrust the supposedly virtuous and respectable side; he recognizes and explores the innate perversity in the mind; he gives the novel a parable-like structure which makes it necessary for a reader to interpret the underlying meaning of the story; and he uses allegory and symbolism more overtly and centrally than ever before. The unconventional and harsh view of the "decent" world and the description of an unnecessary but complete human failure in it make *Cousin Henry* his most anarchic book.

The story describes the disgrace and abject defeat of a little man named Henry Jones, whom the rigidity and resolute intolerance of society terrorize. *Cousin Henry's* Kafkalike atmosphere is striking. Henry, like Joseph K. in *The Trial*, is presumed guilty at the start, but we never know why. He is a timid, furtive, shy person whom everyone automatically despises. From the beginning, all his attempts to ingratiate himself with others are rebuffed. His relatives, acquaintances, and even the servants regard him as a virtual criminal to whom no kindness ought to be shown. They all continually insult him, calling him, for instance, "odious," "vile," a "dog," and a "reptile." To appreciate the originality of this novel, we must realize that the animosity which everyone feels for him, and his own guilt-ridden anxieties, are the absolute *données* of the book for which we can see no explicit cause. There is nothing that Henry could do which would change anyone's opinion about him. And it is this unmotivated persecution which gains our sympathy and pity for the moral outcast rather than for the respectable citizens who make Henry suffer. Trollope's main rhetorical effect is in persuading us to like Henry, the so-called villain, better than the nominally honest and upright characters.

Henry's conservative uncle detests him so much that he makes a new will breaking the tradition of primogeniture and leaves his estate to Isabel, a supposedly virtuous and perfect cousin. Quite by accident, however, the second will is lost, and Henry takes possession of the estate. Everyone believes that he has purposely destroyed the will and robbed Isabel of her inheritance. Though he offers to give money to her, Isabel rejects it and insults him. One day he finds the second will stuck in a book and starts to make the discovery known; but before he can do it, people bully him and frighten him so much that he does not dare tell them about the document for fear they will say that he is lying and punish him for concealing it. In one terrifying passage, he realizes that no matter what he does, people will condemn him. He does not have the courage either to destroy the will and commit a really serious crime or to give it up to the proper authorities and suffer public accusations. Henry is not a criminal; he is only weak and spineless. The prejudice of society, however, and its indictment of him before he has ever done anything specifically wrong thus *force* him to become the guilty sneak which everyone had always thought him. Paralyzed with fear and indecision, Henry waits to be found out, and when the authorities eventually find the will, they denounce him with a vehemence usually reserved for child-slayers. Public opinion drives Henry off the estate and out of the county. He returns, a humiliated and broken man, to his depressing life as a harmless, miserable little London clerk, a permanently lost soul.

Cousin Henry can and should be read as Trollope's note from the Victorian underground complaining against the tyranny of bourgeois respectability and oppressively conformist morality. Like his contemporary, Dostoyevsky, and like Kafka, Trollope, in *Cousin Henry,* was able to elucidate the claustrophobic nature of modern life, the trapped-animal psychology which, to one degree or another, haunts most of us. Henry is a petty sinner, but he is also a harried and doomed victim. Trollope found him, with all his guilt, fear, and anxiety, a more interesting and sympathetic character than anyone else in the novel, and so do we.

Nearly always, in mentioning Henry in the story, Trollope refers to him as "Cousin Henry" in order to emphasize Henry's relationship both to his ostensibly pure and spotless cousin Isabel and to humanity in general. This sly, equivocal, cowardly, unpopular, and lonely fellow who feels both the need and the impossibility of justifying himself to others, who is unjustly picked upon, who has a sense of nebulous guilt, who silently and ineffectually resents the unfairness of life, has a kinship with everybody. Henry is that frail, amoral, scared, repulsive side of human nature which keeps Everyman from living up to a strict and idealistic moral code. Because he is everyone's cousin, his blood flows in all human veins, even those of the rigorous Victorian moralists who tried to disown him. Trollope explicitly turns Henry from a character into a moral personification:

> To be commonly wicked was nothing to him,—nothing to break through all those ordinary rules of life which parents teach their children and pastors their flocks, but as to which the world is so careless. To covet other men's goods, to speak evil of his neighbors, to run after his neighbor's wife if she came in his path, to steal a little in the ordinary way,—such as selling a lame horse or looking over an adversary's hand at whist—to swear a lie, or ridicule the memory of his parents in the novel [Henry actually does none of these things]— these peccadillos had never oppressed his soul.[23]

Henry represents that inherent meanness which, try as we will to keep it down, continually pops up in our lives.

The trouble with the militant and unforgiving war which the other characters wage on Henry is that it neither helps nor reforms him, and it brutalizes all of them. They are so eager to judge and condemn him that they leave him no real alternative but to commit the wrong for which they have already convicted him. Hating sin and moral weakness so passionately that they cannot distinguish between sin and the sinner, they themselves commit the greatest possible sin of omission—much worse than failing to report a will: they live without practising charity. The forces of official morality in the Victorian society which Trollope here depicts are actually immoral. By denying the weaker elements in human nature, they merely pervert the stronger ones. Absolute and fixed standards may become impractical and unworkable. The moral surety of these people leads to arrogance and pride.

---

[23] *Cousin Henry* (London, 1929), chap. xx, p. 233.

The inflexible moral code of the society over which Isabel presides is self-defeating. The community harms itself as well as Henry. Trollope saw that it was neither realistic nor practical merely to condemn and shun sin and sinners. One behaves just as immorally by hating a pitiful little man as by concealing legal evidence. Even self-righteous Isabel participates in sin, and by making society's darling paragon less attractive than Henry, the weak tormented mouse who lives in his underground of psychic guilt and terror, Trollope undermines the notion of moral absolutism and calls in doubt traditional categories of right and wrong.

In *Cousin Henry*, Trollope drew upon his emotional experience of fifty years earlier to represent, intentionally or not, organized morality and "respectable" society as a conspiracy against a weak single man. That craven little boy that he describes in the autobiography remained somewhere inside of him unappeased by success, and finally he let that boy's vision of the world's unfairness come through. The book is not as powerful as it might have been if Trollope were less ashamed of the "cousin Henry" in himself and had been able to make the narrative voice cohere with the vision of the outcast. But there is enough of the outcast point of view to show how morality becomes a weapon and support for the strong. Isabel and the others use Henry; they force him into immoral action in order to assure themselves of their own worthiness and superiority. The "moral" person depends on the existence of the "immoral" man.

Trollope, in *Cousin Henry*, also makes the connection between morality and economic interest. He seems to be saying here and in many of his novels that we take it for granted that whatever threatens our financial status is by definition immoral. Henry is Isabel's rival for property and money; therefore, from her point of view and that of her friends, he is immoral. A moral code and "morality" often have the effect of preserving the economic status quo and defending the property of the relatively rich. They also provide comfortable forts of righteousness from which people can wage economic war. By recognizing and dramatizing these ideas in *Cousin Henry* and in his last novel of consequence, *Mr. Scarborough's Family*, Trollope moved very close to moral relativism and the tolerance it implies.

V

"Judge not lest ye be judged" continues to reappear in one form or another in all these last novels—as a kind of memo from Trollope to himself and as strategic advice to an age in transformation. People who live in aging crystal palaces should not throw stones. Several times in this period he takes up problems of female purity and sexual morality. John Caldigate lives with a woman in Australia before he returns home and marries Hester Bolton. But Trollope now sees sexual morality in relative terms: what might be immoral in England is not necessarily so bad in an Australian mining-camp; what is wrong for a woman may not be wrong for a man. Trollope treats Caldigate sympathetically when his former mistress reappears, and Hester sticks by him in one of the most flagrant assertions of the double standard in "respectable" Victorian fiction.

A character in *Marion Fay* says, "The last thing that a man can abandon of his social idolatries is the sanctity of the women belonging to him.' "[24] We have seen that for Trollope idealization of women was a particularly subtle and destructive form of soul tyranny which violated the individual reality of a human being. In *Kept In the Dark* (1880), Cecelia Western, knowing that her husband believes her a saint, hides the fact that she had once been engaged before she met him. When he finds out, he goes wild: " 'You are not that sweetly innocent creature which I have believed you,' "[25] he says; and he thinks crazily, "When accepting his caresses and returning them with a young wife's ardor, even

---

[24] *Marion Fay* (Leipzig: Tauchnitz, 1882), chap. I, p. 15.
[25] *Kept in the Dark*, 2 vols. (London: Chatto Windus, 1882), I, chap. XI, p. 231.

at that moment she had been a traitor."[26] Only when he can
see *her* and not the two images he created, first, of perfection,
and then of immorality, can he readjust to life. The point
here, in the context of Trollope's last novels, is larger than it
might at first appear: there is nothing for a man to do but
tolerate and accept other people with their flaws or go mad
with rage, disappointment, and feelings of betrayal.

One of the most interesting of these questions about moral
tolerance occurs in *Dr. Wortle's School* (1879). It turns out
that Dr. Wortle's best teacher, Mr. Peacocke, is living with
an American woman who is not legally his wife. In Missouri,
Peacocke had befriended an attractive young woman whose
drunken husband mistreated her. After he had supposedly
died, she married Peacocke. But the first husband showed
up very much alive. After he again disappeared, the Peacockes, deeply in love with each other, returned to England
to live as man and wife. When the book opens, Peacocke is
Dr. Wortle's right-hand man, a popular and splendid teacher, an ordained cleric, and seemingly a model husband. A
blackmailer from America, however, tells Wortle the truth.
Trollope puts the problem this way: "According to the strict
law of right and wrong the two unfortunates should have
parted when they found that they were not in truth married.
And, again, according to the strict law of right and wrong,
Mr. Peacocke should not have brought the woman there,
into his school, as his wife."[27] But because this law is broken,
the interests of humanity and love are served. Against all
prudence, Dr. Wortle defies the moral feelings of the community and the teachings of his Church to support the Peacockes. He refuses to condemn them and instead shelters
the woman, though it means the temporary ruin of his school,
while Peacocke goes to America to prove that the first husband is dead at last.

Dr. Wortle, with his generosity, his materialism, his gruff

---

[26] *Ibid.*, II, chap. xviii, pp. 105–106.
[27] *Dr. Wortle's School* (London, 1928), Part IV, chap. x, p.
101.

stubbornness, his warmth and his loyalty, is very much a self-portrait.[28] After some ambivalent hesitation, Trollope finally comes down on the side of Wortle, who chooses to be merciful against "the strict law of right and wrong." In his understanding of both the inevitability and the desirability of moral relativism, he finally upholds Wortle's tolerance and his belief in "situation ethics." Wortle's battle with a community which has no pity for a Mrs. Peacocke becomes his battle too. When Wortle says, " 'The wife of some religious grocer, who sands his sugar regularly, would have thought her house contaminated by such an inmate,' "[29] or " 'It is often a question to me whether the religion of the world is not more odious than its want of religion,' "[30] we see how much he is like the man who wrote *Cousin Henry*.

Anthony Cockshut, in his provocative discussion of *Doctor Wortle's School*, disagrees, arguing that Trollope accepted the "orthodox moral teaching" and believed, according to the standard of the times, that Wortle's sympathy for the couple and his support was "grotesque." No one has done more to make us understand Trollope's achievement in the later novels than Mr. Cockshut, but here I think he is wrong. If we do not see that Trollope in his last years shows time changing and invalidating the rigid "orthodox" moral teaching of the Victorians, we miss his point. He and his world were finding that it was no longer always possible to rely on moral coercion and castigation to make things go right. Changing conditions required more flexible ideas about morality and made it necessary to live with much more moral ambiguity. As Mrs. Peacocke tells Wortle, " 'It is hard to know sometimes what is right and what is wrong.' "[31] When someone else calls the Peacockes immoral, Wortle says, " 'He

---

[28] See Michael Sadleir, *Trollope: A Commentary* (London, 1951), p. 396.
[29] *Dr. Wortle's School*, Part IV, chap. XI, p. 116.
[30] *Ibid.*, p. 123.
[31] Part V, chap. VII, p. 207.

doesn't know what moral and immoral means.' "[32] Simplistic definitions will no longer do.

The American scenes with Peacocke in the Wild West prove that the absolute moral standards of a rural English village cannot be imposed on a vast world. They completely undercut the provincial assurance of Mr. Puddicombe, an upright Victorian clergyman, who says, " 'He should, of course, have separated from her. There can be no doubt about it. There is no room for any quibble . . . no reference in our own minds to the pity of the thing, to the softness of the moment — should make us doubt it.' "[33] That is certainly not Trollope's view, though he may have had a certain nostalgia for the clear-cut conventional view. Mr. Cockshut quotes lines from early in the novel, which he says show Trollope's orthodoxy: "Should they part? There is not one who reads this but will say that they should have parted. Every day passed together as man and wife must be a falsehood and a sin." But in the rest of the passage Trollope begins to equivocate, to throw in hints of irony and to insist on moral ambiguity:

> There would be absolute misery for both in parting;—but there is no law from God or man entitling a man to escape from misery at the expense of falsehood and sin. Though their hearts might have burst in the doing of it, they should have parted. Though she would have been friendless, alone, utterly despicable in the eyes of the world, abandoning the name which she cherished, as not her own, and going back to that which she utterly abhorred, still she should have done it. And he . . . should have gone his widowed way, and endured as best he might the idea that he had left the woman whom he loved behind, in the desert, all alone.[34]

By the end of the book he shows us pragmatism and tolerance working where a rigorous moral code would have failed.

---

[32] Part V, chap. I, p. 138.
[33] Part III, chap. IX, p. 99.
[34] Part I, chap. III, pp. 32–33.

The moral touchstone of this novel is not Puddicombe but Mrs. Wortle. She, at first, having "no doubt as to the comfort, the beauty and the security of her own position,"[35] judges Mrs. Peacocke harshly, but by the end of the novel, swayed by her husband's logic and mercy and Mrs. Peacocke's goodness, she can ask herself what she would have done "in the same circumstances." For Trollope the root of all morality was the compassionate imagination—the ability, which Wortle has and his wife acquires, to put oneself in another's place and see how it feels.

VI

Though all fiction is hypothetical, the situations in Trollope's last stories almost beg to be stated in hypothetical form. "Suppose," he seems to say, "there were a little man whom everyone automatically hated," or "Suppose a decent couple were not really married." In *Mr. Scarborough's Family* (1881) the hypothesis goes something like this: "Suppose an old man should reject conventional forms of morality and refuse to respect any law beyond his own will and conscience." Is this man immoral? Old Scarborough tells lies, manipulates people, cheats his son's creditors, swindles another son, ruins his dead wife's good name, but he does all this out of benevolent motives. Morever, he gets good results. "In every phase of his life," says Trollope, "he had been actuated by love for others." What one character says of him after his death underscores the moral issue of the novel: "'One cannot make an apology for him without being ready to throw all truth and all morality to the dogs. But if you can imagine for yourself a state of things in which neither truth nor morality shall be thought essential, then old Mr. Scarborough would be your hero. He was the bravest man I ever knew. He was ready to look all opposition in the face, and prepared to bear it down. And whatever he

---

[35] Part III, chap. IX, p. 95.

did, he did with the view of accomplishing what he thought
to be right for other people.' "[36]

People, of course, *were* increasingly ready to throw all
absolute notions of truth and morality to the dogs. Moral
relativism was taking hold of Trollope's world. Another old
man, Mr. Grey, lives by the letter of the law and the common
proprieties, and yet the consequences of his actions are no
more just or right than those of Scarborough's. Grey's absolute moral beliefs tend to protect property just as Scarborough's schemes do. Each old man means well, each does
good and bad things, each defends his way of life, each does
the best he can for posterity, but each finally must let the
young generation run free. There was in Trollope as in most
of his contemporaries the urge to live by a communal moral
code and an opposite urge to defy public opinion and make
his own rules. We have both these sides of him in these two
characters: Scarborough longs for absolute personal freedom
and Grey believes in the absolutely just society. Morality
may serve the interests of property in the book; people may
be fools and knaves; but *Mr. Scarborough's Family* is not a
satire.[37] The mood at the end is one of acceptance. Both
Scarborough and Grey, as they are leaving life, come to treat
with tolerance and sympathy people whom they had previously scorned and belittled. Old men must bless or die
despairing.

These two are men of integrity, though each has a different idea of integrity, and in their merging fates we can see
the larger integrity of their creator. We have said that the
cultural ideal of the Victorians—an ideal which Trollope accepted and helped shape—was individual freedom in a moral
society. They needed both Grey and Scarborough. The faith
of these two and Trollope's own faith come through in the

---

[36] *Mr. Scarborough's Family* (London, 1926), chap. LVIII,
pp. 567–568.
[37] See Anthony Cockshut, *Anthony Trollope, A Critical Study*
(London, 1955), pp. 229–237, for a fine analysis of this novel.

final words of Grey's daughter: " 'We will go on and persevere, and, if we intend to do good, good will come of
it.' "[38] What keeps this from being smug and platitudinous is
Trollope's care in showing how hard it is to "persevere"
against strong opposition, how agonizingly difficult it is to
decide what is "good," how hard it is to control one's motives, and how long it may be between the "good" act and
the "good" result. Finally, he sees that it is now up to a new
generation to "persevere." There is no complacency in his
tone at the end of this book and at the end of his career;
there is, however, a resignation to things as they are and a
reverence for the living. He sees weakness, confusion, and
cruelty, but he knows that people keep trying to make life
good. And because they do, life *is* good.

VII

Erik Erikson, in *Childhood and Society*, describes the last
stage of maturity in a way that seems to fit our impression
of Trollope in his final period:

Only in him who in some way has taken care of things
and people and has adapted himself to the triumphs and
disappointments of products and ideas—only in him may
gradually ripen the fruit of . . . ego integrity. . . . I shall
point to a few constituents of this state of mind. It is the
ego's accrued assurance of its proclivity for order and meaning. It is a post-narcistic love of the human ego—not of the
self—as an experience which conveys some world order and
spiritual sense, no matter how dearly paid for. It is the acceptance of one's one and only life cycle as something that had
to be and that, by necessity, permitted of no substitutions:
it thus means a new, a different love of one's parents [who
also had to die]. It is a comradeship with the ordering of
ways of distant times and sayings of such times and pursuits.
Although aware of the relativity of the various life styles
which have given meaning to human striving, the possessor

---

[38] *Mr. Scarborough's Family*, chap. LXII, p. 608.

of integrity is ready to defend the dignity of his own life style against all physical and economic threats. For he knows that the individual life is the accidental coincidence of but one life cycle with but one segment of history; and that for him all human integrity stands or falls with the one style of integrity of which he partakes. The style of integrity developed by his culture of civilization thus becomes the patrimony of his soul . . .[39]

In fact, the closer we look at Erikson's ideal of maturity, the more it seems to coincide with our impression of Trollope's fiction as a whole. But this is not surprising: the great writer helps create the style or styles of integrity for his civilization.

---

[39] Erik Erikson, *Childhood and Society* (New York, 1963), p. 268.

10
Conclusion

Trollope wrote about his changing world, but he himself
helped to change it. "The nineteenth-century novel," said
Frank O'Connor, "was . . . a great popular art shared by the
whole community in a way inconceivable in either the eigh-
teenth or the twentieth century."[1] This meant that the popular Victorian novelist had a tremendous influence on his
world. We can imagine what reading novels could mean to
a girl living in an English village who knew perhaps fifty
people at most. The novel, for thousands, became an important way of knowing, and a writer like Trollope, to use
Marshall McLuhan's terms, extended the consciousness of
his public. The closest analogy we can make today to the
impact of the novel in the last century is the effect of tele-
vision on our world, and when we have said that, we can
begin to appreciate what a humane and noble enterprise the
Victorian novel was.[2] A popular art which, to a surprising
degree, avoids complacency and does not pander to its
audience appears to us as a kind of miracle. And yet the
major Victorian novelists, like Trollope, involved though

---

[1] *The Mirror in the Roadway*, p. 4.

[2] See Steven Marcus. *The Other Victorians* (New York, 1966),
p. 105: "As one reads through the thousands of pages of *My
Secret Life* . . . one achieves a renewed sense of how immensely
humane a project the Victorian novel was, how it broadened out
the circle of humanity, and how it represented the effort of
Victorian England at its best."

they were in a highly commercial undertaking, sought to change people for the better and make them see their own problems and faults.

Trollope says of the novelist: "He must teach whether he wish to teach or no." He had a strong sense of responsibility because he was sure, in a way that the modern novelist can never be, that he had the power to shape the minds of people—in other words, the power to change the world. "The amusement of time," he writes, "can hardly be the only result of any book that is read, and certainly not so with a novel, which appeals especially to the imagination. . . . A vast proportion of the teaching of the day,—*greater probably than many of us have acknowledged to ourselves,*—comes from these books, *which are in the hands of all readers.*"[3] We can never, of course, precisely answer the question of how a novel changes a person, which probably explains why we have "literary history" and "history" in separate departments—no treaties are signed when a book fires an adolescent's imagination, no troops move at the moment when a writer imagines a new life style. But speaking broadly, it seems safe to say that the nineteenth-century novel created a new and growing psychological awareness among people (twentieth-century psychology seems to be just as much the child of the novelist as of physicians or philosophers). A man like Trollope could make readers understand better the complexity of their own motives and the motives of others, could make them more conscious of not just how people act, but why they act. He changed his world by making it know itself better and by teaching his public the habits of sympathetic imagination. Trollope creates the most valuable illusion that literature has to offer: he makes a reader feel what it is like to be someone else.

The nineteenth-century novel unquestionably abetted the

---

[3] *An Autobiography* (London, 1953), chap. xii, p. 188, italics mine.

growth of democracy, self-esteem, individualism, and personal freedom because it represented so many different kinds of people whose lives have value and meaning. Sometimes its effects were contradictory. It also, by its very nature, fostered relativism, alienation, communal fragmentation, and a sense of the dwindling stature of man: it shows what a small percentage of the truth each person has, how many ways there are of looking at things, how many voices there are in the community, how hard it is to *know*, how infinite the possibilities of life are. On the other hand, by providing models of behavior in their books, the novelists also nurtured common values. Trollope's novels, of course, touched readers in all these ways.

Of the great Victorian novelists—Dickens, Thackeray, Eliot, Hardy, Emily Brontë, and Meredith—Trollope alone was a confirmed antipuritan. Frank O'Connor mentions that he did not write from a "preconceived idea of conduct." He was less concerned than his contemporaries with sin, guilt, divine retribution, and absolute morality. Moral consistency is for gods, and Trollope loves the human inconsistency which he sees as an inevitable part of life. Even in books like *The Prime Minister* or *The Way We Live Now* he is not so much interested in assigning blame or in condemning his characters as he is in pointing out the failure of incorrect procedure. He was trying to persuade his world that its finite goal should be to live with itself in as much peace as possible. People should know that they have to muddle along as best they can, doing as little harm as possible to themselves and others. They must learn to sympathize with other points of view. And above all else his novels show that people must continually face and live with shifting contingency. In his critical portrait of Trollope, Henry James wrote, "There are two kinds of taste in the appreciation of imaginative literature: the taste for emotions of surprise and the taste for recognition. It is the latter that Trollope gratifies." Frederick Karl, quoting this passage, says, "Clearly, all

great writers gratify both tastes," and he uses James's statement to deny Trollope greatness.[4] But at its best, Trollope's
work not only reflects so-called "usual" everyday living, it
recreates the wonder and the astonishment of life itself. By
quoting him at length, I have tried to show how surprising
he is when we look closely at exactly what it is that he is
saying and doing. What after all could be more surprising
than the depth of feeling of an apparently dry man like
Palliser or what his emotions imply about "ordinary" life?
Or what about the insight we get from his startlingly relevant satire in *The Eustace Diamonds*, when at the end he
suddenly makes us see that swelling egotism and egolessness
both have the same causes and both result in the same emptiness? It is not too much to say that Trollope, by finding excitement and unpredictability in what superficially seem the
most placid areas of life, gives us one of the most astounding
visions of experience that we have.

Any final assessment of Trollope is difficult because his
faults and his virtues are so completely intertwined that
they can hardly be separated. His lack of eloquence and his
commonplace use of language (except in dialogue, where
he is a master) are part of a rhetorical attempt to convince
readers that he is giving them unvarnished reality and that
he is not trying to manipulate them. He did not want his
own personality or his own views to "distort" his story or
break the illusion of his objectivity. He can not and does not
illuminate the dark places of the heart and mind—the full
horror of man's imagination—as Dickens and Dostoyevsky
do; he rarely shows us a self that reveals all it knows about
itself. But if his characters have less fully developed inner
lives than those of some other novelists, that is also part of
his vision. He puts people in society and shows them as
others might perceive them because he is so fascinated by
how people interact and how we perceive the personality of

---

[4] Frederick Karl, *An Age of Fiction: The Nineteenth Century
British Novel* (New York, 1964), p. 337.

others. Society is real to him, and he wants us to see how people react to each other, how their obsessions look to others, how they change each other. His moral ambiguity—his sometimes maddening refusal to make necessary choices between moral alternatives—relates directly to his sympathy and tolerence for different life styles. His failure to deal with "fine consciousness" is part of the inherent anti-elitist, democratic thrust of his work.

But Trollope's greatest flaw, the one which has done more harm to his reputation than anything else, was to have written and published so much and to have spent so little time editing and polishing. If Jane Austen had published forty-seven novels, I doubt if her reputation would be nearly as high as it is. Yet it was his fantastic energy and output which allowed him to catch so many of the nuances of one of the most truly revolutionary periods in history.

What in all that mass of Trollope's work deserves to live? A great deal, even after discounting the possibility of special pleading by the harmless drudge who has read all his novels. I do not see how it is possible, if one looks back over the range of Trollope's writing and comprehends the subtle and varied effects of so many of the passages which I have quoted, not to conclude that he is one of the most under-rated novelists of all time. His best and lasting art lies in the Barchester series: *The Warden, Barchester Towers, Doctor Thorne, Framley Parsonage, The Small House at Allington,* and *The Last Chronicle of Barset*; the Palliser books: *Can You Forgive Her? Phineas Finn, The Eustace Diamonds, Phineas Redux, The Prime Minister,* and *The Duke's Children*; and in four other novels, *The Macdermots of Bally-cloran, Orley Farm, The Way We Live Now,* and *Cousin Henry.*

In the Barset books we find a massive and uniquely imagined account of the comic and tragic transformation of a religious, rural society to a modern secular society. The Palliser novels give us one of the greatest renderings in fiction of the relationship between personality and political and social history and of the difficulties that people have in constructing their selves and their society in the flux of time. Out of all the rest of the novels, I choose these four as the most original: *The Macdermots of Ballycloran* for its clear view of the power of history to destroy helpless men; *Orley Farm* for the recognition in it of how the past always changes the present and how tenuous security is, and also for its sensitive treatment of friction between old and young; *The Way We Live Now* for its image of the catastrophic changes that distorted materialistic values can produce; and *Cousin Henry* for the emergence in it of the English underground man, and for the moral relativism which it shows. On these sixteen novels, Trollope's claim to greatness must stand or fall. In them we find his essential vision and range.

His perception of change as the dominant characteristic of his age was anything but unique. The Victorians knew they lived in a changing world, and the Red Queen in *Through the Looking Glass* puts their dilemma succinctly: "Now, *here*, you see, it takes all the running you can do, to keep in the same place." But what Trollope's fiction shows us is that a changing world is never an abstraction. Change always presents itself in specific ways to particular people; and how a person deals with "the changes that come upon him" determines his life. Trollope says in *Rachel Ray*, "A man can not change as men change."[5] But he is doomed to try. That, for Trollope, is man's fate.

---

[5] *Rachel Ray*, chap. XVIII, p. 234.

Index of Trollope's Novels
and Autobiography

(Pages on which central critical discussions appear are set in boldface.)